CAMBRIDGE LIBRARY COLLECTION

Books of enduring scholarly value

Religion

For centuries, scripture and theology were the focus of prodigious amounts of scholarship and publishing, dominated in the English-speaking world by the work of Protestant Christians. Enlightenment philosophy and science, anthropology, ethnology and the colonial experience all brought new perspectives, lively debates and heated controversies to the study of religion and its role in the world, many of which continue to this day. This series explores the editing and interpretation of religious texts, the history of religious ideas and institutions, and not least the encounter between religion and science.

The Book of Revelation in Greek Edited from Ancient Authorities

Samuel Prideaux Tregelles (1813-1875) was a Cornish-born Biblical scholar who travelled to major libraries all over Europe to study ancient manuscripts with the aim of publishing a more reliable Greek New Testament than had been available to Luther and Tyndale. The 1844 edition of the Book of Revelation reissued here was his first major publication, and announced his larger project. Biblical textual scholarship was a burgeoning field at the time, and others working in the field included Tischendorf and Lachmann, both of whom Tregelles subsequently met. This book, containing the Greek text with a meticulous critical apparatus and an English translation provides a window into nineteenth century textual criticism. Tregelles gives a detailed history of the printed editions of Revelation and shows how he went beyond the received text in his own work, examining more than forty thousand variants to establish the most authoritative version of the text. Tregelles' criteria for evaluating the reliability of manuscripts, described in his Introduction, remain of interest to Biblical scholars today.

T0371306

Cambridge University Press has long been a pioneer in the reissuing of out-of-print titles from its own backlist, producing digital reprints of books that are still sought after by scholars and students but could not be reprinted economically using traditional technology. The Cambridge Library Collection extends this activity to a wider range of books which are still of importance to researchers and professionals, either for the source material they contain, or as landmarks in the history of their academic discipline.

Drawing from the world-renowned collections in the Cambridge University Library, and guided by the advice of experts in each subject area, Cambridge University Press is using state-of-the-art scanning machines in its own Printing House to capture the content of each book selected for inclusion. The files are processed to give a consistently clear, crisp image, and the books finished to the high quality standard for which the Press is recognised around the world. The latest print-on-demand technology ensures that the books will remain available indefinitely, and that orders for single or multiple copies can quickly be supplied.

The Cambridge Library Collection will bring back to life books of enduring scholarly value (including out-of-copyright works originally issued by other publishers) across a wide range of disciplines in the humanities and social sciences and in science and technology.

The Book of Revelation in Greek Edited from Ancient Authorities

Samuel Prideaux Tregelles

CAMBRIDGE UNIVERSITY PRESS

Cambridge, New York, Melbourne, Madrid, Cape Town, Singapore,
São Paolo, Delhi, Dubai, Tokyo

Published in the United States of America by Cambridge University Press, New York

www.cambridge.org
Information on this title: www.cambridge.org/9781108007450

© in this compilation Cambridge University Press 2009

This edition first published 1844
This digitally printed version 2009

ISBN 978-1-108-00745-0 Paperback

ΑΠΟΚΑΛΥΨΙΣ ΙΗΣΟΥ ΧΡΙΣΤΟΥ.

THE REVELATION OF JESUS CHRIST.

ΑΠΟΚΑΛΥΨΙΣ ΙΗΣΟΥ ΧΡΙΣΤΟΥ,

ΕΞ ΑΡΧΑΙΩΝ ΑΝΤΙΓΡΑΦΩΝ ΕΚΔΟΘΕΙΣΑ.

THE

BOOK OF REVELATION

IN GREEK,

EDITED FROM ANCIENT AUTHORITIES;

WITH

A NEW ENGLISH VERSION,

AND VARIOUS READINGS.

BY

SAMUEL PRIDEAUX TREGELLES.

LONDON:

SAMUEL BAGSTER AND SONS,

WAREHOUSE FOR BIBLES, NEW TESTAMENTS, PRAYER BOOKS, LEXICONS, GRAMMARS,
CONCORDANCES, AND PSALTERS, IN ANCIENT AND MODERN LANGUAGES.

PATERNOSTER ROW.

ΠΟΛΛΑΙ μεν θνητοις ΓΛΩΤΤΑΙ μια δ'αθανατοισιν.

M.DCCC.XLIV.

NOTICE.

THIS edition of the book of Revelation contains—

1. The Greek Text edited on the authority of ancient MSS. and Versions.

2. An English translation of the Greek Text.

3. The readings which may be considered as *probable*, whether more or less so.

4. The readings of the Elzevir edition of 1624.

5. A selection of all the various readings which are at all supported by ancient MSS., by *many* more recent copies, or by the earliest printed editions;—together with a classified statement of the authorities for such readings.

Also, an Introduction stating in full the principles on which the text has been formed, and an outline of Biblical Criticism as applicable to the text of the Revelation.

CONTENTS OF THE INTRODUCTION.

INTRODUCTION.

I. THE OBJECT AND PLAN OF THE PRESENT WORK.

1. EVERY one who really values Scripture as the word of God, must regard the book of Revelation as being of considerable importance to Christians; this importance must be felt to exist wholly apart from any real or supposed ability to interpret the things which are written therein. No book of the New Testament is pressed upon our attention with more solemn sanctions; " Blessed is he that readeth, and they that hear the words of this prophecy, and keep the things which are written in it;" this alone is sufficient to show us that if we desire, as believers in Christ, to have fellowship with the mind of God and to have our thoughts subject to His will, this book will occupy no small share of our attention. It may be that we have but little intelligence of its general structure, or of its specific interpretation, but still it is our place *to keep* the things written in it, even as Mary who though she little understood the things which were told her, yet kept them and pondered them in her heart. Surely as we hold fast the word of God in all its parts, we may expect, through prayer and the teaching of the Holy Ghost, to become more acquainted with the truths therein written both in their detail and their practical power.

These considerations will, I trust, suffice to show that an adequate motive exists for an attempt to exhibit the Greek text of the book of Revelation as correctly as possible, together with an English version suited to that corrected text. The *object* and *plan* will, I believe, be best understood from a brief account of the motives which led to the preparation and publication of the present work.

2. Several years have elapsed since my mind was particularly turned to the state of the Greek text of the New Testament,

and the various revisions by Griesbach, Scholz, and others: this course of study brought before me very vividly the remarkable difference which exists between the condition of the common text of the book of Revelation and that of the rest of the New Testament: for whether we take Griesbach's or Scholz's text, (my examination was at the time pretty much confined to these), we find more corrections given as resting on critical data in this one book than we do in all the epistles of St. Paul taken together. This raised two thoughts in my mind, first,—what were the actual authorities on which the Greek text of this book was edited, and whether they really differed thus widely from the rest of the New Testament; and, second, when I was satisfied with the need that existed of using critical data for the correction of the text, I was impressed with the desirableness of giving the mere English reader the *results* of such revision, either by publishing a list of passages in which the reading in our authorised version ought to be emended, or else by publishing the English version of the book with the passages so corrected.

My desire to bring the results of critical labour before the mere English reader, arose from feeling how important it is for those who value the word of God to have it set before them as correctly as possible; and this will be especially seen to be the case when the fact is borne in mind (see § II. 5) that in several places the ordinary Greek text of the Revelation (and consequently of our version) rests upon no MS. authority whatever.

3. In carefully examining the authorities of MSS. and versions as given by Griesbach, I found however that in not a few cases I differed in judgment as to the readings to be preferred both from him and from Scholz; they both appeared to me to retain the readings of the common text in several passages, in which the evidence seemed to me very decisive against them; there were also other points on which I found that my judgment could not accord with either of these critics.

Hence it became needful to form a basis for the English translation which I contemplated; to this end I prepared a Greek text of this book, forming it according to the critical principles which I believe to be the most accurate. (see § IV. 2). This led me to a careful examination of the authorities cited by Griesbach and Scholz; and thus I found that in many cases so few of these were given, and in other cases they were stated with so little accuracy and precision, that it required a very

careful revision (see § IV. 1) before I could use them satis-
factorily.

After I had arranged the *authorities* and again revised the
Greek text, I made the English translation; in which I did not
seek to depart from the authorised version, except in cases in
which this was necessary either on account of variation in the
Greek text, or else because of something which was obviously
capable of improvement.

4. It would have been unsuitable to have published the
English translation alone; for as it contained many variations
from any critical text with which I was then acquainted, it was
obviously incumbent on me to give that text together with the
version; neither could the text itself have been properly given
without a statement of the authorities on which it rests; hence
the various readings became a needful accompaniment. (On the
revision of collations and the formation of the Greek text, see
§ IV. 1, 2). It has also been necessary to go into some critical
detail by way of introduction.

5. I do not think that it is needful in this place to enter into
any disquisition on the divine origin and authority of the book;
I am writing for Christians, for those who through grace have
believed in the name of the Son of God, and who believing
have life through His name, and not as addressing those who
wish to cavil and question as to the authority of Scripture.

I am perfectly aware that many feel a dread of any criticism
being applied to the text of Scripture, regarding it as too sacred
to be touched; now I wish most distinctly to state that because I reverence Scripture as being the word of God, I believe
it to be of importance to bring every aid in our power to bear
upon its text, in order that we may as accurately as possible read
it in the very words in which it was given by the Holy Ghost.

I avow my full belief in the absolute, plenary inspiration of
Scripture, 2 Tim. 3. 16. I believe the sixty-six books of the Old
and New Testaments to be verbally the word of God, as absolutely
as were the ten commandments written by the finger of God on
the two tables of stone : and *because* I thus fully believe in its
verbal inspiration, I judge that it is not labour ill bestowed to
endeavour to search into the evidence which is obtainable as to
what those words are, and to exhibit the results of such investi-
gation. I trust that this may suffice to hinder charges being
brought of want of reverence for the book designed to make wise
unto salvation; although I freely own that I have much more

reverence for the more ancient copies, and for the text which they contain, than I have for those which are in common use.

Many have regarded attempts at critical revision of the text of the New Testament, as being connected not only with a want of reverence for the word of God, but also in a certain measure with unsoundness of doctrine as to the Godhead of Christ and other fundamental points. Such charges have no necessary connection with critical revision of the text, or with the results of such revisions, let the conductors of them be whoever they may. Bengel who led the way in such critical revision was free from every suspicion of being opposed to orthodox belief: Wetstein, a laborious collector of critical materials, can hardly be said to have formed a critical text, as he only noted in the *margin* such readings as he preferred; it is most true that his sentiments were decidedly *Arian*, and that his heterodoxy shows itself in his Prolegomena and notes. Griesbach was probably tainted with the rationalism of modern Germany to a considerable degree, but it would be very difficult to prove that his neology has influenced him in his critical text. Scholz, as being a Roman Catholic Professor at Bonn, may be supposed simply to adhere to the doctrines of that church. It is probable that most of the modern German editors are more or less imbued with *rationalism;* but still however incapable we may regard them of forming a true judgment of any subject connected with the word of God, it would be difficult to show that, in their choice of readings, they have rejected or adopted any except on critical grounds, whether sufficient or not.

If there were then any reason for connecting Biblical criticism with unsoundness of doctrine, it could only have arisen from persons who held such views having also paid attention to this subject. But this, instead of leading those who hold orthodox sentiments to avoid the subject, ought to induce them to take it up themselves, in order that they might not be under the necessity of receiving critical texts from doubtful hands.

It is perfectly true that passages *may* have been rested on, and used in argument for the support of the most important doctrines,—such as the Trinity, and the person of Christ,— which may on examination be found to rest on very slight critical authority; but this does not affect the *doctrines* themselves,—nay they may be said to stand by this means on a more sure basis of Scripture testimony, when everything which was insecure in itself has been taken away: sound criticism rightly applied will be a safeguard to the text of the word of God against the encroachments of ignorance and heterodoxy. A disputant may be found to uphold true doctrine by *misquoted* Scripture; in every such case it will be well to open the Bible, quote the passage fairly, and let the *doctrine* itself rest for support upon the passages which really apply:—just so with regard to any doctrinal statements in which the readings are doubtful:—let criticism in a Christian spirit and in true subjection to God's authority come in, let the passages be fairly read, and let testimonies to true doctrine be taken up from that which will bear the test of full examination. It is proper, however, to remark that *very few* passages will receive *any* doctrinal alteration, so that the reader need not suppose these observations to have at all an extensive application. Honest criticism will never touch one atom of orthodox or evangelical truth; it may exhibit the text of the word of God with more exactness, but the doctrines will be found the same, unchanged and unshaken. It is indeed a cause for thankfulness that God has preserved the Scripture unto us in such substantial integrity: it has been subjected to many casualties, it has passed through the hands of many copyists, but in doctrine and precept it is unchanged. I believe that it may most truly be said that the most faulty copy presents to us the doctrines and the duties of Christianity devoid of any material alteration. Of course the more exactly we know the very words of Scripture as originally inspired by the Holy Ghost, the more exactly have we the declaration of His mind set before us.

Men who are possessed of human learning and intellectual power may exercise their own minds on subjects of criticism; but those who through faith in the Lord Jesus Christ possess the knowledge of God, are alone able to look to Him for the blessed guidance of the Holy Ghost, who can give ability in forming an accurate judgment on evidence connected with the criticism of the sacred text.

Ungodly men may make an evil use of the word of God, and of the most blessed truths which it contains; this ought not to hinder Christians from using it aright; and just so do I deem should be our judgment with regard to Biblical criticism; *if* this has been misused by impugners of orthodoxy and truth, it only shows that we who fully acknowledge the Godhead and atonement of the Lord Jesus Christ, and the Gospel of God's grace in His name, and the Personality and Godhead of the Holy Ghost, ought to take good heed that we use this weapon aright, lest it should be supposed to *belong* to unhallowed hands.

The object of textual criticism is of quite sufficient importance to interest Christians; namely the statement of the evidence as to the true reading of the text of Scripture; and it might have been almost expected that they would have regarded it as a subject peculiarly their own.

It will be necessary to give some account of the critical details which relate to the book of Revelation, in order to make the basis of the present work fully intelligible. These details are given at some length in order that they may afford the needful information to those who are not familiar with the subject,* and also because in a more condensed form it would be difficult to be really perspicuous.

II. STATE OF THE GREEK TEXT OF THE BOOK OF REVELATION.

1. Ancient writings, whether sacred or profane, have been transmitted to us by means of transcribers. The autographs of such works have long ago been lost. Hence various casualties may affect the state of the text and the readings, which never could have arisen had the works remained in existence in the handwriting of the authors. Copies which had been made from the originals were used as the exemplars from which others were again taken, and so the work of transcription continued during the successive centuries which preceded the invention of printing. Thus there are many works of great and undoubted antiquity of which there does not exist a single really *very ancient* MS. This does not affect the antiquity of the book, however much it may the state of the *text*.

The Inspired writings of the Old and New Testaments have been transmitted to us just in the same manner as other books; they have been liable to the same casualties in transcription, and the correctness of copies made has depended upon the diligence and accuracy of the transcriber. The fact of their having been " given by inspiration of God," has not and could not ensure

---

* On the subject of Biblical Criticism in general I may mention, "Lectures on Biblical Criticism. By Samuel Davidson, LL.D. Edinburgh, 1839." I know of no volume in English which gives so much information on the subject, and with as much correctness. Of course I do not vouch for *every* fact or *every* conclusion.

perfection in the transcripts made, unless the copyists were also inspired;—as given by inspiration the whole was of God, the words were His as completely as were the two tables of stone " written by the finger of God." But just as a copyist might err in transcribing the letters and words of the decalogue which God had thus written, so might he with respect to any other portion of Scripture; and it must not be looked at as want of reverence for the word of God, or want of belief in its verbal inspiration *in the fullest sense*, for this fact to be fully admitted.

2. *Various readings* are thus found in the copies of the Holy Scriptures as well as in other writings. Various readings are in their origin to works in MS. just what mistakes of the press are in printed books. They are the differences existing between different copies; the places in which the words or phrases vary, or are found in a different order, or in which one copy contains more or less than another.

Every one who has had any connection with the operations of printing, must be practically conscious of the sources of various readings. If a page of MS. were put into the hands of a compositor, he would almost undoubtedly make 'some errors in setting it up in type. In some places he might read the copy wrongly, in others might omit, in others might repeat some of the words before him, and there would probably be several errors in punctuation and orthography. The page of letter-press would on these accounts require a good deal of revision to make it accurately represent the page of MS. which had been sent to the printing office.

But if the page set up in type instead of being corrected were at once worked off with all its errors, and the copies so printed were put into the hands of fresh compositors, then new variations would undoubtedly arise. Some of the compositors might notice unquestionable mistakes and try to rectify them; in doing this they would not improbably depart yet farther from the original MS., and each one perhaps in a different way:—they would also be subject to the same causes of error as was the first compositor, and this too in a still greater degree from their having something more defective to work upon. Let the same operation go on a few times more, and we should have copies of the page, the general texture remaining the same, but with variations in particular parts,—some of them probably very considerable.

Now if the MS. page originally used had been lost, so that it could not be applied for the revision of the incorrect copies, the only way would be to take the copies such as they are, and by examining them amongst themselves to restore if possible the original readings. To this end the page as set up by the first compositor would be the most helpful, and would undoubtedly be nearest to the MS.; it would therefore be important to trace the *genealogy* of these printed copies. If the MS. copy had been put into the hands of more than one compositor, the page as set up by each of these would be a separate and important witness: the united testimony of such pages would lead one to something like a *certainty* as to the original reading.

This may serve to illustrate the causes and character of various readings, and the mode of critically dealing with them.

All the various readings to the New Testament must be ascribed either to *inadvertence* or *design; very few* however can be attributed to this latter cause: except, indeed, such as may have sprung from an attempt at *correction:* but probably *not one* (such attempts excepted) which can come under consideration with regard to the Apocalypse.

Various readings arising from inadvertence all belong to one class in general;—the transcriber having departed from his copy. Sometimes this was occasioned by the eye mistaking a word or phrase,—by *similar* words in appearance and sound being interchanged,—

(*e. g.* ὁμοίως & ὁ μισῶ, Rev. 2. 15,—μέλλει & ἔμελλον, 3. 2,—οὗτος & οὕτως, 3. 5,—ὁράσει σμαραγδίνῳ & ὄρασις σμαραγδίνων, 4. 3, &c.)

by expressions being substituted for others which were synonymous or were so regarded by the copyist,—

(*e. g.* the interchange of κοινωνὸς & συγκοινωνὸς, Rev. 1. 9,—πρῶτος & πρωτότοκος, 1. 17,—Ἐφεσίνης & ἐν Ἐφέσῳ, 2. 1,—φάσκοντας εἶναι ἀποστόλους & λέγοντας ἑαυτοὺς ἀποστόλους, 2. 2,—δυνατοὶ & ἰσχυροὶ, 6. 15, &c.)

by omissions δι᾽ ὁμοιοτέλευτον, *i. e.* when two words or sentences *end* alike, the eye passing on to the *second* termination, and thus omitting a word or phrase altogether;—

(*e. g.* τοῦ θανάτου omitted because of the following αὐτοῦ, Rev. 13. 12, —the words omitted from τοῦ θηρίου to τοῦ θηρίου, 13. 15,—from ὄνομα to ὄνομα in the common text, 14. 1;—the omission of ver. 4 of ch. 5, &c.)

by a similar mistake from words or phrases *commencing* with the same letters,—

(*e. g.* the omission of the words from καὶ ἐδόθη to καὶ ἐδόθη, Rev. 13. 7;—the omission of τοῦ γάμου in 19, 9, &c.)

Sometimes the copyist made too much use of his mind and memory, so that he inserted words in a passage where they did not belong, owing to their being found elsewhere in a similar connection;—

(*e. g.* the insertion of ὁ πλανῶν τὴν οἰκουμένην ὅλην after Σατανᾶς in Rev. 20. 2, out of 12. 9,—δίστομος after ῥομφαία in 19. 15, out of 1. 16, —ταῖς ἐν Ἀσίᾳ after ἐκκλησίαις in 1. 11, out of 1. 4, &c.)

sometimes a copyist inserted an explanatory word or phrase, expressive of the thought which the copy before him conveyed to his own mind;—this led to the substitution of easy readings for those which were more difficult.

Hence such readings as κεκοπίακας καὶ οὐ κέκμηκας, Rev. 2. 3,—τὴν λέγουσαν, 2. 20,—ἣ καταβαίνει, 3. 12,—οὐδενὸς, 3. 17,—λέγουσα, 4. 1, —ὁμοία, 4. 3,—εἶδον τοὺς inserted 4. 4,—εἶχον or ἔχον, 4. 8,—ἡμᾶς & βασιλεύσομεν, 5. 10.

Scholia which had been written in the margin of a copy sometimes were partially blended by a transcriber with the text; this has caused several erroneons readings, some of which are extraordinary and hardly credible.

Hence ζῶντι εἰς τοὺς αἰῶνας τῶν αἰώνων added to the end of Rev. 5. 14,—καὶ ὁ ἄγγελος εἰστήκει in 11. 1,—ἐνώπιον τοῦ θρόνου τοῦ θεοῦ, 14. 5, &c.—the following may be taken as instances of *strange* readings arising from scholia, 2 Cor. 8. 4, δέξασθαι ἡμᾶς ἐν πολλοῖς τῶν ἀντιγράφων οὕτως εὕρηται καὶ οὐ καθὼς ἠλπίσαμεν, so in the Codex Corsendoncensis; see Alter's Gr. Test. vol. 2. p. 594,—of a similar kind is Heb. 7. 3, ἐν ᾧ ὅτι καὶ τοῦ ἀβραὰμ προετιμήθη. θεωρεῖτε κ. τ. λ. in the Complutensian text.

In the most ancient MSS. the interchange of vowels and diphthongs is very frequent, such as ε and αι, η and ει, ο and ω, η and ι, υ and η, αυ and αη, ει and ι, ου and υ. Some of these interchanges are of frequent occurrence, some are comparatively rare; they are, however, the source of many important variations.

Hence has arisen confusion between ἔγειρε & ἔγειραι, Rev. 11. 1;—and many other variations of the same kind; most of which, however, make no possible sense.

Abbreviations have also led to mistakes; I͞C, K͞C, Θ͞C, X͞C, Y͞C, have been thus written for one another, or for other words which they resembled in appearance.

Additions were often made, such as Κύριος before or Χριστὸς after Ἰησοῦς: and short phrases of *common occurrence* were very often interchanged with equally common synonyms.

The *order* of words was very frequently changed, of which instances may be seen among the various readings on almost every page. The termination of a word was often assimilated to that which precedes or follows it.

The *ear* of a transcriber has sometimes misled him, for we find words or clauses substituted for one another which have nothing in common except *sound*.

(*e. g.* in Rev. 22. 14, μακάριοι οἱ πλύνοντες τὰς στολὰς αὐτῶν is the reading of the best authorities; in most copies this is changed into μακ. οἱ ποιοῦντες τὰς ἐντολὰς αὐτοῦ, a reading which resembles the other in nothing but *sound*.)

In estimating the difficulty which a transcriber must have had to encounter, we must bear in mind the fact that ancient writing consisted of *undivided* capitals; thus a far greater labour of the eye and the attention was needful in producing a correct copy. The undivided words were much more difficult to read, and an unskilful copyist often made such blunders, as to render passages of his transcript wholly void of meaning. The following three lines from the Codex Ephræmi will manifest the comparative difficulty of reading the undivided uncial writing.

ΕΓΩΙΩΑΝΝΗΣΟΑΔΕΛΦΟΣΥΜΩΝΚΑΙΣΥΝΚΟΙΝΩΝΟΣΕΝΤΗ
ΘΑΙΨΕΙ·ΚΑΙΒΑΣΙΛΕΙΑΚΑΙΥΠΟΜΟΝΗΕΝΙΥ͞ΕΓΕΝΟΜΗΝΕΝΤΗ
ΣΩΤΗΚΑΛΟΥΜΕΝΗΠΑΤΜΩ·ΚΑΙΤΟΝΛΟΓΟΝΤΟΥΘ͞ΥΚΑΙΤΗ͞

It will be observed that ΝΗ is omitted at the beginning of the third line, probably on account of the ΤΗ which had immediately preceded.

3. The book of Revelation presents, as to its external history and its transmission, some features distinct from the rest of the New Testament. The number of copies which have come down to us, is far fewer than those of any other of the books. This may be accounted for in various ways : it was, probably, written at a later period than any other book of the New Testament, (for no objection can, I believe, be really brought against the testimony of Irenæus*), and thus the other portions of the Christian Scriptures were in use and circulation, most of them for forty, and some of them for fifty years previously.

It is very clear that this book was received and used both in the east and west, and was recognised both as to inspiration and apostolic authorship, for more than a century after it was written ; and yet at a later period some objected, especially in the east, to admit its divine authority. The grounds of this objection were most trifling in themselves,—they were not based upon any appeal to facts or testimonies, and they directly contradicted what had been previously laid down by competent witnesses ;—I mean witnesses who were competent to state what they knew to be the truth, (e. g. Justin Martyr and Irenæus).

In consequence of this book having been for a time comparatively disregarded, transcripts became of course less numerous ; and although, before any very long time had elapsed, its authenticity and authority were owned by all who called themselves Christians, yet, from mistaken ideas as to the mysteriousness of its contents, &c. it was not commonly used like the rest of Holy Scripture in public assemblies.

Transcripts of the various parts of the New Testament were made just as there might exist demand ; thus the copies of the four Gospels are very numerous, from their having been used both in public and private, but especially the former. Copies of the Epistles of St. Paul have also come down to us in considerable number ; of the Acts of the Apostles and Catholic Epistles there are far fewer copies ; but even these are numerous when compared with those of the Revelation.

It seems, indeed, surprising that a book which God has so emphatically pressed upon the attention of those who believe in the name of His Son, should have been for so long a period treated with comparative neglect ; as if, although acknowledged to be of divine authority, it was not to be used and honoured as being indeed the word of God.

The copies being thus comparatively few, those which are *ancient* are

---

* "'Οὐδὲ γὰρ πρὸ πολλοῦ χρόνου ἑωράθη, ἀλλὰ σχεδὸν ἐπὶ τῆς ἡμετέρας γενεᾶς, πρὸς τῷ τέλει τῆς Δομετιανοῦ ἀρχῆς."—i. e. A. D. 96.

peculiarly rare; indeed, for more than a century after the printing of the Greek text no ancient copy of this book was known in the western part of Europe. Thus the history of the unprinted text of the Apocalypse presents to us much fewer facts than that of the other parts of the New Testament; and the scarcity of copies, instead of being favourable to the text being in a tolerably correct condition, was just the contrary; transcribers made more errors in their copies, and these were the less noticed from the book being read so little in public. The commentaries of Andreas and Arethas, which were written in the margin of some MSS., occasioned errors, from passages in the margin having often been confounded with the text.

Thus at the time when printing was employed to multiply and perpetuate books, there were hinderances in the way of a correct text of the Revelation being diffused in this manner, which did not apply in the same degree to the rest of the New Testament.

4. The first *printed* edition of the book of Revelation, as well as of the rest of the New Testament in Greek, was that contained in the Polyglott Bible which was edited and printed at the expense, and under the auspices of Cardinal Ximenes. This Polyglott Bible was printed at Alcala, in Spain; and it is from the Latin name of that town, (Complutum), that the work has been ordinarily called the Complutensian Polyglott.

The portion of the work which contains the New Testament,* was edited by Ælius Antonius Nebrissensis, Demetrius Cretensis, Ferdinandus Pitianus, and Lopez de Stunica; the last mentioned being apparently the most learned of the whole.

The volume which contains the New Testament in Greek and Latin appears, from the subscription at the end of the Revelation, to have been completed January 10, 1514.

The actual *publication* of the work did not, however, take place for some years; hinderances appear to have been thrown in the way previous to the death of Cardinal Ximenes, and it was not until March 22, 1520, that Pope Leo the Tenth gave his formal sanction to the publication taking place. The Pope speaks of the Cardinal having died without obtaining his permission for the publication, and he mentions this as a necessary preliminary; it is not, however, probable that he would have made any objection, for the work was dedicated in the prologue to himself, and he was thanked for having furnished MSS. from the library of the Vatican to aid in its execution: and further, when Erasmus's Greek and Latin New Testament was published, Pope Leo had shown, by a letter expressive of his approbation, how much he esteemed such a work. In this, as well as in most other things, he manifested how desirous he was to be esteemed a patron and promoter both of the arts and of *literature:* into the questions of the circulation of the word of God, whether in the original languages or in translations, and what the effects of their circulation might be, he does not seem to have inquired.

* Nouum testamentum grece & latine in academia complutensi, nouiter impressum.

The *publication* of the Complutensian text of the New Testament may be dated from the time when the sanction of Pope Leo, addressed to the Cardinal's executors, was received in Spain ; it appears, however, that for about two years from the date of the sanction, the copies were not at all widely diffused ; this may be judged from the fact that Erasmus had not, in 1522, yet seen this edition.

The first edition which was *published*, was that of Erasmus, in 1516 ; for although it was not *printed* until after the Complutensian edition, it was the first to be circulated, no hinderances having been thrown in the way.

The first edition of the New Testament, edited by Erasmus, contains the Greek text, a Latin version corrected from the Vulgate, and in the latter part of the volume copious annotations.* The date on the back of the title-page is, " Sexto Calendas Martias, anno M.D.XVI. ;" that at the end of the dedication to Pope Leo the Tenth is, " M.D.XVI. Calendis Februariis ;" at the end of the annotations, " M.D.XVI. Kalendis Martiis ;" although at the conclusion of the whole volume there is " Mense Februario." It was printed at Bâsle by Froben.

It is not a little remarkable, and it shows, I think, the overruling providence of God, that at so short a time before the commencement of the Reformation these two editions of the original text of the New Testament should have been published ; both of them sanctioned and approved by Rome, though really among the most important instruments for the establishment of evangelical doctrine.

This first edition of Erasmus appears to have been sold and circulated very quickly ; it was dedicated to Pope Leo, who expressed his approval in a letter which Erasmus prefixed to his succeeding editions. Its execution, however, was extremely hurried ; it was first proposed to Erasmus that he should edit such an edition on April 17, 1515, only nine months and a half before the printing was completed. It also appears that the printing had not commenced in September, 1515, for at that time it had not been settled whether the Greek and Latin texts should be placed in parallel columns, or whether they should stand separately. Thus the whole period for the printing of the text and the annotations was less than *six months*, and during this time Erasmus was distracted with the multiplicity of editorial labour which he had in hand; so that he might well say of this Greek Testament, " Præcipitatum fuit, verius quam editum." The marks of this extreme haste are traceable in many parts, in the book of Revelation very particularly.

This edition was reprinted at Venice, in 1518, in the same volume as the Aldine LXX. The second edition of Erasmus is dated 1519; the third 1522; in both of these there are some slight alterations in the text ; (1 John v. 7, was first inserted in the third edition); in 1527 Erasmus's fourth edition

---

* Novvm Instrumentum omne, diligenter ab Erasmo Roterodamo reognitum & emendatum, non solum ad græcam ueritatem, uerumetiam ad multorum utriusq; linguæ codicum, eorumq; ueterum simul et emendatorum fidem, postremo ad probatissimorum autorum citationem, emendationem et interpretationem, præcipue, Origenis, Chrysostomi, Cyrilli, Vulgarij, Hieronymi, Cypriani, Ambrosij, Hilarij, Augustini, una cum Annotationibus quæ lectorem doceant, quid qua ratione mutatum sit.

appeared, in the preparation of which he was aided by the Complutensian text; this he used especially in the Revelation; for out of one hundred changes of reading which he made in this edition, Mill states that *ninety* relate to this book alone. Erasmus's fifth and last edition appeared in 1535.

5. The primary printed editions from which those in common use have sprung, being thus the Complutensian and that of Erasmus, it becomes a point of some importance to inquire what the respective sources were from which these editions flowed.

The Complutensian editors speak in high terms of the antiquity and value of the MSS. which they used; it may, however, be safely questioned whether they were good judges on a point of criticism such as this is. We are now much more competent than they were to judge of the age as well as the value of MSS. ; and the character of the readings found in their edition is such as to show plainly that the copies which they used were pretty fair samples of the more modern Greek MSS., such as were currently circulated from the tenth century and onward.

They have been accused of altering the Greek text in order to conform it to the Latin, which stands by the side. If this be brought as a general charge it is undoubtedly false ; but if it be only applied to the text, 1 John v. 7, and a very few other passages, I suppose that every one who knows anything of biblical criticism, and has examined the subject, will now acknowledge it to be true.

In the book of Revelation their text differs considerably from that in common use ; this book has been spoken of as the best executed part of their edition. This may, however, be regarded as very doubtful ; they appear throughout to have followed the ordinary Greek copies, and these in the Revelation were decidedly more correct than that which afterwards obtained general circulation. Very little is known of the MSS. used by the Complutensian editors ; they are, however, *now* supposed to be preserved in the university of Alcala.

The MSS. used by Erasmus are better known ; the greater part of them still remain at Bâsle ; that, however, which was used for the Revelation is now wholly lost : it was one which he had borrowed from Reuchlin, the only MS. of this book which he could procure.

It is certain that he did not make the best use of the MSS. to which he had access ; in fact it was impossible for him to do so in the hurried manner in which the work had to be executed ; and in some places in which he supposed his Greek MS. of the Acts to be defective, it is almost certain that he translated words from the Latin Vulgate into Greek, and inserted them in his text.

In editing the Revelation he laboured under great disadvantages. The one MS. of which he had the use appears to have been in a mutilated condition. It contained the Greek text with a commentary interspersed, and he had to separate the words of the text as well as he could. In not a few places he clearly took the commentary for the text, and thus inserted readings found in no Greek MS. ; where his MS. was altogether illegible he appears to have relied on the Latin Vulgate, and to have supplied words in the Greek

by retranslating them from it.   We *know* that this was the case with the last
six verses of the book ; in his MS. they were wholly wanting, owing to its
mutilated condition, and he ventured on the bold expedient of supplying
them by his own translation from the Latin : this he acknowledges himself,
(see § V. 3).   Hence we cannot wonder that in his fourth edition he should
have made several alterations in the text of this book on the authority of the
Complutensian copy ; and yet there are readings in the last six verses, only
springing from his translation, which are still retained in the commonly used
text of this book.

It must be obvious to the Christian reader that the word of God ought
never to have been edited with such precipitancy, or with such liberties taken
with the text :   indeed it may be regarded as a cause for thankfulness that
more incorrect readings were not thus introduced into the printed copies than
was actually the case.

The fourth and fifth editions of Erasmus are *substantially* the Greek text
now in common use ; the fifth edition was followed with very little variation
by Robert Stephens in his third edition, 1550.*   Stephens's third edition
was the basis of the five published by Beza, and also of the Elzevir editions
of which the first was published in 1624.†

In this country Mill's Greek Testament is the text most commonly reprinted and used ; this *text* is merely a repetition of Stephens's third edition,
with a few errata corrected.   On the continent, until of late, the Elzevir
text was professedly followed; but from examination I find very few
of these editions (probably not one) really follow throughout the Elzevir
text ; in places in which it differs from the Stephanic they sometimes follow
the latter; and sometimes they differ from both.

The ordinary copies of the Greek Testament spring thus from the fifth
edition of Erasmus, in which the book of Revelation was (as has just been
shown) in a very unsatisfactory state.

6. It is not surprising that labour should have been bestowed,
from time to time, in collecting critical materials for a more
correct text of the New Testament in general, and of the Revelation in particular.

The third edition of Robert Stephens (just mentioned) contains various
readings from the Complutensian edition, and from MSS. which might have
been used to advantage for the correction of the text.   Beza often mentions
various readings, and sometimes has followed them.   The first considerable
collection of various readings to the Greek Testament is that contained in the

---

* Τῆς Καινῆς Διαθήκης Ἅπαντα . . . . Novum JESU Christi D. N. Testamentum.   Ex
Bibliotheca Regia. Lvtetiae, MDL.

† H' Καινὴ Διαθήκη. Novum Testamentum. Ex Regiis aliisque optimis editionibus cum
curâ expressum. Lugduni Batavorum, Ex Officinâ Elzeviriana. CIƆIƆCXXIV. It has been
said that wherever Beza's text differs from that of Stephens, it is followed by the Elzevir
editions; this is very incorrect; in the Revelation alone the Elzevir text agrees with Stephens
in TWELVE places in which Beza differs; in NINE places the Elzevir text follows neither
Stephens nor Beza. On this as well as many other questions as to detail of facts, the critical
sketch given by Professor Moses Stuart in his recent notice of Hahn's Greek Te⁸tament in
the " Bibliotheca Sacra," requires *much* correction.

sixth volume of Walton's Polyglott (1657); in the Revelation, however, from the paucity of MSS. these are very meagre. Bishop Fell followed in this course of making critical collections in his edition (1675).* A great advance was made by Mill, whose edition, published in 1707, prepared with long and patient labour, laid the basis of critical emendation of the Greek text.† The first, however, who really *applied* the various readings which had been collected from MSS. and ancient versions was Bengel, in 1734. He had true reverence for the Scripture as being the word of God, and this was the motive which induced him to edit his Greek Testament. ‡ In the Revelation he followed the MS. authorities which had then been collated; this was done on the express ground that it had been originally edited on such very insufficient authority of MSS., and in part on the authority of none. In the other books of the New Testament he selected readings for his text from the different printed editions, and placed those which he judged still better on critical grounds in the margin. Bengel was the first to call attention to the connexion of certain MSS. with others, so that they might be divided into *families*.

The materials for the criticism of the text were greatly increased by the publication of Wetstein's Greek Testament in 1751-2.§ His critical ability in forming a text, and even in judging of the value of MSS., was probably very much below his industry in collation, and in bringing together critical materials. The readings which he prefers he has placed in the margin.

In the latter part of the last century and the commencement of this, the stock of critical materials was greatly increased, and the labours of Griesbach led the way to a more general revision of the common Greek text. ‖ His

* Της Καινης Διαθηκης απαντα. Novi Testamenti Libri Omnes. Accesserunt Parallela Scripturæ Loca, nec non variantes Lectiones ex plus 100 MSS. Codicibus, et Antiquis Versionibus Collectæ. Oxonii. M.DC.LXXV. The collation of the Alexandrian MS. was the most important part of the critical apparatus here given, as was the case also in Walton's Polyglott, where its readings (so far as they were given) were placed throughout under the Greek text.

† Η Καινη Διαθηκη . . . . Cum Lectionibus Variantibus MSS. Exemplarium Versionum, Editionum, SS. Patrum et Scriptorum Ecclesiasticorum; et in easdem notis, &c. Studio et Labore Joannis Millii S. T. P. Oxonii. MDCCVII.

‡ Novvm Testamentvm Graecvm ita adornatvm vt Textvs probatarvm editionvm medvllam Margo variantivm lectionvm in svas classes distribvtarvm locorvmqve parallelorvm delectvm Apparatvs svbivnctvs criseos sacrae Millianae praesertim compendivm, limam, svpplementvm ac frvctvm exhibeat inserviente Io. Alberto Bengelio. Tubingae . . MDCCXXXIV.

§ Novum Testamentum Graecum editionis receptae cum lectionibus variantibus Codicum MSS., Editionum aliarum, versionum et Patrum . . . . Opera et studio Joannis Jacobi Wetstenii. Amstelaedami. MDCCLI. Tom. ii. MDCCLII.

‖ It is altogether foreign to my present object to enter into any particular account of Griesbach's System of Recensions of the Greek Text. It will suffice to say that he tried to carry out the hints proposed by Bengel as to the *families* into which Greek MSS. might be distributed. He divided them into three classes *Alexandrian*, *Western* and *Constantinopolitan*. Almost all the very ancient MSS. belong to the two former of these divisions, the mass of modern copies to the last. This system of Recensions is wholly inapplicable to the Revelation of which we have so few ancient MSS. Various other systems have since been proposed; Scholz divides all MSS. into *Alexandrian* and *Constantinopolitan*,—uniting the two first of Griesbach's classes. He professes almost invariably to prefer the readings of the latter class, *i. e.* of the mass of modern MSS. I believe that his classification is pretty correct in point of fact; though it would be more truly stated if the division were between *ancient* readings (which may themselves admit of *classes*) and *later* readings; contrary to Scholz I should decidedly prefer the *former*.

first edition was published in 1775–7; his second and principal edition in 1796–1806.*

The following additions were made to the stock of critical materials for the text of the Revelation. In 1785 Matthæi published, in the twelfth volume of his Greek Test., the collations of *six* MSS. mostly at Moscow. In 1786 those of *four* MSS. at Vienna were published by Alter. About the same time Birch made his collations, which have a peculiar value on account of their importance; in this book these extend to *ten* MSS.; they were not published until 1801. Various single MSS. were also collated and published by different individuals; and one of the most important steps was the publication of the Codex Alexandrinus by Dr. Woide in 1786.

From the time of Griesbach many editors have published texts differing from that which had been in common use; few of these require any particular notice in this place. Scholz, after making an extensive examination of MSS. not previously collated, published an edition in 1830–36;† in this his endeavour was to establish a text on the authority of the mass of consenting MSS.; this led him in general to prefer the many later copies to those which are the most ancient. In his second volume, however, he appears to have departed from this principle, commonly for the better.

In 1831, Lachmann, acting in partial conformity to a plan laid down by the celebrated Bentley, published an edition in which the authority of ancient MSS. was absolutely followed.‡ In this, however, he acted rather mechanically than critically, especially in the Revelation, of which there are so few ancient copies. Bentley's principle, however, I believe to be perfectly sound; that in the text of the New Testament, the authority of the ancient MSS. is to be taken as of *primary* authority, and especially when connected with the most ancient and most literal versions; so much so that it is only the necessity of the case which can warrant our departing therefrom, and even then we must have competent witnesses, such as versions and other MSS. Indeed, except in the Revelation, I suppose that we should not be obliged ever to resort to the more modern copies as the ground of a reading.

This was the principle upon which I had in some measure acted before I

---

* Novvm Testamentvm Graece. Textvm ad fidem Codicvm Versionvm et Patrvm Recensuit et Lectionis Varietatem adjecit D. Jo. Jac. Griesbach. Tom. i. 1796. Tom. ii. 1806. Griesbach also published a manual edition in 1805; this was reprinted in 1825 and it is stated on the title-page to be ".editio nova non tamen mutata," it is however "mutata" very seriously; the errata are of considerable importance.

† Novum Testamentum Graece. Textum ad fidem testium criticorum recensuit, lectionum familias subiecit, e graecis codicibus manuscriptis, qui in Europae et Asiae bibliothecis reperiuntur fere omnibus, e versionibus antiquis, conciliis, sanctis Patribus et scriptoribus ecclesiasticis quibuscunque vel primo vel iterum collatis copias criticas addidit, &c. Dr. J. Mart. Augustinus Scholz. The *text* of Scholz corrected as to errata, punctuation, &c. has been twice printed in England, in "the English Hexapla," 1840, and in the "Critical Greek and English Testament," 1841; in this latter edition collations are subjoined of the texts of Griesbach and others. Although I can by no means admit that Scholz has proved the superiority of the Greek MSS. which he prefers, and although many things connected with his edition are unsatisfactory, yet it must be admitted that his *text* is really preferable to that in common use.

‡ Novum Testamentum Graece, ex recensione Caroli Lachmanni. 1831. He has since commenced another edition in which he appears to attempt more fully to carry out Bentley's plan of comparing the Greek and Latin texts: Novvm Testamentvm Graece et Latine. Carolvs Lachmannvs recensvit. Philippvs Bvttmannus Ph. F. Graecae Lectionis Avctoritates Apposvit: Tomvs Prior. 1842. If the second volume of this edition be yet published I do not know, but I have not seen it.

knew of or had attended to Lachmann's edition, although since its publication;* and to this book (see § I. 2, 3) I have first sought to apply these
principles of criticism.   I was compelled to lay aside, for a time at least,
my labour connected with the Greek Testament as a whole.†

When the present work was nearly completed, the Greek Testament of
Tischendorf was published.‡   This has certainly in the Revelation met my
judgment far more than any critical text with which I am acquainted; it led
me to examine the authorities with particular care in the places in which my
text differs from his.   Tischendorf has since edited the Codex Ephraemi
(§ III. 2, C), which was published just when the printing of the present work
(after some unavoidable delays) was about to commence.   This has been of
peculiar importance to me while giving the whole another revision; indeed
the importance of this MS. has been far more than compensation to me for
previous hinderances.   It was published just as I was meditating how I might
procure from Paris certain information as to the reading of this MS. in
several passages in which it was not cited by Wetstein.

The mode in which the critical materials were brought together and used,
will be detailed below. (See § IV. 1, 2).

---

* I paid no very particular attention to Lachmann's text after I knew of his edition in consequence of having mistaken his choice of critical materials. He has termed the authorities
eastern or *Asiatic* which others have usually called Alexandrian (and Western); hence I supposed that his critical system was in some measure identical with that of Scholz, whereas in
fact it is the direct contrary. Lachmann's new nomenclature misled me as well it might; nor
have I been alone in this; Dr. Davidson (Biblical Criticism, p. 28) says in speaking of MSS.;
—" Scholz, Lachmann, Rink, &c. favour the *Asiatic*." Lachmann is here placed in the very
juxta-position which he would wish to shun, but it is all in consequence of his own contra-
dictory nomenclature. On the whole subject of recensions and classification of MSS. a good
and lucid account will be found in Dr. Davidson's work, p. 227, *sq*.

† I still, however, have this object before me, for which I commenced my] preparations
several years ago. I still trust, "if the Lord will and I live," to prepare a manual edition of
the Greek New Testament, containing the text edited on ancient authority, entirely irrespec-
tive of modern and commonly received readings, together with a careful collation of all the
more ancient MSS. so far as they are attainable. The plan, which at a considerable time
since occurred to my mind, was to give the Greek text together with the readings of ancient
authorities *only;*—this led me to examine the principles on which such a text should be
formed, and I have no hesitation in stating that I believe the combined use of ancient MSS.
such as A B C D L &c. with versions (as witnesses of the insertion of *clauses*, &c.) would set
such a text on a satisfactory critical basis.

‡ Novum Testamentum Graece. Textum ad fidem antiquorum testium recensuit, brevem
apparatum criticum una cum variis lectionibus Elzeviriorum, Knappii, Scholzii, Lachmanni sub-
junxit; argumenta et locos parallelos indicavit; Commentationem isagogicam notatis propriis
lectionibus Edd. Stephanicae tertiae atque Millianae, Matthaeianae, Griesbachianae premisit
Aenoth. Frid. Const. Tischendorf. 1841. The Prolegomena contain a valuable discussion
on the critical principles laid down by Scholz, with a statement of the *facts* by which those
principles are controverted. In mentioning Tischendorf's name it is in a manner incumbent
to protest against his subsequent conduct as a New Testament editor;—he has published at
Paris an edition in Greek and Latin in which the Vulgate is made the standard to which the
Greek text is 'conformed in every place in which *any* MS. authority accords with the Latin
readings. He has not taken the ancient copies of the Vulgate, but the modern Clementine
text as sanctioned by Romish authority; and yet Tischendorf can elsewhere boast about the
Reformation. In a postscript which he has since appended to the unsold copies of his previous edition, (dated from Naples, the feast of St. John the Baptist, 1843), he states that his
Paris edition (meaning I believe *another* which I have not seen) was particularly intended
for the use of the French and *English;* I trust that we may be preserved from using Greek
Testaments avowedly conformed to a Romish standard, such as the Paris edition of Tischendorf now before me. No Romanist ever ventured to publish such an edition. I am
under considerable obligation to Tischendorf for his critical labours in publishing the Codex
Ephraemi, but I have felt myself obliged for the sake of truth and the integrity of God's
word to speak faithfully of his Paris edition in Greek and Latin.

d

III. SOURCES OF EMENDATION OF THE GREEK TEXT.

1. The sources of emendation of the text, or of editing it more correctly, are MSS., ancient versions, and the quotations of early writers; in other words, these are the channels through which the New Testament Scriptures, as unprinted, have been transmittted to us.

In the Revelation, since the *ancient* MSS. which we have are very few, our evidence of this kind for the true reading is proportionally scanty; the later MSS. also are comparatively not numerous; several of these afford valuable aid.

The more ancient MSS. are written in large or uncial letters, without any divisions between the words;—the later MSS. are written in *cursive* letters, with breathings and accents, the words divided;—they appear to be all of later date than the ninth century, most of them much more recent; some of these, however, (such as 38), are manifestly transcripts of a much older text. Many MSS. were corrected after they were written, and hence the difference between readings *à primâ manu*, and those proceeding *à correctore*. These corrections are often much more recent than the text, and the readings are often very inferior; sometimes corrections proceeded from the copyist himself.

Ancient versions are more to be regarded as evidences of the general contents of a book, and of its several parts, than of the *words* themselves; with respect to whole clauses their testimony is very important, and so too with regard often to more minute points; but still it is not unfrequently doubtful which of two readings a version supports; and it must also be borne in mind that versions like the original have come down to us through the hands of copyists, so that we are often glad to have recourse to the most ancient MSS. of these which we can procure.

Ancient citations would be of much more importance, if we could be sure that writers quoted from the Greek text as they had it; it is pretty certain that they often relied on their memory, and besides this the copyists and editors of their works often altered citations so as to adapt them to the readings with which they were familiar. With these cautions, such citations may be used as subsidiary evidence. (See on

this subject Dr. Davidson's " Biblical Criticism," p. 118, *sq.*)
On these accounts citations from ecclesiastical writings have
not been here given amongst the various readings, although
their testimony has not been overlooked in the formation of
the text ; in the Revelation, however, they afford singularly
little aid.

To these three sources of emendation, or rather of transmission, some have
had the temerity to add *critical conjecture;* this *may* be tolerable in editing
profane writings ; but even there it would be a great liberty if many copies of
the author were in existence.   But to use critical conjecture with regard to
the word of God is to act in a manner wholly unjustifiable.   When this is
done, then charges of innovation and want of reverence for God's holy word
may indeed be brought.   Nothing of the kind will be found in the text here
given.   I mention this expressly, because it is not long since a Greek text
was edited in this country, with a preface, in which the needlessness and
temerity of critical conjecture was strongly stated, (together with some
objections to the free use of MSS. authorities), and yet *in the text* words
were marked in a few places as "probably spurious," wholly on *conjectural*
grounds, and some suggestions of the same kind were inserted in the notes.

2. The following is a list of those Greek MSS. which contain
the Apocalypse, either in whole or in part, which are written in
large or uncial letters.

A. Codex Alexandrinus, preserved in the British Museum.   This
MS., which contains all the books of the Old and New Testaments, either
entire or mutilated, was presented by Cyrillus Lucaris, patriarch of Con-
stantinople, to king Charles I.   Its supposed date is the *fifth century*, and it
appears probable that it was written at Alexandria.   The New Testament was
published from this MS. in types cast so as in some measure to resemble the
writing of the MS. in 1786, under the editorial care of Dr. Woide, whose
prolegomena contain much valuable information relative to ancient MSS. in
general.*   The Old Testament has been also published from this MS. more
recently under the superintendence of the Rev. H. H. Baber.

This MS. contains the Apocalypse entire ; its readings present a *general
agreement* with the other very ancient authorities ; so that in those portions of
the Apocalypse which are contained in no other *ancient* copy, its readings,
especially when supported by other authorities, are entitled to considerable
attention.   For this present work the readings of this MS. have been taken
from the printed edition.

B. A MS. formerly belonging to the monks of the convent of St. Basil in
Urbe, and numbered in their library CV.   It is now, according to Scholz, in
the Vatican Library.   In Blanchini's Evangeliarium Quadruplex, Part I.

* Novum Testamentum Græcum e codice MS. Alexandrino qui Londini in Bibliotheca
Musei Britannici asservatur, descriptum a Carolo Godofredo Woide. MDCCLXXXVI.

p. DV. there is a fac-simile of the MS., which is commonly referred to the seventh century. This MS. contains homilies of Basil and Gregory of Nyssa, amongst which (from p. 249 to 268) stands the book of the Revelation. The Greek text has the accents, which are said to be *à primâ manu ;* but if a judgment may be formed from the specimen given by Blanchini, they are not placed with much precision.

A correct description and examination of this MS. is yet a desideratum ; for although it was professedly collated for Wetstein by order of Cardinal Quirini, yet the mere inspection of the variations noted, (which are given in one place in Wetstein's Greek Testament, vol. 2, p. 894–6), suffices to show either that the MS. must have many chasms, or else that it has been very imperfectly collated ; I should think it probable that *both* of these deductions were true.

I have used the collation as printed in Wetstein, where the variations of the first few verses (from Blanchini) and of the last two chapters stand in their place under the text ; the rest of the collation (from its not having arrived in time) stands as a kind of Appendix.

Care must be taken not to confound this MS. with the celebrated and very valuable Codex Vaticanus, 1209, which in the Gospels, Acts, and Epistles, is designated by Wetstein, and those who have adopted his notation, by the same letter B.* The Codex Vaticanus, 1209, is defective in the Revelation, (which has been supplied by a modern hand, see No. 91); *this* MS. is far more recent, (probably by three centuries), and much less valuable.

This MS. can of course be only regarded as an authority in places where it has been *expressly cited ;* no inference can be deduced from its silence.

C. CODEX EPHRAEMI, in the Royal Library at Paris. This MS. is so named from its being a *codex rescriptus,*† of which the later writing contains some of the works of Ephraem the Syrian. This MS. appears to have originally contained the Old and New Testaments, but it is now in a very mutilated condition. Wetstein employed a great deal of labour in deciphering the ancient writing and collating the text,—a work of no small difficulty. His collations have been used by subsequent editors, but they are now wholly superseded by the publication of the MS. itself. This took place subsequently to the preparation of the present work, and the readings thus brought to light have in several instances modified the results to which I had previously arrived, partly misled by want of evidence, partly by that which was erroneous.

Before the publication of the MS. means had been taken for bringing the ancient writing to light more effectually. This was apparently done at the instance of Fleck, who visited Paris in 1834. The MS. was subjected to a chemical process, and the object desired was very successfully accomplished.

The text of the MS. was edited by Tischendorf in 1843. He has prefixed

---

* This mistake has been actually made: from the manner in which it is mentioned in Tischendorf's Prolegomena (p. lxxix) a reader would be in great danger of identifying these very different MSS. Dr. Davidson appears to have overlooked this MS.

† Scarcity of writing materials led copyists not unfrequently to erase older MSS. in order to substitute something more modern. Of all the codices rescripti of the New Testament this is by far the most important ; the rest are mere fragments ; it is worthy of notice, however, that they all, or almost all, are authorities which confirm the readings of the other most ancient documents.

valuable critical Prolegomena, and there is an interesting fac-simile appended, exhibiting both the ancient and the more recent writing.*

This MS. is probably the most ancient of those which have come down to us that contain this book; its text exhibits a very general agreement with the Alexandrian MS., so that they serve in a great measure to confirm each other as transmitting the ancient text.   It is, however, defective in many places ; the hiati in the Revelation are the following :—

The 1st verse of chapter 1 is obliterated; it commences ὃς ἐμαρτύρησεν.

From ζήλευε οὖν καὶ μετα—iii. 19, to -κύνησαν (in προσεκύνησαν), v. 14.

From οὗτοί εἰσιν, vii. 14, to καὶ οὕτως, ix. 17.

(From vii. 17, δάκρυον to viii. 4, ἐνώπιον τοῦ Θεοῦ stands in the place of chap. x. 10, ἔφαγον to xi. 3, χιλίας; the latter passage being in consequence entirely wanting.)

From πνεύματα τρία ἀκάθαρ—xvi. 13, to παντὸς ὀρνέου, xviii. 2.

From οἱ μικροὶ, xix. 5, to the end.

[These hiati have been specified very inaccurately by Scholz.]

Hence it will be seen that about *nine* of the chapters of this book are deficient in this MS. ; the ancient vellum having been destroyed probably at the time when the parts of the book which still exist were erased for the purpose of being devoted to a new object.

Thus the Revelation has only come down to us in three ancient MSS. ; one of these (in itself the most valuable) is grievously mutilated ; another is but partially described and collated, so that in a considerable portion of this book the Alexandrian MS. is the only *ancient MS.* authority to which we can have recourse.

3. The following is a list of the Greek MSS. in *cursive* letters which contain the Revelation.

(1.) A MS. formerly belonging to Reuchlin ; what has now become of it is wholly unknown.   It was the only one of the Revelation used by Erasmus for his first edition ; (§ II. 5) ; he describes it as very ancient : it appears, however, to have had a commentary (either that of Arethas or Andreas) with the text interspersed, so that Erasmus had to separate as well as he could the Greek words which belong to the text ; in doing this he was aided by the Vulgate Latin.   This MS. appears to have wanted the six concluding verses.   Its readings can only be known from the first edition of Erasmus.

(2.) CODEX REGIUS 237 (formerly 2869) in the Royal Library at Paris. It contains the Acts, Epistles, and Revelation, with Scholia.   It was one of the MSS. used by Robt. Stephens for his third edition.   He denotes it ιε΄. Collated by Wetstein, and examined by Scholz.   It is supposed to belong to the tenth century.

(3.) The MS. used by Stephens, ις΄, now unknown.   The readings have been taken from the margin of Stephens's third edition.

* Codex Ephraemi Syri Rescriptus sive Fragmenta Novi Testamenti e codice Graeco Parisiensi celeberrimo quinti ut videtur post Christum seculi; eruit atque edidit Constantinus Tischendorf. 1843.

(4.) CODEX REGIUS 219 (formerly 1886) at Paris, on vellum. It contains the Acts, Epistles, and Revelation, with Scholia. Of the tenth century, or later. Collated by Wetstein.

(5.) CODICES used by Laurentius Valla, (who died in 1458). These are cited in his annotations published by Erasmus in 1505. What these MSS. were, and where they now are, is wholly unknown.

(6.) CODEX BAROCCIANUS 3, (in the Bodleian Library), on vellum. It contains part of the Acts, the Epistles, and the Revelation. In the latter book it is defective from· chap. 17. 10, to 18. 7, and also the three last chapters. Perhaps of the twelfth century.

(7.) CODEX HARLEIANUS 5537, on vellum. It contains the Acts, Epistles, and Revelation. It was written in the year 1087. It appears to be one of the best MSS. of the Revelation.

(8.) CODEX HARLEIANUS 5778, on vellum. It contains the Acts, Epistles, and Revelation; in this last book the last lines are defaced.

(9.) CODEX BODLEIANUS 131, (formerly Huntingdon). It contains the Acts, Epistles, and Revelation. Perhaps of the thirteenth century.

(10.) CODEX MORI 1, (now in the Cambridge Public Library D d 8, 49); it contains the Gospels written in 1297, and the Revelation by a more modern hand.

(11.) CODEX PETAVII 2. It contains the Acts, Epistles, and Revelation. The MS. appears to be much mutilated.

(12.) CODEX ALEX. VAT. 179, on vellum. It contains the Acts, Epistles, and Revelation, and has been but imperfectly collated. It is defective from 17. 9, to 14. Cent. XI. [Wetstein, Birch.]

(13.) CODEX SEIDELIANUS, on vellum. It contains the Acts, Epistles, and Revelation. Cent. XI. Defective from 18. 3—13.

(14.) CODEX LEICESTRENSIS. A MS. partly on vellum, partly on paper, containing the New Testament, but mutilated in parts. Cent. XIV. In the Revelation it ends at chap. 21. 1.

(15.) A fragment of the third and fourth chapters, written on a MS. of the four Gospels, CODEX BASILIENSIS. B. vi. 21.

(16.) CODEX UFFENBACHIANUS. It contains the Acts, Epistles, and Revelation. Cent. XV.

(17.) CODEX COISLINIANUS 199, on vellum. It contains the whole of the New Testament. Cent. XI.

(18.) CODEX COISLINIANUS 202, partly on vellum, partly on cotton paper. It contains the Acts, Epistles, and Revelation, the latter book being written on vellum. Cent. XI.

(19.) CODEX COISLINIANUS 205, on vellum. It contains the Acts, Epistles, and Revelation, written in the year 1079. The commencement of the Revelation, (as far as 2. 5), has been supplied by a later hand.

(20.) CODEX VAT. 2080, (formerly Monachorum S. Basilii, cxix.), Blanchini gives the *two last verses* of this MS. (Wetstein cites 20. 21. on chap. 22, ver. 11, perhaps for 21. 22.)

(21.)} Wetstein gives under these numbers two French MSS. cited by
(22.)} Bentley in his specimen of the last chapter of the Revelation.

Scholz has substitued for these, two Codices Vallicelliani D 20, & B 86 *but he has not once cited them;* the references which he gives to 21 and 22 are taken from Wetstein.

(23.) Wetstein gives under this number *Codex Mediceus*, a MS. or MSS., the readings of which were written by some unknown Dutchman on the margin of a Greek Testament, and thus came into Wetstein's hands. What this MS. may be, is very doubtful. (See Birch, Var. Lect. in Apoc. p. xvii.) Scholz substitutes for this MS. Coisl. 200; but in the only places in which he cites the number 23, he gives the readings of the Codex Mediceus, *taken from Wetstein.*

(24.) Codex Vat. 2062, (formerly Bas. 101). Part of the two last *verses* (not *chapters* as stated by Scholz) are cited by Blanchini; Scholz speaks of having collated the MS., but he only cites it *seven* times.

(25.) Codex Palat. Vat. 171, on vellum. It contains the whole of the New Testament. Cent. XIV. Partially collated. [Birch.]

(26.) Codex Wakianus 1, on vellum. It contains the Revelation and other parts of the New Testament. Cent. XI.

(27.) Codex Wakianus 2, on vellum. It contains great part of the New Testament. Cent. XI. or XII.

(28.) Codex Baroccianus 48, on paper. It contains the Revelation as far as chap. xvii. 6.

[All the following MSS. are additions to Wetstein's list.]

(29.) Codex Harleianus, 5613, on paper. It contains the Acts, Epistles, and Revelation, written in the year 1407. It is defective from chap. 22. 2, ἕκαστον κάρπον to the end. [Griesbach.]*

(30.) Codex Guelpherbytanus XVI. 7, on paper. It contains the Acts, Epistles, and Revelation. Cent. XIV. Collated by Knittel, whose collation was republished by *Matthæi* in his Greek Testament, vol. 12.

(31.) Codex Harl. 5678, on paper. It contains Revelation and other works. Cent. XV. A collation of the eight first chapters was communicated to *Griesbach*, who inserted the readings in his second edition.

(32.) Codex Dresdensis, on vellum. It contains Revelation. Cent. XV. Collated by *Matthæi*, who designates it by the letter t.

(33.) Codex Vindobonensis; Lambecii, 1. It contains the Old and New Testaments in Greek. Cent. XII. or XIII. The New Testament of this MS. was published by *Alter* in 1787. In the Revelation it is deficient from chap. 13. 5, to 14. 8. From chap. 15. 7, to 17. 2. From chap. 18, 10, to 19. 15. It ends with λυθήσεται, 20. 7. The text of Alter's edition of this MS. was collated for this work.

(34.) Codex Vindobonensis; Lambecii 34, on vellum. It contains the Acts, Epistles, and Revelation. Cent. XII. This MS. is not mutilated in the Revelation as is erroneously stated by Griesbach and Scholz: the deficiencies of 34 are supplied in *Alter's* edition from this MS., a collation of which with the text of the edition is given at the end of vol. 2.

(35.) Codex Vindobonensis; Lambecii 248, on vellum. Cent. XIV. It contains the Revelation with a commentary, besides other works; collated with the text of 33 by *Alter*.

(36.) Codex Vindobonensis; Forlosiæ 29, on vellum. It contains the Revelation with a commentary. Cent. XIV. It ends at 19. 20. Collated by *Alter* with 33.

* Symbolae Criticae, vol. 2, p. 191.

(37.) CODEX VAT. 366, on paper. It contains the Acts, Epistles, and Revelation. Cent. XIII. Collated by *Birch.**

(38.) CODEX VAT. 579, on cotton paper. It contains the Revelation with some other works. Cent. XIII. This MS. appears to be of more importance and authority than any of the others which are written in cursive characters : this is shown by the very marked agreement between it and the most ancient MSS. A & C ; this is often manifested by the readings which are common only to this MS., and one or both of those. Hence, as C is defective in so considerable a part of this book, the testimony of this MS. is very important as a witness of the ancient text. Collated by *Birch*, inspected by Scholz.

(39.) CODEX VAT. 1136, on vellum. It contains the Epistles of St. Paul and the Revelation. Cent. XIII. It is defective at the beginning as far as 4. 7; and also from 6. 18, to 13. 11. Collated by *Birch*, inspected by Scholz.

(40.) CODEX VAT. 1160, on vellum. It contains the whole of the New Testament. Cent. XI. Collated by *Birch*, inspected by Scholz.

(41.) CODEX ALEX. VAT. 68, on paper. It contains the Revelation with some other works. Cent. XIV. Collated by *Birch*, inspected by Scholz.

(42.) CODEX PIO. VAT. 50, on vellum. It contains the Acts, Epistles, and Revelation. Cent. XII. Collated by *Birch*, inspected by Scholz.

(43.) CODEX BARBERINUS 23, on vellum. It contains amongst other works a fragment of the Revelation from chap. 14. 17, to 18. 20. Cent. XIV. Collated by *Birch*, inspected by Scholz.

(44.) CODEX BORGIÆ, on vellum. It contains the Acts, Epistles, and Revelation. Cent. XIII. Collated by Engelbreth, (whose collation is published by *Birch*), and inspected by Scholz.

(45.) CODEX LAURENTIANUS, IV. 32, on vellum. It contains the Acts, Epistles, and Revelation, written in the year 1093. The three first chapters of the Revelation were collated by *Birch*.

(46.) CODEX VENETUS 10, on vellum. It contains the whole of the New Testament. Cent. XV. Collated in select places by Engelbreth, whose collation was published by *Birch*.

(47.) CODEX DRESDENSIS, (Matthæi k), on vellum. It contains the whole of the New Testament. Cent. XI. Collated by *Matthæi*.†

(48.) CODEX MOSQUENSIS 380, (Matthæi l), on vellum. It contains the whole of the New Testament. Cent. XII. Collated by *Matthæi*.

(49.) CODEX MOSQUENSIS 67, (Matthæi o), on paper. It contains the Revelation, with a Commentary, besides other works. Cent. XV. Collated by *Matthæi*.

(50.) CODEX MOSQUENSIS 206, (Matthæi p), partly on vellum, partly on paper. It contains the Revelation, and other works. Cent. XV.

(50².) In Scholz's list, see 90.

---

* Variae Lectiones ad Textum Apocalypseos ex Codd. graecis MSS. Bibliothecae Vaticanae, Barberinianae, Borgianae Velitris, Laurentianae atque S. Marci Venetorum, collectae et editae ab Andrea Birch. Hauniæ. 1800.

† Joannis Apocalypsis Graece et Latine. Ex codicibus nvnqvam antea examinatis edidit et animadversiones criticas adiecit Christianvs Fridericvs Matthaei. 1785. This is the twelfth volume of Matthaei's larger Greek Test. (the seventh in the order of publication); from this have been taken the collations of 30. 32. 47—50. 90.

The MSS. from 51 to 89 inclusive have been used by Scholz only. In the following list those only are mentioned which he sometimes actually cites ; the greater part merely occupying a place in his catalogue, without any readings being given so as to form a judgment of the nature of the MSS. themselves.* Scholz numbers the next MS. after 86, 86² ; this I call 89. For the libraries in which the *twenty-nine* uncited MSS. are to be found, see Scholz's list.

(51.) Codex Regius (Paris) 47 (formerly 2241). It contains the New Testament, written in the year 1364. Scholz states that he has collated the Revelation entirely: he has cited from it thirty-seven readings in the two first chapters, and thirty-six in the rest of the book.

(52—54 uncited.)

(55.) Codex Regius 101, (formerly 2869), on cotton paper. It contains the Acts, Epistles, and Revelation. Cent. XIII. Collated *cursim* by Scholz, who cites from it twenty-two readings in chap. 1, and twenty-eight in the rest of the book.

(56.) Codex Regius 102 A, on vellum. It contains the Acts, Epistles, and Revelation ; this latter book of Cent. XIII. collated *cursim* by Scholz, who cites from it five readings.

(57—63 uncited.)

(64.) Codex Regius 224, (formerly 2245²), on vellum. It contains St. Paul's Epistles and Revelation. Cent. XI. Scholz cites from it thirty-three readings, all in the first two chapters.

(65—67 uncited.)

(68.) Codex Vat. 1904, on vellum. Some fragments. Cent. XI. Containing Revelation 7. 17 ;—8. 12 ; and 20. 1, to the end. Scholz cites fourteen readings.

(69.) Codex Vat. Ottob. 258, on paper. It contains the Acts, Epistles, and Revelation, with a Latin version. Cent. XIII. and XIV. Defective in the latter part of the Revelation. Cited by Scholz sixty times in the first two chapters, and twice afterwards.

(70—79 uncited.)

(80.) Codex Monacensis 544, on cotton paper. It contains the Revelation and a commentary. Cent. XIV. Cited by Scholz thirty-three times.

(81 uncited.)

(82.) Codex Monacensis 211, on vellum. It contains the Acts, Epistles, and Revelation. Cent. XI. Cited by Scholz sixty-four times in the two first chapters, and eighteen times in other places.

---

* The catalogue of MSS. in Scholz's Greek Testament is very valuable as indicating the places in which they may be found for future use. He cites, however, but a few of those which no one had previously collated. He states that he has entirely collated many from which he has printed very few extracts in his notes;—many citations would have occupied too much room on the pages of his Greek Testament. It would be well if he were to publish his own collations apart from the text and from all other critical materials in the same manner as was done by Birch; we should then know what he actually performed, and be able rightly to appreciate his labour as a collator, in which he probably stands much higher than as a critical editor. In some respects Scholz has erred from too close a dependence upon Griesbach's edition even in its mere errata, to these he has even given in some places *various readings*.

(83—85 uncited.)*

(86.) A MS. (10) in the Greek convent of St. Saba in Judæa, on vellum. It contains the New Testament. Cited three times by Scholz in the beginning of the Revelation.

(86² see 89 ; 87 uncited.)

(88.) CODEX VENETUS 5, on vellum. It contains the Old and New Testaments. Cent. XV. Scholz cites in the Revelation forty-seven readings, all of which, except two, are in the two first chapters.

(89 or 86² uncited.)

(90.) CODEX MOSQUENSIS (Matthæi r, Sch. 50²) on vellum. It contains the Revelation. Cent. X. Collated by *Matthæi*.

(91.) CODEX VAT. 1209. The modern supplement to this most ancient and important MS.; the Revelation is said to have been copied from a MS. which formerly belonged to Card. Bessarion. Cent. XV. The whole of this MS., both ancient and modern, was collated for Bentley, and the collation was published by Ford, in the Appendix to the Codex Alexandrinus, Oxford, 1799, and it has been used throughout for this work.

(92.) CODEX MONTFORTIANUS, preserved in Trinity College, Dublin. This MS., which contains the New Testament, is the Codex Britannicus, on the authority of which Erasmus inserted in his third edition the text 1 John 5. 7. When the authenticity of that text was still defended by critics, this MS. acquired a peculiar degree of celebrity. It was probably written in the sixteenth century, and though in some places (as 1 John 5. 7) the Latin Vulgate may have lent its aid, yet in general it was undoubtedly copied from Greek Manuscripts. It has the *Latin* chapters, and it is strongly suspected that it was written out for the purpose of producing a MS. which should contain 1 John 5. 7, in Greek; this text stands in the MS. in wholly incorrect phraseology, with the article omitted, just as might be expected from an ignorant transcriber forming the Greek text from the Latin. The collation of a considerable part of this MS. was published by Dr. Barrett in the Appendix to the Dublin Codex Rescriptus, and from this I have taken the readings of the Revelation. This MS. has never before been used for this book in any critical edition; the same is likewise the case with 91, except its having been a few times cited by Tischendorf.

This catalogue of MSS. has been drawn up from Wetstein, the collations of different MSS. as published, Marsh's Michælis, and Scholz.

4. The Manuscript Authorities may be divided into *four* classes :—

a. Perfect MSS. which have been collated throughout.

 A. 2. 4. 7. 8. 9. 10. 16. 17. 18. 19. 26. 27. 30. 32. 34. 35. 37. 38. 40. 41. 42. 47. 48. 49. 50. 90. 91. 92. = 29.

---

* Scholz on his critical principles would have no particular regard to the readings of A. & C. or of a MS. which mostly agrees with them; had it been otherwise he would certainly have given many citations from 83, for he says of it, "Textus ab eo codd. A. C. rarissime recedit." Tischendorf (Prolegomena, p. xlvi.) speaks of 83 as one of the more important MSS. of this book; probably from Scholz's testimony, but he may have other information relative to this MS.

β. MSS. with defects which are noted, but which have been collated throughout in the parts where they are perfect ; also some MSS. of which a *known
part* has been collated.
    C. 6. 13. 14. 15. 28. 29. 33. 36. 39. 43. 45. = 12.
γ. MSS. which are only occasionally cited ; either partially collated or partially defective ; the *silence* of these MSS., with regard to any particular
reading, cannot of course be regarded as affording any evidence.
    B. 1. 3. 5. 11. 12. 20. 21. 22. 23. 24. 25. 31. 44. 46. 51. 55. 56. 64. 68.
        69. 80. 82. 86. 88. = 25.
δ. MSS. which are known to exist, but are altogether uncited.
    52. 53. 54. 57. 58. 59. 60. 61. 62. 63. 65. 66. 67. 70. 71. 72. 73. 74. 75.
        76. 77. 78. 79. 81. 83. 84. 85. 87. 89. = 29.
    To these may be added Scholz's 21. 22. 23.
    The uncial MSS., A. B. C., are cited in the various readings to the present
work by these designations ; the other MSS., when many support a particular
reading, are cited by their classes, *e. g.* α 17. β 7. γ 3., would imply so many
MSS. of these several classes as containing the cited reading ; when but a
few MSS. support a reading, they are cited *nominatim.*

5. List of the Ancient Versions which contain the Revelation.

    1. The Latin Vulgate.   This version executed by Jerome about the end of
the 4th century, is that still used by the Church of Rome.   It was declared
authentic by the Council of Trent ;—the edition regarded as the standard by
Romanists was issued by Clement VIII. in 1592.   This version is exceedingly
useful as an authority in the textual criticism of the New Testament.   It is
true that in the lapse of years, it has suffered in many respects from transcription, but even as it is it has great value.   Citations of MSS. of this version have been taken from Wetstein, Griesbach, and Matthæi.
    A collation of a very ancient MS. of the Vulgate was published by Fleck
in 1840 ;* this MS., *Codex Amiatinus*, preserved at Florence, appears to have
been written in the 6th century ; it often confirms the readings of the most
ancient Greek MSS.
    The readings of the *Codex Toletanus* are cited by Griesbach from Blan-
chini, Vindiciæ Canonicarum Scripturarum.
    The Codex Harleianus, 1772, contains the Epistles and Revelation (to chap.
14. 16) in Latin ; it appears to be an Ante-hieronymian version, altered in
many places so as to be conformed to more modern readings.   The collation given in Griesbach's Symbolæ Criticæ, has been here used.†

    2. The Coptic Version, probably executed in the 3rd or 4th century ;—

---

* Novum Testamentum Vulgatae Editionis . . . . cum variantibus in margine lectionibus
Antiquissimi et Praestantissimi Codicis olim Monasterii montis Amiatae in Etruria, nunc
Bibliothecae Florentinae Laurentianae Mediceae: saec. VI. P. Chr. Scripti. Praemissa est
Commentatio de codice Amiatino et versione Latina Vulgata.   Edente Ferdinando Flo-
rente Fleck.   1840.

    † I have purposely omitted the readings of the ancient Latin version cited by Sabatier out
of Primasius ;—many of the readings so cited are undoubtedly really ancient, but many of them
have been *indubitably* modernized,—perhaps by transcribers and editors.

published by Wilkins, 1716 ; the readings of this version have been principally adopted from Wetstein and Griesbach. [Scholz gives a list of fragments of the Sahidic Version in the Borgian MSS., some of which contain
part of the Revelation, but he cites no readings from them in this book.]

3. The Æthiopic Version, probably executed in the 4th century, the readings of this translation have here been taken from Wetstein and Griesbach.

4. The Syriac Version of the Revelation ; this must not be confounded
with the *Peshito*, executed probably in the 2nd century, in which this book
forms no part : the version of the Revelation may perhaps be assigned to the
6th century.

It is uncertain whether the Philoxenian, or later Syriac Version (made in
the year 508), contained this book ; if it did, it is no longer extant.

5. The Armenian Version ; this was completed in the year 410 by Miesrob
and his coadjutors. It was collated for Griesbach, by Bredencamp of
Hamburgh.

6. The Arabic Versions. There are two which contain the Revelation,
that in Walton's Polyglott, and that published by Erpenius, in 1616. Both
of these versions were probably made in the 7th century or later. The readings have here been taken from Wetstein and Griesbach.

7. The Slavonic Version ; this was made in the 9th century, by Cyrillus
and Methodius. The printed editions, as well as several MSS., (principally
of the Revelation), were collated for Griesbach, by Dobrowsky of Prague.

IV. MODE OF ARRANGING THE CRITICAL MATERIALS IN PREPARING THIS EDITION.

1. In order to form an estimate of the evidence with regard
to each particular reading, it was needful to bring them all
together into such a form as to admit of their being examined
with facility. Griesbach in his edition *selected* some of Wetstein's readings, to which he added others from different
sources ; Scholz followed Griesbach, and added in this book
402 readings from *ten* of the MSS. which he was the first to examine. But in using Griesbach's and Scholz's editions, I soon
found that in not a few places the great mass of authorities for
a reading were altogether overlooked ; a *few* modern copies are
sometimes cited for a reading in this book, which is really that
of ancient MSS. A. or C., and *many* of the more recent copies ;
hence it became evident that it would not do to rely on the

readings given in either of these editions, and therefore I had resort to the following plan : —

i. Wetstein's various readings were taken as a basis, and carefully examined and compared with any other collations of the MSS. cited by him.   To this end the published Alexandrian MS. was used ; the readings of B. were copied from Wetstein's Appendix; the readings of Stephens's *ις'* were taken from the margin of his edition ; the MSS. in Wetstein's list, which have since been examined by Birch or Scholz, were compared as to their extracts with the citations previously given.

ij. The various readings of Wetstein having been thus revised, those found in other MSS. were added ; they were always if possible taken from the readings published by the actual collator.   29 from Griesbach ; 30 from Knittel as reprinted by Matthæi ; 31 from Griesbach ; 32 from Matthæi ; 33—36 from Alter ; 37—46 Birch ; 47—50 Matthæi ; then the four hundred and two citations given by Scholz from the MSS. which he collated took their place ; 90 from Matthæi ; 91 from the collation published by Ford ; 92 from that by Barrett.

In doing this it was necessary for me to ascertain if possible what edition was used by the collator, and to keep the same before me while copying his citations.   To this end it was necessary to use Stephens's third edition ; the Elzevir, 1624 ; Bp. Fell's, 1675 ; Mill's, 1707 ; and also that of Cephalæus, 1524.

iij. A copious list of authorities having been thus made out, the whole was revised so as to verify every citation.   The number of references to MSS. altogether had amounted to about 40,000, of which but a very small proportion had been found ready to my hand in Scholz.   This number collected from so many different sources will give some idea of the unexpected labour of comparison ; I say *unexpected* because I had supposed that little more would be needed than the revision of Scholz's various readings with Griesbach and Wetstein ; the delay caused by the transcription and verification of *forty thousand* citations had not entered into my calculations, but when it was found needful I was glad to undertake whatever might tend to give correctness and completeness to the work.

iv. The various readings from ancient versions were next examined, and (when it appeared necessary) corrected, particular care being taken to notice what support was thus given to readings which had not been previously cited from MSS.

v. The Complutensian Polyglott was twice collated, as also was the first edition of Erasmus, in order that the readings of these primary editions, made from MSS. now inaccessible, might be given accurately.

The *data* having been thus collected, it remained for me to use them in forming a critical text.

2. In forming the Text, no *prescriptive right* was allowed to the Received Text ; the principles on which readings were

approved, were the same that I should have adopted, had the
critical materials been before me without such a thing as a
printed edition being in existence ;—in fact, I put myself in the
place in which the Complutensian editors or Erasmus would
have been, had they the various collations before them; and it
was now my place to act as they, according to my judgment,
ought in such circumstances to have acted.

I had, previous to my revision and collection of the various
readings of this book, prepared a kind of rough draught of this
Greek text, (§ I. 3); this had been formed in order to make
from it an English translation, before I felt it to be indis-
pensable that such a translation should be accompanied by
the original.

This draught of a Greek text was now altogether thrown
aside, and the whole was wrought *de novo* from my arranged
critical materials.

The following are the principal rules by which I judged of
various readings in forming the text:—

(1.) Whatever rests on the *unanimous* consent of MSS. both ancient and
modern, and versions must of course be taken as an integral and unquestionable portion of the text.

(2.) In cases of variation of reading, that is to be preferred *cæteris paribus*
which is supported by the nearest approximation to unanimous testimony.

(3.) The authority of *ancient* MSS. (A. C.) is superior to that of the whole
mass of *modern* copies;

(4.) But there may be cases in which the most ancient MSS. agree in a
certainly incorrect reading; this may be shown by such reading being altogether incongruous, entirely unsupported by ancient versions, and being one
which might naturally arise from transcriptural error ; this is particularly the
case with regard to interchange of vowels.

(5.) In doubtful cases the testimony of ancient versions is a very valuable
auxiliary ; particularly with regard to the insertion or the non-insertion of
members of sentences or important words. The versions, however, in the
book of Revelation are generally speaking in a much worse condition than in
other parts of the New Testament.

(6.) A reading is to be rejected which is found only in a few modern
copies.

(7.) A reading is to be rejected which appears clearly to have sprung from
one which is well supported by authorities of all classes.

(8.) Omissions δι᾽ ὁμοιοτέλευτον may be found even in the oldest
and best MSS., such readings would be regarded as mere errata.

(9.) Generally speaking a *more difficult* reading, *cæteris paribus* as to evidence, is to be preferred to one which is altogether *easy;* " *Proclivi Lectioni præstat ardua.*" Bengel. Transcribers would naturally change that which is obscure for that which is simple, and not *vice versâ.*

(10.) But a more simple reading may be supported by evidence so full that the more difficult reading must be attributed to the mere error of a transcriber. In the Revelation the readings which appear ungrammatical must be referred to the class of *difficult readings.* The same remarks will hold good with regard to passages which are found in some copies in a more ample form than in others,—the shorter reading being *primâ facie* the more probable.

(11.) A reading may justly be suspected which appears to have been inserted from another part of the New Testament. This applies especially to the three first Gospels, but there are also instances in the Revelation. The same remark will apply to a *verbal agreement* produced in different parts by transcribers ; in such cases the more ancient copies afford great aid.

(12.) In cases of *great difficulty* the most ancient MSS. are especially to be relied on ; in cases in which *probabilities* alone can be arrived at, such probabilities should be stated; this may apply to *insertion, omission,* or the balance of authority between two conflicting readings.*

I may here again remark that I believe it to be the privilege and duty of a Christian editor to pray that he may be enabled to collect the evidence which is needful, and to form a right judgment on evidence so collected. It is true that this will not make him infallible ; but just as in every matter of daily life it is our place to pray for Divine guidance that we may act as disciples of Christ, and just as every Christian must acknowledge that this has been often vouchsafed to him, so surely we may seek in this matter to be guided aright in judgment on evidence, both as to the principles and their application in particular instances. Whatever *approximation* to truth may be made in the statement of results or probabilities may be thus thankfully ascribed to Him who can bestow the needful diligence, application, and vigilance.

Thus it will be seen that the text of the Revelation as here given is substantially that of the most ancient MSS.; the authority of which has been followed, except in cases in which there was a palpable reason to the contrary.

3. On these principles the text was formed, and to this there is subjoined in the inner margin those readings of the " Received Text," from which those here given differ; and also readings which are supported by *probable* authorities, though inferior in my judgment to those adopted in the text, these are marked ∾ : cases in which the omission of certain words is very probable,

---

* In connection with this subject see also the remarks on the *causes* of various readings, ♦. II. 2.

are indicated by brackets; when less probable, by dotted brackets.

4. To these are subjoined a selection of various readings, with the authorities compendiously stated, (§ III. 4): in making this selection from the mass that was before me, I acted on the principle of choosing (1.) those which are the authorities for the text as here given; (2.) those which are supported by any ancient copies; (3.) those which are supported by several copies; and (4.) those which are found in the Complutensian edition, and the first of Erasmus.

In all the various readings those of the "Received Text" stand first; when such readings differ from the text here given, an asterisk (*) is prefixed. This mark will indicate at once the places in which the Received Text has not been followed, and the authorities which are opposed to it.

There will be no difficulty in finding what MSS. read differently from those cited, as the amount of those entirely collated is given, and an enumeration of all of each class will be found in § III. 4.

It may, however, be well to remark that too much must not be attributed to the *silence* of a collator as to a particular reading; it is often far from being conclusive.

All the readings of the most ancient MSS. are given, except a few which relate wholly to matters of orthography which seemed unworthy of being noticed; such as the continual insertion of ν ἐφελκυστικὸν, as in ἐμαρτύρησεΝ τὸν; it is a matter of question whether in the Greek Testament this ν ought always to be inserted or not,* the text is otherwise wholly unaffected by it. νικοῦντι for νικῶντι and other similar forms have also been unnoticed as being mere orthographical errors.

I do not wish to present the text here given in such a manner as to seem to press it dogmatically; the results to which my own mind has come are stated, and the evidence on which such conclusions rest is also presented; so that the Christian reader may have the opportunity of *weighing* the whole matter and forming his own judgment: one thing I ask,—that no one will suppose that he is competent without any previous knowledge of the subject, to form a hasty opinion on the readings which he may examine.

---

    * This νῦ ἐφελκυστικὸν is inserted throughout by Lachmann and Tischendorf; it is of little importance in itself, but as found in the more ancient copies it cannot be looked at as an unsuitable insertion. A reader can omit or insert such a little orthographical distinction just as he may see fit.

V. CONCLUDING MEMORANDA.

There are some subjects which it is proper to notice in this place, partly relating to critical detail, and partly to other matters.

1. A list of the passages in which the MSS. A. and C. have not been followed where they unite in a reading.

READING ADOPTED.	READING IN A. & C.
1. 5. λούσαντι	λύσαντι ∿; a reading which has a good deal of probability, as the vowels might have been interchanged either way; but it is much less supported by *Versions*; and also as to sense, it is the *easier* reading.
11. Θυάτειρα	Θυάτειραν (a mere orthographical error.)
13. ἐν μέσῳ	ἐμμέσῳ (a mere orthographical error.)
χρυσῆν	-σᾶν (mere orthographical variation.)
15. πεπυρωμένοι	-νης (mere erratum.)
2. 1. τῆς	τῷ (see the series of addresses; the most ancient MSS. often give a similar ending to two following words; see the passage.)
ἐν μέσῳ	ἐμμέσῳ (mere orthographical error.)
χρυσῶν	-σεῶν (mere orthographical variation.)
13. πιστὸς	πιστός μου
3. 9. δίδωμι	διδῶ (orthographical error.)
6. 6. ἐν μέσῳ	ἐμμέσῳ („)
11. 18. τοῖς μικροῖς καὶ τοῖς μεγαλοῖς	τοὺς μικροὺς κ. τοὺς μεγαλούς. (interchange of vowels.)
12. 2. κράζει	κράζει καὶ
5. ἄῤῥενα	ἄρσεν
13. 7. καὶ ἐδόθη ... νικῆσαι αὐτους	omitted from the similar beginning of two clauses; the transcriber's eye must have passed from one καὶ ἐδόθη to the other.
8. ὄνομα	ὄνομα αὐτοῦ ∿
14. ὃ	ὃς ∿
15. αὐτῷ	αὐτῇ (mere erratum.)
14. 1. ἑστὼς	ἑστὸς (mere interchange of vowels.)
4. ὑπάγῃ	-γει (η and ει are often confounded in MSS.)
15. 4. δοξάσῃ	-σει

f

READING ADOPTED.	READING IN A. & C.
6. λίνον	λίθον (a singular erratum, found in several MSS.)
18. 3. πεπώκασι	πέπτωκαν
16. μαργαρίταις . . .	-τῃ

These *twenty-three* passages are all the places in which the consenting testimony of A. C. is not followed, besides a few most unimportant cases of orthography; and indeed about half those here given are little more than variations in this respect. Also in some passages an *omission* in these two MSS. is marked as *probable*, the word or words being in brackets in the text: these passages are ii. 5, iii. 2, 3, vii. 5—8, 9, x. 4, xiv. 4, 5, xviii. 3.

Besides these passages there are others in which A. & C. *differ*, and in which neither of them is followed; also those in which one of the two is followed; also passages in the parts in which C. is defective in which A. is not followed;—it did not appear necessary to draw up a list of these classes of passages, as the especial object of that here given is to show how *rarely* the most ancient copies *agree* in a reading which is either false or improbable, or not sufficiently certain.

2. Variations of the Elzevir text, 1624, and that of Stephens's 3rd edition, 1550.

The "Received Text" is a name commonly given to the Elzevir editions, to the second of which (1633) the editor or printer has appended the appellation "Textus ab omnibus receptus." The common editions of the Greek Testament follow either these editions or that of Stephens, 1550. The readings of the first Elzevir edition, 1624, have been placed in brackets in the inner margin when they differ from the text adopted; for purposes of reference a list is here given of the places in which the text of Stephens, 1550, differs from the Elzevir editions. In all of these places the Stephanic reading follows Erasmus.

ELZEVIR.	STEPHENS.
2. 5. ταχύ	τάχει
14. τὸν Βαλ.	ἐν τῷ Βαλ.
3. 1. ἑπτὰ (1st)	om.
12. ἡ καταβαίνει	ἡ καταβαίνουσα
4. 3. ὁμοία	ὅμοιος
10. προσκυνήσουσι . . .	προσκυνοῦσι
βαλοῦσι	βάλλουσι
5. 11. καὶ ἦν . . . μυριάδων .	om.
7. 3. σφραγίσωμεν	-ζωμεν
10. τῷ Θεῷ ἡμῶν τῷ καθημένῳ ἐπὶ τοῦ θρόνου	τῷ καθ. ἐπὶ τ. θρόνου τοῦ Θ. ἡμῶν.

Elzevir.	Stephens.
8. 5. τὸν . . . αὐτὸν . . .	τὸ . . . αὐτὸ
11. τῶν ὑδάτων	om.
11. 1. καὶ ὁ ἄγγελος εἰστήκει .	om.
2. ἔξωθεν	ἔσωθεν
13. 3. ἐθαύμασεν ὅλη ἡ γῆ . .	ἐθαυμάσθη ἐν ὅλῃ τῇ γῇ
5. πόλεμον ποι.	om. πόλεμον
14. 18. τῆς ἀμπέλου	om.
16. 14. ἃ ἐκπορεύεται	ἐκπορεύεσθαι
19. 1. ὡς	om.
6. λεγόντων	λέγοντας
14. τὰ ἐν	om. τὰ
20. 4. τῇ εἰκόνι	τὴν εἰκόνα
τοῦ Χριστοῦ	om. τοῦ
21. 16. σταδίους	σταδίων
22. 8. ἔπεσον	ἔπεσα

It may also be noticed that in Rev. 16. 5, Elz. 1624, has the reading ὅσιος, while that of 1633 has ἐσόμενος; this latter reading was adopted from Beza and is followed by our Authorised Version; it is not found in any *known* MS.

I believe that the comparison given above (which was made from actual collation) is more exact than any that has been published. Mill noticed *twelve* places in the whole New Testament in which these two texts differed; Wetstein pointed out several more. Birch in his collations gives a list of the variations; by comparison I find that he has inserted several incorrectly, the two texts *agreeing* precisely in the places cited: he probably used some *reprints* of the two texts which were not quite accurate:—he has also omitted several readings. In comparing this list with Tischendorf's (Prolegomena, p. lxiij), I find that he has omitted *nine* of the passages here given.

Most collations of Greek MSS. have been made with one or the other of these two texts or those which spring from them; and this it is which makes it of importance to know where they differ; because there is otherwise considerable danger of falling into error as to the readings which we may suppose to be found in MSS.

3. The last six verses from the 1st edition of Erasmus, 1516.

The last six verses of this book, (or rather perhaps the latter half of ver. 16, and the whole of the five which follow), having been supplied by Erasmus in his first edition by a *retranslation* from the Latin, it may be well to give them in this place, in order to show that some readings which rest *solely* upon this *guess-work* authority were not excluded by Erasmus even after he had seen the Complutensian Polyglott, and hence they are still found in the copies commonly used.

I give the text of Erasmus *between* the Complutensian and that here
adopted, indicating the latter as agreeing with both, or else specifying it when
necessary.

C. ἐγώ ιησούς ἔπεμψα τον ἀγγελόν μου μαρτυρήσαι υμίν ταῦτα
E. Ἐγὼ ΙΗΣΟΥΣ ἔπεμψα τὸν ἄγγελόν μου μαρτυρῆσαι ὑμῖν ταῦτα
T. „   „   „   „   „   „   „   „   „

C. ἐπί ταις ἐκκλησίαις. ἐγώ εἰμί η ρίζα και το γένος του δαυίδ,
E. — ταῖς ἐκκλησίαις. ἐγὼ εἰμῒ — ρίζα καὶ τὸ γένος του δαβίδ,
T. ἐν „   „   „   „ ἡ „   „   „   „ — Δαυὶδ

C. ο αστήρ ο λαμπρός — ο πρωϊνός. και το πνεύμα και η
E. ὁ ἀστὴρ — λαμπρός, καὶ — ὀρθρινὸς. καὶ τὸ πνεῦμα καὶ ἡ
T. „   „ ὁ „   [καὶ] ὁ πρωϊνός. „   „   „   „   „

C. νύμφη λέγουσιν ἔρχου. και ο ακούων ειπάτω ἔρχου. και ο
E. νύμφη λέγουσιν, ἔλθὲ. καὶ ὁ ἀκούων εἰπάτω, ἐλθὲ. καὶ ὁ
T. „   „ Ἔρχου· „   „   „   „ Ἔρχου. „   „

C. διψῶν ερχέσθω — ο θέλων λαβέτω — ὕδωρ ζωής δωρεάν.
E. διψῶν, ἐλθέτω. καί ὁ θέλων, λαμβανέτω τὸ ὕδωρ ζωῆς δωρεὰν,
T. „ ἐρχέσθω — „   „ λαβέτω — „   „   „

C.   μαρτυρώ ἐγώ παντί — ακούοντι τους λόγους της προφητείας
E. συμμαρτυροῦμαι γὰρ παντὶ — ἀκούοντι τοὺς λόγους — προφητείας
T.   Μαρτυρῶ ἐγὼ „ τῷ „   „   „ τῆς „

C. του βιβλίου τούτου εάν τις επιθή επ αυτά επιθήσαι επ
E. — βιβλίου τούτου. ἔι τις ἐπιτιθῆ πρὸς ταῦτα ἐπιθήσει ὁ
T. τοῦ „   „ ἐάν τις ἐπιθῇ ἐπ’ αὐτὰ, ἐπιθήσει ὁ

C. αυτόν ο θεός τας επτά πληγάς τας γεγραμμένας εν τω
E. θεὸς ἐπ’ αὐτὸν τὰς — πληγὰς τὰς γεγραμμένας ἐν —
T. Θεὸς ἐπ’ αὐτὸν „ — „   „   „   „ τῷ

C. βιβλίω τούτω. και εάν τις αφέλη από των λόγων του βιβλίου
E. βιβλίῳ τούτῳ. καὶ ἔι τίς ἀφαιρῇ ἀπὸ τῶν λόγων — βίβλου
T. „   „   „ ἐάν „ ἀφέλῃ ἀπὸ „   „ τοῦ βιβλίου

C. της προφητείας ταύτης αφέλοι ο θεός το μέρος αυτού από του
E. τῆς προφητείας ταύτης. ἀφαιρήσει ὁ θεὸς τὸ μέρος αὐτοῦ ἀπὸ —
T. „   „   „ ἀφελεῖ „   „ „   „   „ „ τοῦ

C. ξύλου της ζωής και εκ της πόλεως της αγίας — των γεγραμμέ-
E. βίβλου — ζωῆς, και — — πόλεως — ἁγίας, καὶ τῶν γεγραμμέ-
T. ξύλου τῆς „   „ ἐκ τῆς „ τῆς „   — „   „

C. νων εν τω βιβλίω τούτω. λέγει ο μαρτυρών ταύτα ναι έρχομαι
E. νων ἐν — βιβλίῳ τούτῳ. λέγει ὁ μαρτυρῶν ταῦτα. ναὶ ἔρχομαι
T. „ „ τῷ „ „ „ „ „ „ „ „

C. ταχύ, αμήν ναι έρχου κύριε ιησού. η χάρις του κυρίου —
E. ταχὺ, ἀμὴν. ναὶ, ἔρχου κύριε ΙΗΣΟΥ. ἡ χάρις τοῦ κυρίου ἡμῶν
T. „ „ — „ „ „ „ „ „ „ —

C. ιησού χριστού μετά πάντων τῶν αγίων. αμήν.
E. ΙΗΣΟΥ ΧΡΙΣΤΟΥ μετὰ πάντων ὑμῶν. Ἀμὴν.
T. „ „ „ „ τῶν ἀγίων. [ἀμήν.]

4. I have now done with the critical part of this Introduction; and, I trust, that sufficient grounds have been shown for the present work having been undertaken, and also for the principles on which it has been executed. In addition to what has been said above, (§ I. 5), I may here remark, that no charge of *innovation* can be fairly brought against the text here adopted. The *innovation* really has been the adoption and use of modern readings instead of ancient; this arose from modern copies having been most known at the time of the invention of printing. I do not judge it needful to make any apology for departures from the "Received Text," the only particulars in which any justification could be needed, are the places in which the most ancient copies, A. and C. agree, in what appears to me to be an erroneous reading. These places I have specified above. Of course I do not mean for a moment to allege that this text is perfect; I know too well the difficulties which encompass the subject for me to imagine that; but I give my conclusions accompanied by my principles and data in order that they may be examined, and that the text be not condemned previously to this being done.

No one will, I believe, expect any apology for an English text adapted to the Greek here given; I have sought to give an accurate rendering throughout, and not merely in the places in which this Greek text differs from that on which our Authorised Version is based.

In this introduction I have avoided anything which might relate to the *interpretation* of the Revelation; this was not my object, but it was to supply a text which might aid those who in subjection of mind to the word of God are seeking the teaching of the Spirit to know the things that are here written. No thoughts of my own on the subject of *interpretation* have, I believe, in a single instance influenced my judgment as to the adoption of readings ; on the contrary in many places preconceived thoughts on particular passages had to give way before what I saw, on sufficient grounds of evidence, to be " the words of the Holy Ghost."

And now, in conclusion, it is my earnest desire that this revised text and version may, through the blessing of God, be for the profit and instruction of some of those who may use it. This was what I sought in undertaking the work; this was what I bore in mind in the various stages of labour in connection with it. In the course of its execution I have had much cause for thankfulness; the critical materials which I most wanted have come to my hand just when they were especially needed, and in many ways I have had to trace the providential and overruling care of God. He has enabled me to bring to a conclusion this little work in connection with a portion of His word ;—may He graciously forgive all that is defective therein, and vouchsafe His Holy Spirit's blessing thereon, through Jesus Christ our Lord.

S. PRIDEAUX TREGELLES.

Islington, May 27, 1844.

EXPLANATION OF THE MARKS USED.

1. IN THE GREEK TEXT.

A reading for the omission of which *probable* reasons may be given, is included within brackets: *e. g.* [ἐπ σε] iii. 3. A less probable omission is included within *dotted* brackets: *e. g.* ⸢καὶ εἰδον⸣ vi. 5.

A *letter* in the text refers to the inner margin; a perpendicular line **ı** shows *how far* the marginal reading would extend: in case the marginal reading is an *addition*, it is put immediately after the letter, as *ᵃ* ı.

2. IN THE ENGLISH TEXT.

Brackets are employed in the same manner as in the Greek text.

A *letter* refers to the inner margin; when such a mark is found, it indicates a various reading of some degree of probability.

3. IN THE INNER MARGIN.

The letters answer to those in the Greek or English text.

A reading in *brackets* marks it as belonging to the Elzevir edition, 1624.

∾ marks a reading supported by some probable authorities, but apparently *inferior* to that given in the text.

+ marks an addition.

— marks an omission.

4. IN THE LOWER MARGIN.

The words of the " Received Text," (Elzevir 1624), stand first; then the authorities which differ from them.

An asterisk * is prefixed to readings from which the text here adopted differs.

The MSS. in *uncial* letters are cited A. B. C. (see § III. 2.)

Those in *cursive* letters are commonly cited compendiously in classes.

α denotes those MSS. which are perfect and collated throughout. Of these there are 28 in cursive letters.

β those which are defective, but with the defects noted, and which have been collated throughout; of these there are 11 in cursive letters.

γ MSS. partially collated. The silence of these is no authority *against* a reading. (See § III. 4.)

An asterisk after the designation of a MS. *e.g.* A* denotes a reading *à primâ manu*, afterwards altered.

Two asterisks thus:—A** mark a reading from correction.

When in the citation of authorities a figure is marked with † as 9† it denotes not that the particular MS. so designated is intended, but that *number* of MSS. of different classes. This is only used in cases which might have been ambiguous.

The abbreviations by which the *versions* are denoted, require in general no explanation beside the remark that abbreviations in italics, as *Am. Tol. Harl.*, denote Latin MSS. mentioned in § III. 5, and that Erp. is here used, (as has commonly been done), to denote the Arabic Version published by *Erpenius.* Ar. P. is the Arabic version of Walton's Polyglott. Arr. denotes both the Arabic versions.

ΑΠΟΚΑΛΥΨΙΣ

ΙΗΣΟΥ ΧΡΙΣΤΟΥ.

ΑΠΟΚΑΛΥΨΙΣ.

ἈΠΟΚΑΛΥΨΙΣ ἸΗΣΟΥ ΧΡΙΣΤΟΥ, ἣν
ἔδωκεν αὐτῷ ὁ Θεὸς, δεῖξαι τοῖς δούλοις αὐτοῦ ἃ
δεῖ γενέσθαι ἐν τάχει, καὶ ἐσήμανεν ἀποστείλας
διὰ τοῦ ἀγγέλου αὐτοῦ τῷ δούλῳ αὐτοῦ Ἰωάννῃ,
2 ὃς ἐμαρτύρησε τὸν λόγον τοῦ Θεοῦ καὶ τὴν μαρ-
3 τυρίαν Ἰησοῦ Χριστοῦ, ὅσα ᵃ| εἶδε. μακάριος ὁ
ἀναγινώσκων, καὶ οἱ ἀκούοντες τοὺς λόγους τῆς
προφητείας, καὶ τηροῦντες τὰ ἐν αὐτῇ γεγραμ-
μένα· ὁ γὰρ καιρὸς ἐγγύς.
4 Ἰωάννης ταῖς ἑπτὰ ἐκκλησίαις ταῖς ἐν τῇ
Ἀσίᾳ· χάρις ὑμῖν καὶ εἰρήνη ἀπὸ ᵇ| ὁ ὢν καὶ ὁ ἦν
καὶ ὁ ἐρχόμενος· καὶ ἀπὸ τῶν ἑπτὰ πνευμά-
5 των ἃ ᶜ| ἐνώπιον τοῦ θρόνου αὐτοῦ· καὶ ἀπὸ

ᵃ [+ τε.]   ᵇ [+ τοῦ.]

---

1. τῷ δούλῳ) τοῦ δούλου A.
2. *ὅσα τε) — τε, A. B. C. α 27. β 7. γ 8. Compl.   Vulg. Copt. Æth.
    Syr. Arm. Erp. Slav.
    εἶδε.) + καὶ ἅτινα εἰσι (ἐστι), καὶ ἃ (ἅτινα 4†) χρῆ γενέσθαι μετὰ
    ταῦτα. α 9. β 3. γ 6. Compl.   Arm. Ar. P.

THE REVELATION.

THE REVELATION OF JESUS CHRIST, which God gave unto him, to show unto his servants things which must come to pass shortly; and *which* having sent by his angel he signified unto his servant John: who testified the word of God, and the 2 testimony of Jesus Christ, *concerning* all things that he saw. Blessed *is* he that readeth, and they that 3 hear the words of this prophecy, and keep the things which are written in it: for the time *is* at hand.

JOHN to the seven churches which are in Asia: 4 Grace *be* unto you, and peace, from him who is, and who was, and who is to come; and from the seven Spirits that *are* before his throne; and from 5

---

c [+ ἐστιν.]

---

3. τοὺς λόγους.) τὸν λόγον B.   + τούτους C.
4. *ἀπὸ τοῦ) — τοῦ A. C. 6. *a* 10. γ 4. Compl.   Θεοῦ B. *a* 18. β 4. γ 9.
  Arm.
  ὁ ἦν) ὃς ἦν Er.
  *ἅ ἐστιν) τῶν A. 47. — ἐστιν B. C. *a* 20. β 4. γ 11.

Ἰησοῦ Χριστοῦ, ὁ μάρτυς ὁ πιστὸς, ὁ πρωτό-
τοκος ^a| τῶν νεκρῶν, καὶ ὁ ἄρχων τῶν βασιλέων
τῆς γῆς·

Τῷ ^b ἀγαπῶντι| ἡμᾶς, καὶ ^c λούσαντι| ἡμᾶς ^d ἐκ|
6 τῶν ἁμαρτιῶν ἡμῶν ἐν τῷ αἵματι αὐτοῦ· καὶ
ἐποίησεν ἡμᾶς ^eβασιλείαν| ἱερεῖς τῷ Θεῷ καὶ
πατρὶ αὐτοῦ· αὐτῷ ἡ δόξα καὶ τὸ κράτος εἰς
τοὺς αἰῶνας τῶν αἰώνων. ἀμήν.

7 Ἰδοὺ ἔρχεται μετὰ τῶν νεφελῶν, καὶ ὄψεται
αὐτὸν πᾶς ὀφθαλμὸς, καὶ οἵτινες αὐτὸν ἐξεκέν-
τησαν· καὶ κόψονται ἐπ' αὐτὸν πᾶσαι αἱ φυλαὶ
τῆς γῆς. ναὶ, ἀμήν.

8 Ἐγώ εἰμι τὸ ^f"Αλφα| καὶ τὸ ^g"Ω|, λέγει ^hΚύριος
ὁ Θεός·| ὁ ὢν καὶ ὁ ἦν καὶ ὁ ἐρχόμενος, ὁ παντο-
κράτωρ.

9 Ἐγὼ Ἰωάννης, ὁ ⁱ| ἀδελφὸς ὑμῶν καὶ συγκοι-
νωνὸς ἐν τῇ θλίψει καὶ ^k| βασιλείᾳ καὶ ὑπομονῇ
^l ἐν Ἰησοῦ,| ἐγενόμην ἐν τῇ νήσῳ τῇ καλουμένῃ

^a [+ ἐκ.] ^b [ἀγαπήσαντι.] ^c ∿λύσαντι. ^d [ἀπὸ.] ^e [βασιλεῖς καὶ.] ^f ['Α]

5. *πρωτότ. ἐκ) — ἐκ A. B. C. a 24. β 6. γ 10. Vulg. Copt. Syr. Arr.
*ἀγαπήσαντι) ἀγαπῶντι A. C. a 22. β 6. γ 10.
λούσαντι) λύσαντι A. C. 6. 7. 12*. 28. 36. 69. Syr. Slav. MSS.
* ἀπὸ) ἐκ A. C. 12. 28. 36. 38. Er.
ἡμῶν) — A. 12. 16. Er.
6. ἐποίησεν) ποιήσαντι B. & 9.†
ἡμᾶς) ἡμῖν A. 13. 23. 27. 31. 55. ἡμῶν C. nostrum regnum, Tol.
Harl. Am.
*βασιλεῖς καὶ) βασιλείαν A. C. a 27. β 4. γ 8. Compl. (Vulg.)
Am. Harl. Copt. Æth. Syr. Ar. P. Slav. MSS. — καὶ B. 30*.
(vdtr.) βασίλειον ἱεράτευμα 13. 14. 23. 27. 55. 92.
τῶν αἰώνων) — A. 9. Copt. Slav. MSS.
7. μετὰ) ἐπὶ C.
ὀψ. αὐτὸν) — αὐτ. 46. 88. Er.

Jesus Christ, the faithful Witness, the first begotten of the dead, and the Prince of the kings of the earth.

Unto him that loveth us, and hath "washed us from our sins in his own blood, and hath made 6 us a kingdom,—priests unto his God and Father; to him *be* glory and dominion for ever and ever. Amen.

Behold, he cometh with clouds; and every eye 7 shall see him, and those who pierced him: and all the tribes of the land shall mourn at him. Even so, Amen.

I am Alpha and Omega, saith the Lord God, 8 who is, and who was, and who is to come, the Almighty.

I John, who am your brother, and fellow-partaker 9 in the tribulation and kingdom and patience in Jesus, was in the isle that is called Patmos because of the

---

g [+ ἀρχὴ καὶ τέλος.] h [ὁ κύριος.] i [+ καὶ.] k [ἐν τῇ.] l ['Ιησοῦ Χριστοῦ.] m ⁀ freed.

7. ἐπ αὐτὸν) — 47*. Er.
8. *τὸ⁷Α) τὸ ἄλφα A. C. a 15. β 4. γ 3. Compl.
   *ἀρχὴ καὶ τέλος) — A. B. C. a 23. β 6. γ 9. Compl.   Æth. Syr. Arm. Slav. MS.
   *ὁ κύριος) κύριος ὁ θεὸς A. B. C. a 24. β 8. γ 12. Compl.   Vulg. Copt. Syr. Arm. Arr. Slav. MS.
9. *καὶ ἀδελ.) — καὶ A. C. a 27. β 5. γ 11. Compl.   Vulg. Copt. Æth. Syr. Arm. Arr. Slav. MSS.
   συγκοινωνὸς) κοινωνὸς. a 22. β 4. γ 6. Compl.
   *ἐν τῇ βασ.) — ἐν τῇ A.B.C. a23. β6. γ5. Compl. Vulg. Copt. Erp.
   *'Ιησοῦ Χριστοῦ) ἐν 'Ιησοῦ. C. 38.   Am. Tol. Copt.   ἐν Χριστῷ A. B. 25.   ἐν Χριστῶ 'Ιησοῦ. a 27. β 7. γ 6. Compl.   Vulg. Syr. Arm. Arr.
   τῇ καλουμένῃ) — Er.

Πάτμῳ, διὰ τὸν λόγον τοῦ Θεοῦ καὶ ^a|τὴν μαρ-
10 τυρίαν Ἰησοῦ^b|. ἐγενόμην ἐν Πνεύματι ἐν τῇ
κυριακῇ ἡμέρᾳ· καὶ ἤκουσα ὀπίσω μου φωνὴν
11 μεγάλην ὡς σάλπιγγος, λεγούσης·^c| Ὃ βλέπεις
γράψον εἰς βιβλίον, καὶ πέμψον ταῖς ^dἑπτὰ| ἐκ-
κλησίαις^e|, εἰς Ἔφεσον, καὶ εἰς Σμύρναν, καὶ εἰς
Πέργαμον, καὶ εἰς Θυάτειρα, καὶ εἰς Σάρδεις, καὶ
εἰς Φιλαδέλφειαν, καὶ εἰς Λαοδίκειαν.
12 Καὶ ἐπέστρεψα βλέπειν τὴν φωνὴν ἥτις ^f ἐλά-
λει| μετ᾽ ἐμοῦ· καὶ ἐπιστρέψας εἶδον ἑπτὰ λυχνίας
13 χρυσᾶς, καὶ ἐν μέσῳ τῶν^g| λυχνιῶν ὅμοιον υἱῷ
ἀνθρώπου, ἐνδεδυμένον ποδήρη, καὶ περιεζωσμέ-
14 νον πρὸς τοῖς μαστοῖς ζώνην χρυσῆν· ἡ δὲ κεφαλὴ
αὐτοῦ καὶ αἱ τρίχες λευκαὶ ^hὡς| ἔριον λευκὸν,
ὡς χιών· καὶ οἱ ὀφθαλμοὶ αὐτοῦ ὡς φλὸξ πυρός·
15 καὶ οἱ πόδες αὐτοῦ ὅμοιοι χαλκολιβάνῳ, ὡς ἐν
καμίνῳ πεπυρωμένοι· καὶ ἡ φωνὴ αὐτοῦ ὡς φωνὴ
16 ὑδάτων πολλῶν· καὶ ἔχων ἐν τῇ δεξιᾷⁱ χειρὶ αὐτοῦ|
ἀστέρας ἑπτά· καὶ ἐκ τοῦ στόματος αὐτοῦ ῥομ-

---

^a [+ διὰ.]　^b [+ Χριστοῦ.]　^c [+ ἐγώ εἰμι τὸ Α καὶ τὸ Ω, ὁ πρῶτος καὶ ὁ ἔσχατος, καὶ.]

9. διὰ τ. λ.) καὶ τ. λ. C.
　*διὰ τ. μ.) — διὰ A. C. 4. 9. 31. 34. 35. 37. 38. 48. Er.　Vulg.
　Copt. Arm.
　*χριστοῦ) — A. C. 12. 28. 36.　Vulg.
10. ἐγενόμην) ἐγὼ ἔγεν. A.
　ὀπ. μ. φω.) φω. ὀπ. μ. a 17. β 3. γ 5. Compl. φω. μεγ. ὄπισθεν μον A.
11. *ἐγώ εἰμι τὸ Α καὶ τὸ Ω, ὁ πρῶτος καὶ ὁ ἔσχατος, καὶ) — A. B. C. a 24.
　β 5. γ 6. Compl.　Vulg. Copt. Æth. Syr. Arm. Slav. MSS.
　*ἐκκλη.) ἑπτὰ ἐκκλη. A. B. C. a 27. β 5. γ 10. Compl.　Vulg.
　Copt. Æth. Syr. Arm. Arr. Slav. MSS.
　*ταῖς ἐν Ἀσίᾳ) — A. B. C. a 28. β 7. γ 6. Compl.　Am. Harl. Tol.
　Æth. Syr. Ar. P.
　Θυάτειρα·) -ραν A. C. 8. 11. 14. 34. 35. 92.　-ρας. 12. Er.
12. καὶ ἐπέστ.) κ. ἐκεῖ ἐπέστ. B. a 22. β 4. γ 7. Compl.　Ar. P.

word of God and the testimony of Jesus.   I was in 10
the Spirit on the Lord's day, and heard behind me a
great voice, as of a trumpet, saying, What thou seest, 11
write in a book, and send unto the seven churches;
unto Ephesus, and unto Smyrna, and unto Pergamos,
and unto Thyatira, and unto Sardis, and unto Philadelphia, and unto Laodicea.

And I turned to see the voice that was speaking 12
with me.   And being turned, I saw seven candlesticks of gold ; and in the midst of the candlesticks 13
one like unto the Son of man, clothed with a garment
down to the foot, and girt about the paps with a
girdle of gold.   And his head and *his* hairs *were* white 14
as white wool, as snow ; and his eyes *were* as a
flame of fire ; and his feet like unto fine brass, as if 15
they had been refined in a furnace ; and his voice
as the sound of many waters.   And he had in his 16
right hand seven stars : and out of his mouth went

ᵈ Rec.—   ᵉ [+ ταῖς ἐν 'Ασίᾳ.]   ᶠ [ἐλάλησε.]   ᵍ [+ ἑπτὰ.]   ʰ [ὡσεὶ.]   ⁱ [αὐτοῦ χειρὶ.]

12. *ἐλάλησε) ἐλάλει. B. C. a 26. β 4. γ 6. Compl.   λαλεῖ A.

13. ἐν μέσῳ) ἐμμέσῳ A. C.
     *ἑπτὰ) — A. C. 12. 28. 38. 46. Er.   *Am.* Copt. Æth. Syr. Arm. Erp.
     ὅμοιον) ὁμοίωμα A.   *Harl.* Slav. MS.
     υἱῷ) υἱὸν a 18. β 5. γ 4.
     ποδήρη) -ρην A. 11.
     μαστοῖς) μαζοῖς A. 10. 17. 28. 37. 49. 80*. 91. Compl.
     χρυσῆν) -σᾶν A. C.

14. *ὡσεὶ) καὶ ὡς a 11. β 3. γ 2.   ὡς A. 14. a 10. γ 2.

15. πεπυρωμένοι) -μένης A. C. -μένω 16. 46. 69. 88.   Vulg. Æth. Syr.
     Arr. Slav. MSS.

16. ἔχων) — A. 41.
     *αὐτ. χειρὶ) χειρὶ αὐτοῦ A. C. a 9. β 2. γ 4.

φαία δίστομος ὀξεῖα ἐκπορευομένη· καὶ ἡ ὄψις
αὐτοῦ ὡς ὁ ἥλιος φαίνει ἐν τῇ δυνάμει αὐτοῦ.
17 Καὶ ὅτε εἶδον αὐτὸν, ἔπεσα πρὸς τοὺς πόδας
αὐτοῦ ὡς νεκρός· καὶ "ἔθηκε¹ τὴν δεξιὰν αὐτοῦᵇ¹
ἐπ' ἐμὲ λέγωνᶜ¹. Μὴ φοβοῦ· ἐγώ εἰμι ὁ πρῶτος
καὶ ὁ ἔσχατος, καὶ ὁ ζῶν· καὶ ἐγενόμην νεκρὸς,
18 καὶ ἰδοὺ ζῶν εἰμὶ εἰς τοὺς αἰῶνας τῶν αἰώνων·ᵈ¹
καὶ ἔχω τὰς κλεῖς τοῦ ᵉθανάτου καὶ τοῦ ᾅδου.¹
19 γράψον ᶠοὖν¹ ἃ εἶδες, καὶ ἅ εἰσι, καὶ ἃ μέλλει
20 γίνεσθαι μετὰ ταῦτα· τὸ μυστήριον τῶν ἑπτὰ
ἀστέρων ᵍ οὓς¹ εἶδες ἐπὶ τῆς δεξιᾶς μου, καὶ τὰς
ἑπτὰ λυχνίας τὰς χρυσᾶς. οἱ ἑπτὰ ἀστέρες,
ἄγγελοι τῶν ἑπτὰ ἐκκλησιῶν εἰσι· καὶ ʰαἱ λυχνίαι
αἱ ἑπτὰ,¹ ἑπτὰ ἐκκλησίαι εἰσί.

II. Τῷ ἀγγέλῳ τῆς ⁱἐν Ἐφέσῳ¹ ἐκκλησίας
γράψον· Τάδε λέγει ὁ κρατῶν τοὺς ἑπτὰ ἀστέρας
ἐν τῇ δεξιᾷ αὐτοῦ, ὁ περιπατῶν ἐν μέσῳ τῶν ἑπτὰ
2 λυχνιῶν τῶν χρυσῶν· Οἶδα τὰ ἔργα σου, καὶ

ᵃ [ἐπέθηκε.]   ᵇ [+ χεῖρα.]   ᶜ [+ μοι.]   ᵈ [+ ἀμήν.]   ᵉ [ᾅδου καὶ

17. ὅτε) ὅτι Compl.
    ἔπεσα) -σον a 6. & 13. 25.
    *ἐπέθηκε) ἔθηκε A. C. α 22. β 6. γ 6.
    *χεῖρα) — A. C. α 22. β 6. γ 6.   Vulg. Arm. Æth. Slav. MS.
    *μοι) — A. C. α 22. β 8. γ 9. Compl.   Vulg. Syr. Arm. Arr.
    Slav. MSS.
    πρῶτος) πρωτότοκος A.
18. *ἀμήν.) — A. C. 36. 38. Er.   Vulg. Copt. Æth. Ar. P.
    κλεῖς) κλεῖδας) α 13. β 4. γ 3.
    *τοῦ ᾅδου καὶ τοῦ θανάτου) τ. θαν. κ. τ. ᾅδου. A. C. α 24. β 6. γ 8.
    Compl. Verss.
19. *γράψον) + οὖν A. C. α 25. β 7. γ 9. Compl.   Vulg. Copt. Æth.
    Syr. Ar. P. Slav.

forth a sharp two-edged sword: and his countenance *was* as the sun shineth in his strength.

And when I saw him, I fell at his feet as dead. 17 And he laid his right hand upon me, saying, Fear not; I am the first and the last: and he that liveth, and was dead; and behold, I am alive for ever and 18 ever: and I have the keys of death and of hades. Write therefore the things which thou hast seen, and 19 the things which are, and the things which shall be hereafter; the mystery of the seven stars which 20 thou sawest upon my right hand, and the seven candlesticks of gold.   The seven stars are the angels of the seven churches: and the seven candlesticks are the seven churches.

II. Unto the angel of the church in Ephesus write; These things saith he that holdeth the seven stars in his right hand, who walketh in the midst of the seven candlesticks of gold; I know thy works, and 2

τοῦ θανάτου.]   ᶠ Rec.—   ᵍ [ὧν.]   ʰ [αἱ ἑπτὰ λυχνίαι ἃς εἶδες.]   ⁱ ['Εφεσίνης.]

ἃ μέλ.) ἃ δεῖ μέλ: C.
γίνεσθαι) γένεσθαι C. 6. 11. 14. 28. 91. Compl.
20. *ὧν) οὓς. A. C. 8. 12. 46. 80**. 88. Er.
ἐπὶ τῆς δεξιᾶς) ἐν τῃ δεξιᾷ A.
*αἱ ἑπτὰ λυχνίαι) αἱ λυχ. αἱ ἑπτὰ. A.B.C. a 9. β 4. γ6.   αἱ λυχ. ἑπτὰ.
    30. 33. 35. 36.   ἑπτὰ λυχ. 23. Er.
*ἃς εἶδες) —A.B.C. a 21. β 5. γ 6.   Vulg. Æth. Syr. Arm. Ar. P.
    Slav. MS.

1. τῆς) τῷ A. C. τῷ τῆς 36.
*'Εφεσίνης) ἐν 'Εφέσῳ A.C. a 26. β 7. γ 9.   Vulg. (Syr. Arr.)
    ἐκκλ. 'Εφέσῳ Compl.
ἐν μέσῳ) ἐμμέσῳ A. C. ἐπὶ μ. Er.
χρυσῶν) — σεῶν A. C.

3

τὸν κόπον[a] καὶ τὴν ὑπομονήν σου, καὶ ὅτι οὐ
δύνῃ βαστάσαι κακοὺς, καὶ [b] ἐπείρασας τοὺς
λέγοντας ἑαυτοὺς ἀποστόλους καὶ οὐκ εἰσὶ, καὶ
3 εὗρες αὐτοὺς ψευδεῖς, καὶ [c] ὑπομονὴν ἔχεις καὶ
ἐβάστασας διὰ τὸ ὄνομά μου, [d] καὶ οὐ κεκοπία-
4 κας[e]. ἀλλ' ἔχω κατὰ σοῦ, ὅτι τὴν ἀγάπην σου
5 τὴν πρώτην ἀφῆκας. μνημόνευε οὖν πόθεν
[f] πέπτωκας, καὶ μετανόησον, καὶ τὰ πρῶτα ἔργα
ποίησον· εἰ δὲ μὴ, ἔρχομαί σοι [ταχὺ,] καὶ κινή-
σω τὴν λυχνίαν σου ἐκ τοῦ τόπου αὐτῆς, ἐὰν μὴ
6 μετανοήσῃς. ἀλλὰ τοῦτο ἔχεις, ὅτι μισεῖς τὰ
ἔργα τῶν Νικολαϊτῶν, ἃ κἀγὼ μισῶ.
7 Ὁ ἔχων οὖς ἀκουσάτω τί τὸ Πνεῦμα λέγει
ταῖς ἐκκλησίαις· τῷ νικῶντι δώσω αὐτῷ φαγεῖν
ἐκ τοῦ ξύλου τῆς ζωῆς, ὅ ἐστιν ἐν [g] τῷ παραδείσῳ
τοῦ Θεοῦ[h].
8 Καὶ τῷ ἀγγέλῳ τῆς [i] ἐν Σμύρνῃ ἐκκλησίας

---

[a] + [σου.]   [b] [ἐπειράσω τοὺς φάσκοντας εἶναι ἀποστόλους.]   [c] [ἐβάστασας
[g] [μέσῳ τοῦ παραδείσου.]   [h] ∾ + μου.

2. *κόπον σου) — σου A. C. a 5. β 2. γ 2. Compl.   Vulg. Syr. Arm.
καὶ ὅτι) — καὶ A.   Copt. Æth.
*ἐπειράσω) ἐπείρασας A. B. C. a 26. β 7. γ 8. Compl.
*φάσκοντας εἶναι ἀποστόλους) λέγοντας ἑαυτοὺς ἀποστόλους. A. B. C.
18. 25. Slav.   id. + εἶναι a 24. β 8. γ 7. Compl.   Vulg. Æth.
Syr. Arm. Arr.
3. *ἐβάστασας καὶ ὑπομονὴν ἔχεις καὶ) ὑπομ. ἔχ. κ. ἐβάστ. A. B. C. a 17.
β 5. γ 7.   Vulg. Copt. Æth. Arm. Slav. MS.
ἐβαστ.) ἐβάπτισας Er.
*καὶ δια) — καὶ 17. 18. 25. 26. 27. 49. 88. Compl. Arm.
*μου) + καὶ οὐ (or οὐκ) A. (B.) C. a 23. β 8. γ 9. Compl.   Vulg.
Æth. Syr. Arm. Slav. MSS.
*κεκοπίακας καὶ οὐ κέκμηκας) κεκοπίακας (-κες A. C.),16. 37. 38. 69.
ἐκοπίασας B. a 23. β 8. γ 9. Compl.   Vulg. Æth. Syr. Arr.
Slav. MSS.

labour, and thy patience, and that thou canst not bear those who are evil : and thou hast tried those who call themselves apostles, and are not, and hast found them liars : and thou hast patience, and hast borne 3 for my name's sake, and hast not been wearied. Nevertheless I have *this* against thee, that thou hast 4 left thy first love. Remember therefore whence thou 5 hast fallen, and repent, and do the first works ; or else I am coming unto thee [quickly,] and I will remove thy candlestick out of its place, except thou repent. But this thou hast, that thou hatest the 6 deeds of the Nicolaitanes, which I also hate.

He that hath an ear, let him hear what the Spirit 7 saith unto the churches ; To him that overcometh will I give to eat of the tree of life, which is in the paradise of ^{k}God.

And unto the angel of the church in Smyrna 8

καὶ ὑπομονὴν ἔχεις καὶ.] ^{d} Rec. — ^{e} + [καὶ οὐ κέκμηκας.] ^{f} [ἐκπέπτωκας.]
     ^{i} [ἐκκλησίας Σμυρναίων.] ^{k} ~ my God.

4. ἀγάπην σου τ. πρώτην.) πρώ. σ. ἀγάπ. A.   ἀφῆκας) -κες C.

5. *ἐκπέπτωκας) πέπτωκας A. C. *a* 21. β 6. γ 6.
     ταχὺ) — A. C.   Vulg. (*not* Harl.) Copt. Æth.   τάχει. Er.

6. ἅ) — A.   Copt.

7. ταῖς ἐκκλ.) τ. ἑπτὰ ἐκκλ. A.   τ. ἐκκλ. ταῖς ἑπτὰ C.
     αὐτῷ) — 6† Compl.
     *μέσῳ τοῦ παραδείσου) τῷ παραδείσῳ A. B. C. *a* 20. β 6. γ 6.
         Vulg. Æth. Syr. Slav. MS.
     Θεοῦ) + μου B. *a* 26. β 5. γ 7. Compl.   Vulg. Copt. Æth. Syr.
         Erp. Slav. MS.

8. τῆς.) τῷ A.
     *ἐκκλησίας Σμυρναίων) ἐν Σμύρνῃ ἐκκλησίας. (A.) C. *a* 28. β 7. γ 8.
         Compl.   Vulg. Æth. Syr. Arm. Arr. Slav. MS.   ἐν
         Σμυρνῆς A

γράψον· Τάδε λέγει ὁ πρῶτος καὶ ὁ ἔσχατος, ὃς
9 ἐγένετο νεκρὸς καὶ ἔζησεν· Οἶδά σου[a] τὴν θλίψιν
καὶ τὴν πτωχείαν· ([b]ἀλλὰ πλούσιος[1] εἶ·) καὶ τὴν
βλασφημίαν [c]ἐκ[1] τῶν λεγόντων Ἰουδαίους εἶναι
ἑαυτούς, καὶ οὐκ εἰσίν, ἀλλὰ συναγωγὴ τοῦ
10 Σατανᾶ. [d]μὴ[1] φοβοῦ ἃ μέλλεις πάσχειν· ἰδοὺ
μέλλει [e]βάλλειν[1] [f]ὁ διάβολος ἐξ ὑμῶν[1] εἰς φυλα-
κήν, ἵνα πειρασθῆτε· καὶ ἕξετε θλίψιν [g]ἡμερῶν[1]
δέκα. γίνου πιστὸς ἄχρι θανάτου, καὶ δώσω σοι
τὸν στέφανον τῆς ζωῆς·
11 Ὁ ἔχων οὖς ἀκουσάτω τί τὸ Πνεῦμα λέγει
ταῖς ἐκκλησίαις· ὁ νικῶν οὐ μὴ ἀδικηθῇ ἐκ τοῦ
θανάτου τοῦ δευτέρου.
12 Καὶ τῷ ἀγγέλῳ τῆς ἐν Περγάμῳ ἐκκλησίας
γράψον· Τάδε λέγει ὁ ἔχων τὴν ῥομφαίαν τὴν
13 δίστομον τὴν ὀξεῖαν· Οἶδα[h] ποῦ κατοικεῖς, ὅπου
ὁ θρόνος τοῦ Σατανᾶ, καὶ κρατεῖς τὸ ὄνομά μου,
καὶ οὐκ ἠρνήσω τὴν πίστιν μου· [i]καὶ ἐν ταῖς
ἡμέραις[1] [k]Ἀντίπας ὁ μάρτυς μου ὁ πιστός, ὃς
ἀπεκτάνθη παρ᾽ ὑμῖν, ὅπου [l]ὁ Σατανᾶς κατοικεῖ.[1]

---

[a] + [τὰ ἔργα καὶ, ver. 2, 19.]   [b] [πλούσιος δὲ.]   [c] Rec.—   [d] [μηδὲν.]
[i] ∾ ἐν ταῖς ἡμέραις ἐν αἷς.   [k] + [ἐν αἷς.]

8. πρῶτος) πρωτότοκος A.
   ὃς) —a 9. β 2. γ 3.
9. *τὰ ἔργα καὶ) — A. C. 19. 47.   Vulg. Copt. Æth.
   *πλούσιος δὲ) ἀλλὰ πλούσιος A. B. C. a 28. β 8. γ 9. Compl.
   *τῶν λεγ.) ἐκ τ. λ. A. B. C. a 21. β 5. γ 6.   Vulg. Copt. Syr.
     Arm. Slav. MSS.
   Ἰουδαίους) -ων C.
10. *μηδὲν) μὴ A. B. C. 8. 49.   Æth.
   πάσχειν) παθεῖν. B. a 15. β 5. γ 4.
   ἰδοὺ) + δὴ a 19. β 3. γ 4. Compl.   Slav. MS.
   *βαλεῖν) βάλλειν A. C. a 8. β 2. γ 3.

THE REVELATION.   13

write; These things saith the first and the last, who
was dead, and hath lived; I know thy tribulation, 9
and poverty, (but thou art rich,) and *I know* the
blasphemy of those who say that they are Jews, and
are not, but *are* the synagogue of Satan.   Fear not 10
the things which thou shalt suffer : behold, the
devil shall cast *some* of you into prison, that ye
may be tried ; and ye shall have tribulation ten
days : be thou faithful unto death, and I will give
thee the crown of life.

He that hath an ear, let him hear what the Spirit 11
saith unto the churches ; He that overcometh shall
not be hurt of the second death.

And to the angel of the church in Pergamos 12
write ; These things saith he which hath the sharp
sword with two edges; I know where thou dwellest, 13
even where Satan's throne *is :* and thou holdest fast
my name, and hast not denied my faith; ᵃand in
those days *was* Antipas my faithful witness, who was
slain among you, where Satan dwelleth.   But I 14

ᵉ [βαλεῖν.]   ᶠ [ἐξ ὑμῶν ὁ διάβολος.]   ᵍ ∼ ἡμέρας.   ʰ + [τὰ ἔργα σου καὶ, ver. 2, 19.]
ˡ [κατοικεῖ ὁ Σατανᾶς.]   ᵐ ∿ in the days in which.

---

10. *ἐξ ὑμῶν ὁ διάβολος) ὁ διαβ. ἐξ ὑμ. A. C. a 20. β 8. γ 8. Compl.
    πειρασθῆτε) παραθῆτε Er.
    ἔξετε) ἔχητε A. 36. ἔχετε C. 11. 12.
    ἡμερων) ἡμέρας B. a 17. β 5. γ 5.
13. *τὰ ἔργα σου καὶ) — A. C. 38.   Vulg. Copt. Æth. Slav. MSS.
    καὶ ἐν τ. ἡμ.) — καὶ a 28. β 7. γ 6. Compl.   Vulg. MS. Æth.
        Syr. Arr.
    *ἐν αἷς) — A. C.   Vulg. MS. *Am. Harl.* Copt.   ἐμαῖς 91**. Er.
        ἐν — a 19. β 4. γ 5.
    πιστὸς) + μου A. C. 14. 92.   Syr.
    *κατοικεῖ ὁ Σατανᾶς) ὁ Σατ. κατοικ. A. C. a 20. β 8. γ 5. Compl.

14 ἀλλ᾽ ἔχω κατὰ σοῦ ὀλίγα, [ὅτι] ἔχεις ἐκεῖ κρατοῦντας τὴν διδαχὴν Βαλαάμ, ὃς ἐδίδασκε ᵃτῷ| Βαλὰκ βαλεῖν σκάνδαλον ἐνώπιον τῶν υἱῶν Ἰσραὴλ, φαγεῖν εἰδωλόθυτα καὶ πορνεῦσαι.

15 οὕτως ἔχεις καὶ σὺ κρατοῦντας τὴν διδαχὴνᵇ|

16 Νικολαϊτῶν ᶜὁμοίως.| μετανόησον ᵈ[οὖν·]| εἰ δὲ μὴ, ἔρχομαί σοι ταχὺ, καὶ πολεμήσω μετ᾽ αὐτῶν ἐν τῇ ῥομφαίᾳ τοῦ στόματός μου.

17 Ὁ ἔχων οὖς ἀκουσάτω τί τὸ Πνεῦμα λέγει ταῖς ἐκκλησίαις· τῷ νικῶντι δώσω αὐτῷᵉ| τοῦ μάννα τοῦ κεκρυμμένου, καὶ δώσω αὐτῷ ψῆφον λευκὴν, καὶ ἐπὶ τὴν ψῆφον ὄνομα καινὸν γεγραμμένον, ὃ οὐδεὶς ᶠοἶδεν| εἰ μὴ ὁ λαμβάνων.

18 Καὶ τῷ ἀγγέλῳ τῆς ἐν Θυατείροις ἐκκλησίας γράψον· Τάδε λέγει ὁ υἱὸς τοῦ Θεοῦ, ὁ ἔχων τοὺς ὀφθαλμοὺς αὐτοῦ ὡς φλόγα πυρὸς, καὶ οἱ 19 πόδες αὐτοῦ ὅμοιοι χαλκολιβάνῳ. Οἶδά σου τὰ ἔργα καὶ τὴν ἀγάπην ᵍ καὶ τὴν πίστιν, καὶ τὴν διακονίαν,| καὶ τὴν ὑπομονήν σου, καὶ τὰ ἔργα σουʰ| τὰ ἔσχατα πλείονα τῶν πρώτων.

ᵃ [τὸν.]   ᵇ + [τῶν.]   ᶜ [ὁ μισῶ, ver. 6.]   ᵈ Rec.—

14. ὅτι) — C. Am. Tol. Harl.* Copt. Syr.
  ἐδίδασκε) ἐδίδαξε) a 21. β 6. γ 6. Compl.
  *τὸν Βαλ.) τῷ Βαλ. A. C. 11.   ἐν τῷ Βαλ. 18. 92**. Er.
  βαλεῖν) βασιλεῖ A.
  φαγεῖν) καὶ φαγ. a 14. β 3. γ 3. Slav. MS.
15. *τῶν Νικολ.) — τῶν A. C. a 13. β 6. γ 2.
  *ὃ μισῶ) ὁμοίως A. C. a 27. β 7. γ 8. Compl.   Vulg. Copt. Syr.
    Slav. MS.   ὁμοίως ὃ μισῶ. 3†.
16. *μετανόησον) + οὖν A. C. a 23. β 5. γ 8.   Æth. Arm. Arr. Slav. MS.
17. *φαγεῖν ἀπὸ) —A. B. C. a 18. β 4. γ 4.   Vulg. Copt. Æth.
  καινὸν) κενὸν Compl.

have a few things against thee, that thou hast there
them that hold the doctrine of Balaam, who taught
Balak to cast a stumblingblock before the children
of Israel, to eat things sacrificed unto idols, and to
commit fornication. So thou also hast those that hold 15
the doctrine of the Nicolaitanes in like manner. 16
Repent therefore ; or else I am coming unto thee
quickly, and will fight against them with the sword
of my mouth.

He that hath an ear, let him hear what the Spirit 17
saith unto the churches ; To him that overcometh
will I give of the hidden manna, and I will give him
a white stone, and on the stone a new name written,
which none knoweth save he that receiveth *it*.

And unto the angel of the church in Thyatira 18
write ; These things saith the Son of God, who hath
his eyes as a flame of fire, and his feet *are* like unto
fine brass ; I know thy works, and love, and faith, 19
and service, and thy patience ; and thy last works
to be more than the first. Notwithstanding I 20

ᵉ + [φαγεῖν ἀπὸ.]   ᶠ [ἔγνω.]   ᵍ [καὶ τὴν διακονίαν καὶ τὴν πίστιν.]   ʰ + [καὶ.]

---

17. *ἔγνω) οἶδεν A. B. C. a 28. β 7. γ 7. Compl.

18. τῆς.) — C. τῷ A.
   Θυατείροις) -ραις Er. (so ver. 24) -ρῃ B. a 9. β 3. γ 2.
   αὐτοῦ (1st) — A. 36. 38.

19. *καὶ τὴν διακονίαν καὶ τὴν πίστιν) κ. τ. πίστ. κ. τ. διακον. A. C. a 17.
   β 7. γ 9. Compl.   Vulg. MS. Copt. Æth. Syr. Arm. Arr.
   Slav. MSS.   τὴν πιστ.) — τὴν C.
   τὴν ὑπομ.) — τὴν A. 36.
   *καὶ τὰ ἔσχ.) — καὶ A. C. a 21. β 7. γ 7. Compl.   Vulg. Copt. Æth.
   Syr. Arr. Slav. MS.

20 ^aἀλλὰ| ἔχω κατὰ σοῦ^b| ὅτι ^c ἀφεῖς| τὴν ^dγυναῖκα|
^eἸεζάβελ,|^f ἡ λέγουσα ἑαυτὴν| προφῆτιν, ^g καὶ
διδάσκει καὶ πλανᾷ τοὺς| ἐμοὺς δούλους, πορ-
21 νεῦσαι καὶ ^h φαγεῖν εἰδωλόθυτα.| καὶ ἔδωκα
αὐτῇ χρόνον ἵνα μετανοήσῃ ⁱ καὶ οὐ θέλει μετα-
22 νοῆσαι ἐκ τῆς πορνείας αὐτῆς.| ἰδοὺ ^k|βάλλω
αὐτὴν εἰς κλίνην, καὶ τοὺς μοιχεύοντας μετ᾽
αὐτῆς εἰς θλίψιν μεγάλην, ἐὰν μὴ μετανοήσωσιν
23 ἐκ τῶν ἔργων ^l αὐτῆς·| καὶ τὰ τέκνα αὐτῆς ἀπο-
κτενῶ ἐν θανάτῳ· καὶ γνώσονται πᾶσαι αἱ ἐκκλησίαι ὅτι ἐγώ εἰμι ὁ ἐρευνῶν νεφροὺς καὶ καρδίας·
καὶ δώσω ὑμῖν ἑκάστῳ κατὰ τὰ ἔργα ὑμῶν.
24 ὑμῖν δὲ λέγω ^m τοῖς| λοιποῖς τοῖς ἐν Θυατείροις,
ὅσοι οὐκ ἔχουσι τὴν διδαχὴν ταύτην, ⁿ| οἵτινες
οὐκ ἔγνωσαν τὰ ^o βαθέα| τοῦ Σατανᾶ, (ὡς λέ-
γουσιν·) Οὐ ^p βάλλω| ἐφ᾽ ὑμᾶς ἄλλο βάρος·
25 πλὴν ὃ ἔχετε κρατήσατε, ἄχρις οὗ ἂν ἥξω.

---

^a [ἀλλ᾽]   ^b + [ὀλίγα, vr. 14.]   ^c [ἐᾷς.]   ^d ∽ γυναῖκα σου.   ^e [Ἰεζαβὴλ.]
ⁱ [ἐκ τῆς πορνείας αὐτῆς καὶ οὐ μετενόησεν.]   ^k + [ἐγώ.]   ^l [αὐτῶν.]

20. * ἀλλ᾽) ἀλλὰ A. 13. 30. 33. 34. 35. 36.
    *ὀλίγα) — A. B. C. a 27. β 5. γ 8. Compl.   Harl. Tol. &c. Copt.
    Æth. Syr. Arr. Slav. MSS.
    *ἐᾷς) ἀφεῖς A. B. C. a 22. β 6. γ 8. Compl.
    γυναῖκα) + σου. A. a 22. β 5. γ 5. Compl.   Syr. Slav. MS.
    *Ἰεζαβὴλ) Ἰεζάβελ. A.B.C. a 17.β 3. γ 6. Er.Compl. τὴν᾽Ιεζ.A.Compl.
    *τὴν λέγουσαν) ἡ λέγουσα A. C.   ἡ λέγει B. a 26. β 6. γ 5. Compl.
    ἑαυτὴν) αὐτὴν B. 16. 40. 69.
    *διδάσκειν καὶ πλανᾶσθαι) καὶ διδάσκει καὶ πλανᾷ τοὺς A. B. C.
    a 27. β 8. γ 8. Compl.   Copt. Æth. Syr. Arr.
    *εἰδωλόθυτα φαγεῖν) φαγ. εἰδ. A. C. a 19. β 8. γ 6. Compl.
21. *ἐκ τῆς πορνείας αὐτῆς, καὶ οὐ μετενόησεν) καὶ οὐ θέλει μετανοῆσαι ἐκ
    τῆς πορνείας αὐτῆς. (A.) B. C. a 27. β 8. γ 8. Compl.   Vulg.
    Copt. Æth. Syr. Arr. Slav. MSS.   θέλει,) ἠθέλησεν A.

have *this* against thee, that thou lettest alone [q] that
woman Jezebel; who calleth herself a prophetess,
and teacheth and seduceth my servants to commit
fornication, and to eat things sacrificed unto idols.
And I gave her space to repent, and she willeth not 21
to repent of her fornication. Behold, I do cast her 22
into a bed, and those that commit adultery with her
into great tribulation, except they repent of her deeds. 23
And I will kill her children with death; and all the
churches shall know that I am he who searcheth
the reins and hearts: and I will give unto every 24
one of you according to your works. But unto you
I say, the rest that are in Thyatira, as many as
have not this doctrine, who have not known the
depths of Satan, (how they speak!) I lay upon you
no other burden. But that which ye have hold fast 25
till I come.

---

[f] [τὴν λέγουσαν ἑαυτὴν.] [g] [διδάσκειν καὶ πλανᾶσθαι.] [h] [εἰδωλόθυτα φαγεῖν.]
[m] [καὶ.] [n] + [καὶ.] [o] [βάθη.] [p] [βαλῶ.] [q] ∾ thy wife.

---

22. *ἐγὼ) — A. C. α 27. β 6. γ 8. Compl. Vulg. Copt. Æth. Syr. Slav. MSS.
κλίνην) φυλακὴν A. μετανοήσωσιν) -σουσιν A.
*αὐτῶν) αὐτῆς B. C. α 27. β 7. γ 6. Compl. Vulg. MS. *Am.* Tol. Harl.* Æth. Syr. MS. Erp. Slav. MS.

23. καὶ τὰ) — καὶ A.
ὑμῶν) αὐτοῦ B. 38. Vulg. ed. (*Am.* "vestra.")

24. *καὶ λοιποῖς) τοῖς λοιποῖς A. C. α 22. β 7. γ 7. Compl. Vulg. MS. *Am.* Copt. Æth. Syr. Arr. λοιποῖς. α 5. (& 3. 6.)
*καὶ οἵτινες.) — καὶ A. C. α 26. β 7. γ 8. Compl. Vulg. MS. *Am.* *Harl.* Copt. Æth. Syr. Arm. Slav. MS.
*βάθη) βαθέα A. C. α 28. β 5. γ 7. Compl.
*βαλῶ) βάλλω A. C. α 20. β 6. γ 8.

25. ἄχρις) ἕως A. 47.
ἂν ἥξω) ἀνοίξω α 15. β 4. γ 2.

26 Καὶ ὁ νικῶν καὶ ὁ τηρῶν ἄχρι τέλους τὰ ἔργα
27 μου, δώσω αὐτῷ ἐξουσίαν ἐπὶ τῶν ἐθνῶν· καὶ
ποιμανεῖ αὐτοὺς ἐν ῥάβδῳ σιδηρᾷ· ὡς τὰ σκεύη
τὰ κεραμικὰ ᵃσυντρίβεται,| ὡς κἀγὼ εἴληφα παρὰ
28 τοῦ πατρός μου· καὶ δώσω αὐτῷ τὸν ἀστέρα
29 τὸν πρωϊνόν. ὁ ἔχων οὖς ἀκουσάτω τί τὸ
Πνεῦμα λέγει ταῖς ἐκκλησίαις.

III. Καὶ τῷ ἀγγέλῳ τῆς ἐν Σάρδεσιν ἐκκλησίας
γράψον· Τάδε λέγει ὁ ἔχων τὰ ἑπτὰ πνεύματα
τοῦ Θεοῦ καὶ τοὺς ἑπτὰ ἀστέρας· Οἶδά σου τὰ
ἔργα, ὅτι ᵇ| ὄνομα ἔχεις ὅτι ζῇς, καὶ νεκρὸς εἶ.
2 γίνου γρηγορῶν, καὶ ᶜ στήρισον |.τὰ λοιπὰ ἃ
ᵈ ἔμελλον| ἀποθανεῖν· οὐ γὰρ εὕρηκά σου [τὰ]
ἔργα πεπληρωμένα ἐνώπιον τοῦ Θεοῦ ᵉ μου.|
3 μνημόνευε οὖν πῶς εἴληφας καὶ ἤκουσας, καὶ
τήρει, καὶ μετανόησον· ἐὰν οὖν μὴ γρηγορήσῃς,
ἥξω [ἐπί σε] ὡς κλέπτης, καὶ οὐ μὴ γνῷς ποίαν
4 ὥραν ἥξω ἐπί σε. ᶠἀλλ᾿| ἔχεις ὀλίγα ὀνόματα
ᵍ| ἐν Σάρδεσιν, ἃ οὐκ ἐμόλυναν τὰ ἱμάτια αὐτῶν·

ᵃ ∾ συντριβήσεται. ᵇ + [τὸ.] ᶜ [στήριξον.] ᵈ [μέλλει.] ᵉ Rec. —

27. συντρίβεται) συντριβήσεται a 24. β 6. γ 8. Compl. Vulg. Copt.
 Æth. Syr. Arm. Arr. Slav. ed.

1. ἑπτὰ πνευ.) — ἑπτὰ 12. Er.
 *τὸ ὄνομα) — τὸ A. C. a 19. β 7. γ 6. Compl.
 ὅτι ζῇς) καὶ ζῇς a 17. β 2.
2. *στήριξον) στήρισον A. C. a 9 & 6. 11. 12. τήρησον a 3. β 3.
 *μέλλει) ἔμελλον A. C. 12. 28. 34. 35. 36. 38. Vulg. Copt. Syr.
 Erp. ἔμελλες B. a 18. β 4. γ 4. ἔμελες Compl.
 ἀποθανεῖν) ἀποβάλλειν B. a 20. β 4. γ 5. Ar. P. ἀποβαλεῖν Compl.
 τὰ ἔργα) — τὰ A. C. Er.

And he that overcometh, and he that keepeth my 26
works unto the end, to him will I give power over the
nations : and he shall rule them with a rod of iron ; 27
as the vessels of a potter *h* are broken to shivers :
even as I received of my Father.   And I will give 28
unto him the morning star.   He that hath an ear, 29
let him hear what the Spirit saith unto the churches.

III. And unto the angel of the church in Sardis
write ; These things saith he that hath the seven
Spirits of God, and the seven stars ; I know thy
works, that thou hast a name that thou livest, and
art dead.   Be watchful, and strengthen the things 2
which remain, that were ready to die : for I have not
found thy works complete before my God.   Remember 3
therefore how thou hast received and heard, and hold
fast, and repent.   If therefore thou shalt not watch,
I will come [on thee] as a thief, and thou shalt not
know what hour I will come upon thee.   But thou 4
hast a few names in Sardis, which have not defiled

---

f Rec.—   *g* + [καί.]   *h* ∾ shall they be broken to shivers.

2. *Θεοῦ) + μου A. C. a 27. β 7. γ 3. Compl. Vulg. Copt. Æth. Syr. Erp.
3. καὶ ἤκουσας καὶ τήρει) — B. a 17. β 4. γ 4.
   ἐπί σε) —A.C. 12. 28. Vulg. MS. *Harl.* *Tol.* Copt. Arm. Slav. MSS.
   γνῷς) γνώσῃ a 17. β 4.
4. *ἔχεις) ἀλλ' ἔχ. A. C. a 28. β 5. Compl.   Vulg. Copt. Æth. Syr.
       Arr. Slav. MSS.
   ἔχεις ὀλίγα) ὀλ. ἔχ. a 15.   Compl.
   *καὶ ἐν Σαρ.) —καὶ A. C. a 28. β 6. γ 4. Compl.   Vulg. Copt. Æth.
       Syr. Arr.
   ᾶ) οἱ 17. 28. 37. 38. 46. 88. Er. Vulg.
   αὐτῶν) ἑαυτῶν C.

καὶ περιπατήσουσι μετ' ἐμοῦ ἐν λευκοῖς, ὅτι
ἄξιοί εἰσιν.

5 Ὁ νικῶν [a] οὕτως | περιβαλεῖται ἐν ἱματίοις
λευκοῖς· καὶ οὐ μὴ ἐξαλείψω τὸ ὄνομα αὐτοῦ ἐκ
τῆς βίβλου τῆς ζωῆς, καὶ [b] ὁμολογήσω | τὸ ὄνομα
αὐτοῦ ἐνώπιον τοῦ πατρός μου καὶ ἐνώπιον τῶν
6 ἀγγέλων αὐτοῦ. ὁ ἔχων οὖς ἀκουσάτω τί τὸ
Πνεῦμα λέγει ταῖς ἐκκλησίαις.

7 Καὶ τῷ ἀγγέλῳ τῆς ἐν Φιλαδελφείᾳ ἐκκλησίας
γράψον· Τάδε λέγει ὁ ἅγιος, ὁ ἀληθινός, ὁ ἔχων
τὴν [c]κλεῖν | [d]Δαυΐδ, | ὁ ἀνοίγων καὶ οὐδεὶς
8 [e]κλείσει, κλείων, | καὶ οὐδεὶς ἀνοίγει· Οἶδά σου
τὰ ἔργα· ἰδοὺ δέδωκα ἐνώπιόν σου θύραν
ἀνεῳγμένην, [f]ἣν | οὐδεὶς δύναται κλεῖσαι αὐτήν·
ὅτι μικρὰν ἔχεις δύναμιν, καὶ ἐτήρησάς μου τὸν
9 λόγον, καὶ οὐκ ἠρνήσω τὸ ὄνομά μου. ἰδοὺ
δίδωμι ἐκ τῆς συναγωγῆς τοῦ Σατανᾶ τῶν
λεγόντων ἑαυτοὺς Ἰουδαίους εἶναι, καὶ οὐκ
εἰσὶν, ἀλλὰ ψεύδονται· ἰδοὺ ποιήσω αὐτοὺς ἵνα
[g]ἥξουσι καὶ προσκυνήσουσιν | ἐνώπιον τῶν ποδῶν
10 σου, καὶ γνῶσιν ὅτι ἐγὼ ἠγάπησά σε. ὅτι

---

[a] [οὗτος.]   [b] [ἐξομολογήσομαι.]   [c] [κλεῖδα.]   [d] [τοῦ Δαβὶδ.]

5. *οὗτος) οὕτως A. C. a 15. β 2.   Vulg. Copt. Syr. Arm. Ar. P.
περιβαλεῖται) - βάλλεται. C.
τῆς βιβ.) — τῆς Er.
*ἐξομολογήσομαι) ὁμολογήσω A. C. a 26. β 7. γ 3. Compl.
7. Φιλαδελφείᾳ) -ας A.
ἅγιος ὁ ἀληθινὸς) ἀληθ. ὁ ἅγ. A.
*κλεῖδα) κλεῖν A. C. a 25. β 3. Compl.
*τοῦ Δαβὶδ) — τοῦ A. C. [Δαυὶδ better orthography, so in Compl.]
Δαβὶδ) ἄδου 7. 16. 33. 45.
*κλείει, καὶ κλείει καὶ οὐδεὶς ἀνοίγει.) κλείσει, κλείων καὶ οὐδεὶς ἀνοίγει

their garments ; and they shall walk with me in white : for they are worthy.

He that overcometh shall thus be clothed in white 5 raiment ; and I will not blot out his name out of the book of life, and I will confess his name before my Father, and before his angels.   He that hath an 6 ear, let him hear what the Spirit saith unto the churches.

And to the angel of the church in Philadelphia 7 write ; These things saith he that is holy, he that is true, he that hath the key of David, he that openeth, and no one will shut, that shutteth, and no one openeth ; I know thy works : behold, I have set 8 before thee an open door, which no one can shut : for thou hast a little strength, and hast kept my word, and hast not denied my name.   Behold, I 9 make those of the synagogue of Satan, who say that they are Jews, and are not, but do lie; behold, I will make them to come and worship before thy feet, and know that I have loved thee.   Because thou hast 10

ᵉ [κλείει, καὶ κλείει.]   ᶠ [καὶ.]   ᵍ [ἤξωσι καὶ προσκυνήσωσιν.]

A. so, but in some, καὶ κλ. a 5, (and 3 others). κλείσει, καὶ κλείει καὶ οὐδὲ εἷς ἀνοίγει C. κλείσει αὐτὴν, εἰ (ὁ Compl.) μὴ ὁ ἀνοίγων, καὶ οὐδεὶς ἀνοίξει. a 22. β 5. γ 3. Compl.   Ar. P.
8. *καὶ οὐδ.) ἦν οὐδ. A. C. a 28. β 8. γ 4. Compl.   Vulg. Copt. Æth. Syr. Arm. Arr.
9. δίδωμι) διδῶ A. C.
      *ἤξωσι) -ουσι A. C. 2. 14. 28. 35. 36. Compl.
      *προσκυνήσωσιν) -σουσιν. A. C. 2. 13. 25.
      ἐγὼ) — a 21 β 6. Compl.
10. ὅτι) καὶ A.   καὶ ὅτι 38.

ἐτήρησας τὸν λόγον τῆς ὑπομονῆς μου, κἀγώ σε
τηρήσω ἐκ τῆς ὥρας τοῦ πειρασμοῦ τῆς μελλούσης
ἔρχεσθαι ἐπὶ τῆς οἰκουμένης ὅλης, πειράσαι τοὺς
11 κατοικοῦντας ἐπὶ τῆς γῆς. ᵃ|ἔρχομαι ταχύ· κρά-
τει ὃ ἔχεις, ἵνα μηδεὶς λάβῃ τὸν στέφανόν σου.

12 Ὁ νικῶν, ποιήσω αὐτὸν στύλον ἐν τῷ ναῷ
τοῦ Θεοῦ μου, καὶ ἔξω οὐ μὴ ἐξέλθῃ ἔτι· καὶ
γράψω ἐπ᾽ αὐτὸν τὸ ὄνομα τοῦ Θεοῦ μου, καὶ τὸ
ὄνομα τῆς πόλεως τοῦ Θεοῦ μου, τῆς καινῆς
Ἱερουσαλὴμ, ᵇἡ καταβαίνουσα| ἐκ τοῦ οὐρανοῦ
ἀπὸ τοῦ Θεοῦ μου, καὶ τὸ ὄνομά μου τὸ καινόν.
13 ὁ ἔχων οὖς ἀκουσάτω τί τὸ Πνεῦμα λέγει ταῖς
ἐκκλησίαις.

14 Καὶ τῷ ἀγγέλῳ τῆς ᶜἐν Λαοδικείᾳ ἐκκλησίας|
γράψον· Τάδε λέγει ὁ Ἀμὴν, ὁ μάρτυς ὁ
πιστὸς καὶ ἀληθινὸς, ἡ ἀρχὴ τῆς κτίσεως τοῦ
15 Θεοῦ. Οἶδά σου τὰ ἔργα, ὅτι οὔτε ψυχρὸς εἶ,
οὔτε ζεστός· ὄφελον ψυχρὸς ᵈἦς,| ἢ ζεστός·
16 οὕτως ὅτι χλιαρὸς·᾽ εἶ, καὶ οὔτε ᵉζεστὸς οὔτε
ψυχρὸς,| μέλλω σε ἐμέσαι ἐκ τοῦ στόματός μου.
17 ὅτι λέγεις· Ὅτι πλούσιός εἰμι, καὶ πεπλούτηκα,
καὶ ᶠοὐδὲν| χρείαν ἔχω· καὶ οὐκ οἶδας ὅτι σὺ εἶ

ᵃ + [ἰδού.]   ᵇ [ἡ καταβαίνει.]   ᶜ [ἐκκλησίας Λαοδικέων.]

11. *ἰδού) — A. C. a 20. β 6. Compl.   Vulg. MS. Am. Tol. Copt. Syr.
     Erp. Slav. MS.
12. ἐπ᾽ αὐτὸν) — C.
     *ἢ καταβαίνει) ἡ καταβαίνουσα. A. C. 12. 15. 25. 28. 37. 38. Er.
     ἐκ) ἀπὸ a 14. β 3. γ 3.
     ὄνομά μου) — μου. a 19. β 5.
14. *ἐκκλησίας Λαοδικέων) ἐν Λαοδικείᾳ ἐκκλησίας A. C. a 28. β 9. γ 2.
     Compl.   Vulg. Æth. Syr. Arr.
     ὁ Ἀ.) — ὁ Er.

kept the word of my patience, I also will keep thee
from the hour of temptation, which shall come upon
all the world, to try them that dwell upon the earth.
I am coming quickly: hold fast that which thou hast, 11
that none take thy crown.

Him that overcometh will I make a pillar in the 12
temple of my God, and he shall go no more out: and
I will write upon him the name of my God, and the
name of the city of my God, the New Jerusalem,
which cometh down out of heaven from my God:
and *I will write upon him* my new name.   He that 13
hath an ear, let him hear what the Spirit saith unto
the churches.

And unto the angel of the church in Laodicea 14
write; These things saith the Amen, the faithful and
true Witness, the beginning of the creation of God;
I know thy works, that thou art neither cold nor hot: 15
I would thou wert cold or hot.   Thus because thou 16
art lukewarm, and neither hot nor cold, I am about
to spue thee out of my mouth.   Because thou sayest, 17
I am rich, and have become enriched, and have need
of nothing; and knowest not that thou art wretched,

---

d [εἴης.]   *e* [ψυχρὸς οὔτε ζεστὸς.]   *f* [οὐδενὸς.]

14. καὶ ἀλη.) καὶ ὁ ἀλη. C. 2.
15. ὄφελον . . . . . ἢ ζεστός) — A. 47.
       *εἴης) ἦς C. a 23. β 7. γ 2. Compl.
16. οὔτε) οὐ a 12. β 3. γ 2. Compl.
       *ψυχρὸς οὔτε ζεστὸς) ζεστ. οὔτε ψυχ. C. a 19. β 7. Compl.   Copt.
       Syr. Arr.
17. ὅτι πλ.) — ὅτι a 21. β 5. Compl.
       *οὐδενὸς) οὐδὲν A. C. 12.

ὁ ταλαίπωρος καὶ ^aὁ[|] ἐλεεινὸς, καὶ πτωχὸς καὶ
18 τυφλὸς καὶ γυμνός· συμβουλεύω σοι ἀγοράσαι
παρ᾽ ἐμοῦ χρυσίον πεπυρωμένον ἐκ πυρὸς, ἵνα
πλουτήσῃς, καὶ ἱμάτια λευκὰ, ἵνα περιβάλῃ, καὶ
μὴ φανερωθῇ ἡ αἰσχύνη τῆς γυμνότητός σου·
καὶ ^bκολλύριον[|] ^cἐγχρίσαι[|] τοὺς ὀφθαλμούς σου,
19 ἵνα βλέπῃς. ἐγὼ ὅσους ἐὰν φιλῶ, ἐλέγχω καὶ
20 παιδεύω· ^dζήλευε[|] οὖν καὶ μετανόησον. ἰδοὺ
ἕστηκα ἐπὶ τὴν θύραν καὶ κρούω· ἐάν τις ἀκούσῃ
τῆς φωνῆς μου, καὶ ἀνοίξῃ τὴν θύραν, εἰσελεύσομαι πρὸς αὐτὸν, καὶ δειπνήσω μετ᾽ αὐτοῦ
καὶ αὐτὸς μετ᾽ ἐμοῦ.
21 Ὁ νικῶν, δώσω αὐτῷ καθίσαι μετ᾽ ἐμοῦ ἐν τῷ
θρόνῳ μοῦ, ὡς κἀγὼ ἐνίκησα, καὶ ἐκάθισα μετὰ
22 τοῦ πατρός μου ἐν τῷ θρόνῳ αὐτοῦ. ὁ ἔχων
οὖς ἀκουσάτω τί τὸ Πνεῦμα λέγει ταῖς ἐκκλησίαις.

IV. Μετὰ ταῦτα εἶδον, καὶ ἰδοὺ θύρα ἠνεῳγμένη ἐν τῷ οὐρανῷ, καὶ ἡ φωνὴ ἡ πρώτη, ἣν
ἤκουσα ὡς σάλπιγγος λαλούσης μετ᾽ ἐμοῦ
^eλέγων·[|] Ἀνάβα ὧδε, καὶ δείξω σοι ἃ δεῖ
γενέσθαι μετὰ ταῦτα.

---

^a Rec. — ^b [κολλούριον.] ^c [ἔγχρισον.]

17. *ἐλεεινὸς) ὁ ἐλε. A. a 17. β 3. Compl.
18. παρ᾽ ἐμοῦ χρυσίον) χρυ. παρ᾽ ἐμ. a 15. β 4. Compl.
   *κολλύριον) κολλύριον. C. a 15. β 4. γ 3. Vulg. κολούριον Compl.
   κουλλούριον Er.
   *ἔγχρισον) ἐγχρίσαι A. C. 7. 16. 18. 28. 36. 45. ἵνα ἐγχρίσῃ a 12
   β 5. γ 2. + ἐπὶ. 10. 37. Compl.

and miserable, and poor, and blind, and naked : I
counsel thee to buy of me gold refined by fire, that 18
thou mayest be enriched ; and white raiment, that
thou mayest be clothed, and *that* the shame of thy
nakedness may not appear ; and anoint thine eyes
with eyesalve, that thou mayest see.   As many as I
love, I rebuke and chasten : be zealous therefore, and 19
repent.   Behold, I stand at the door, and knock : if 20
any one hear my voice, and open the door, I will
come in to him, and will sup with him, and he
with me.

To him that overcometh will I grant to sit with me 21
in my throne, even as I also overcame, and am set
down with my Father in his throne.   He that hath 22
an ear, let him hear what the Spirit saith unto the
churches.

IV. After these things I saw, and, behold, *there was*
a door opened in heaven : and *there was* the first voice
which I heard as it were of a trumpet talking with
me ; saying, Come up hither, and I will show thee
the things which must be hereafter.

---

^{d} [ζήλωσον.] ^{e} [λέγουσα.]

---

19. *ζήλωσον) ζήλευε A. C. a 17. β 4. γ 1.
20. εἰσελεύσομαι) καὶ εἰσελεύσομαι a 18. β 4. γ 2. Compl.   Slav. MS.

1. ἠνεῳγμένη) ἀνεῳγμένη) a 12. β 6. γ 2. Compl.
    *λέγουσα) λέγων A. a 20. β 4.   ἀνάβα) -βηθι. A.
    ἃ δεῖ) ὅσα δεῖ A.
                                                    5

2 ^aΕὐθέως ἐγενόμην ἐν Πνεύματι· καὶ ἰδοὺ
θρόνος ἔκειτο ἐν τῷ οὐρανῷ, καὶ ἐπὶ^bτὸν θρό-
3 νον[|] καθήμενος· [καὶ ὁ καθήμενος] ^cὅμοιος ὁράσει
λίθῳ ἰάσπιδι καὶ ^dσαρδίῳ·[|] καὶ ἶρις κυκλόθεν
4 τοῦ θρόνου ^eὅμοιος[|] ὁράσει σμαραγδίνῳ. καὶ
κυκλόθεν τοῦ θρόνου θρόνοι εἴκοσι^f| τέσσαρες·
καὶ ἐπὶ τοὺς θρόνους^g| εἴκοσι^h| τέσσαρας πρε-
σβυτέρους καθημένους, περιβεβλημένους ἐν ἱμα-
τίοις λευκοῖς· καὶ ⁱ| ἐπὶ τὰς κεφαλὰς αὐτῶν
5 στεφάνους χρυσοῦς. καὶ ἐκ τοῦ θρόνου ἐκπο-
ρεύονται ἀστραπαὶ καὶ ^kφωναὶ καὶ βρονταὶ·[|] καὶ
ἑπτὰ λαμπάδες πυρὸς καιόμεναι ἐνώπιον τοῦ
θρόνου, αἵ εἰσι τὰ ἑπτὰ πνεύματα τοῦ Θεοῦ·
6 καὶ ἐνώπιον τοῦ θρόνου ^lὡς[|] θάλασσα ὑαλίνη,
ὁμοία κρυστάλλῳ. καὶ ἐν μέσῳ τοῦ θρόνου
καὶ κύκλῳ τοῦ θρόνου τέσσαρα ζῶα γέμοντα
7 ὀφθαλμῶν ἔμπροσθεν καὶ ὄπισθεν. καὶ τὸ ζῶον
τὸ πρῶτον ὅμοιον λέοντι, καὶ τὸ δεύτερον ζῶον
ὅμοιον μόσχῳ, καὶ τὸ τρίτον ζῶον ἔχον τὸ πρόσ-

^a +[καὶ.]   ^b [τοῦ θρόνου.]   ^c +[ἦν.]   ^d [σαρδίνῳ,]
ⁱ + [ἔσχον.]   ^k [βρονταὶ καὶ φωναί.]

2. *καὶ εὐθέως) — καὶ A. a 15. β 5.   Vulg. MS. Am. Harl. Syr.
*τοῦ θρόνου) τὸν θρόνον A. a 20. β 5.
3. καὶ ὁ καθήμενος ἦν) — a 23. β 6. Compl.   Æth. Arm. Arr. Slav. MS.
*ἦν) — A. 7. 13. 19. 26. 41. 42. 92.
*σαρδίνῳ) σαρδίῳ (s. σαρδείῳ) A. a 26. β 6. γ 3. Compl.
ἶρις) ἱερεῖς A. 28. Æth. Arm.
*ὁμοία) ὅμοιος. A. 6. 11. 12. 30. 35. 36. Er.   ὁμοίως a 15 β 4.
ὁράσει σμαραγδίνῳ) ὅρασις σμαραγδίνων, a 16. β 3.
4. θρόνοι) θρόνους A. 34. 35.
*εἴκ. καὶ τέσσ. [bis.] — καὶ A. a 12. β 5. Compl. κδ' Er. (and
several MSS.)
θρόνους) after εἴκ. τέσσ. A. 17. 18. 19.

Immediately I was in the Spirit : and, behold, 2 there was a throne set in heaven, and upon the throne *there was* one who sat. ⸢And he that sat⸣ *was* in 3 appearance like a jasper-stone and a sardius : and *there was* a rainbow round about the throne, in appearance like unto an emerald. And round about the throne 4 *were* twenty-four thrones : and upon the thrones *I saw* twenty-four elders sitting, clothed in white raiment ; and *I saw* on their heads crowns of gold. And out of the throne proceed lightnings and 5 voices and thunderings : and *there were* seven lamps of fire burning before the throne, which are the seven Spirits of God. And before the throne 6 *there was* as it were a sea of glass like unto crystal : and in the midst of the throne, and round about the throne, *were* four living creatures full of eyes before and behind. And the first living crea- 7 ture *was* like a lion, and the second living creature like a calf, and the third living creature had a face

---

e [ὁμοία.]   *f* + [καὶ.]   *g* + [εἶδον τοὺς.]   *h* + [καὶ.]
    i Rec. −

---

4. *εἶδον τοὺς) — A. a 11. Er.   Vulg. Copt. Æth. Syr. Arm. Arr.
     Slav. MSS.)   — εἶδον. a 9. β 3.
   ἐν) — A. 28.
   *ἔσχον) — A. a 28. β 8. Compl. Er.   Vulg. Æth. Syr. Arm. Arr.
     Slav. MSS.
5. *βρονταὶ καὶ φωναὶ) φω. κ. βρον. A. a 23. β 6. γ 2. Compl.
   θρόνου) + αὐτοῦ. a 21. β 7. γ 2. Compl.   Syr.
   αἵ εἰσι) ἅ ἐστιν A.
   τὰ) — a 18. β 3. Compl.
6. *θάλασσα) ὡς θαλ. A. 28. β 6. γ 2. Compl.   Vulg. Copt. Syr. Erp.
   ἐν μέσῳ) ἐμμέσῳ A.
7. τὸ πρόσωπον) — τὸ a 13. β 3.

ωπον ὡς ^aἀνθρώπου,[|] καὶ τὸ τέταρτον ζῶον
ὅμοιον ἀετῷ ^bπετομένῳ.[|]

8 Καὶ ^cτὰ[|] τέσσαρα ζῶα, ἓν καθ᾽ ^dἓν αὐτῶν,[|]
^eἔχων[|] ἀνὰ πτέρυγας ἓξ κυκλόθεν, καὶ ἔσωθεν
^fγέμουσιν[|] ὀφθαλμῶν, καὶ ἀνάπαυσιν οὐκ ἔχου-
σιν ἡμέρας καὶ νυκτὸς, ^gλέγοντες·[|] Ἅγιος,
ἅγιος, ἅγιος Κύριος ὁ Θεὸς ὁ παντοκράτωρ, ὁ
9 ἦν καὶ ὁ ὢν καὶ ὁ ἐρχόμενος. Καὶ ὅταν δώσουσι τὰ ζῶα δόξαν καὶ τιμὴν καὶ εὐχαριστίαν
τῷ καθημένῳ ἐπὶ τοῦ θρόνου, τῷ ζῶντι εἰς τοὺς
10 αἰῶνας τῶν αἰώνων, πεσοῦνται οἱ εἴκοσι^h| τεσ-
σαρες πρεσβύτεροι ἐνώπιον τοῦ καθημένου ἐπὶ
τοῦ θρόνου, καὶ προσκυνήσουσι τῷ ζῶντι εἰς
τοὺς αἰῶνας τῶν αἰώνων, καὶ βαλοῦσι τοὺς
στεφάνους αὐτῶν ἐνώπιον τοῦ θρόνου, λέγοντες·
11 Ἄξιος εἶ, ⁱὁ Κύριος καὶ ὁ Θεὸς ἡμῶν,[|] λαβεῖν
τὴν δόξαν καὶ τὴν τιμὴν καὶ τὴν δύναμιν· ὅτι

---

^a [ἄνθρωπος.]   ^b [πετωμένῳ.]   ^c Rec. —   ^d [ἐαυτὸ.]
                                            ^h + [καὶ.]

7. *ὡς ἄνθωρπος) ἀνθρώπου. a 15. β 5.   ὡς ἀνθρώπου. A. 11. 13. 36.
    Vulg. Copt Syr. Arr.

τέταρ. ζῶον) — ζῶον a 12. β 4.
*πετωμένῳ) πετομ. A. a 12. β 3.

8. *τέσσ.) τὰ τεσσ. A. 9. β 5.   Syr.
*ἐαυτὸ) ἐν αὐτῶν A. B. a 10. β 3. γ 2. Compl.   Vulg. Copt. Æth.
    Syr. Arm. Arr. Slav. ed.   ἐν. a 15. β 5.

*εἶχον) ἔχων A. 13. 16. 30. 32. 36. 39.   ἔχον B. a 15. β 2. γ 2.
    Compl.

κυκλόθεν) + καὶ ἔξωθεν B. 12. 33. 35. 91.
*γέμοντα) γέμουσιν A. B. a 26. β 7. γ 4. Compl.
*λέγοντα) λέγοντες A. a 21. β 5. γ 2. Er.

as of a man, and the fourth living creature *was* like a flying eagle.

And the four living creatures had each of them 8 six wings about *him;* and they are full of eyes within: and they have no rest day and night, saying, Holy, holy, holy, Lord God the Almighty, who was, and who is, and who is to come. And 9 when the living creatures give glory and honour and thanks to him that sitteth on the throne, who liveth for ever and ever, the twenty-four elders fall down before him that sitteth on the throne, and worship him that liveth for ever and ever, 10 and cast their crowns before the throne, saying, Thou art worthy, O our Lord, and God, to receive 11 glory and honour and power: for thou hast created

---

^e [εἶχον.]   ^f [γέμοντα.]   ^g [λέγοντα.]
    ⁱ [Κύριε.]

---

8. ἅγιος) nine times B. a 17. β 3. Compl.   Arm.
    ὁ θεὸς) σαβαώθ. 7. 17*. 28. 36. 39.   Ar. P. Slav. MS.

9. δώσουσι) δῶσι a 17. β 2. γ 2.   δώσει 13. 27. 31. 40. Compl.
    εὐχαριστίαν) -τίας A.
    τοῦ θρόνου) τῷ θρόνῳ A.

10. *εἴκ. καὶ τέσσ.) — καὶ A. a 8. β 4. Compl.   κδ. Er.
    προσκυνήσουσι) προσκυνοῦσι 91**. Er.
    βαλοῦσι) βάλλουσι a 5. β 3. Compl. Er.

11. *κύριε) ὁ κύριος καὶ ὁ θεὸς ἡμῶν A. B. a 23. β 5. γ 4. Compl. *Am.*
    Syr. Ar. P.   κύριε ὁ θεὸς ἡμῶν a 5. β 3. Vulg. Copt. Æth.
    Arm. Erp. Slav. MSS. + ὁ ἅγιος. a 24. β 5. γ 4. Compl.
    Syr. Ar. P.
    τὴν δυν.) — τὴν A.

σὺ ἔκτισας τὰ πάντα, καὶ διὰ τὸ θέλημά σου
^aἦσαν¹ καὶ ἐκτίσθησαν.

V. Καὶ εἶδον ἐπὶ τὴν δεξιὰν τοῦ καθημένου
ἐπὶ τοῦ θρόνου βιβλίον γεγραμμένον ἔσωθεν
καὶ ^bὄπισθεν¹ κατεσφραγισμένον σφραγῖσιν ἑπτά.
2 καὶ εἶδον ἄγγελον ἰσχυρὸν κηρύσσοντα ^cἐν¹
φωνῇ μεγάλῃ· Τίς ^d¹ ἄξιος ἀνοῖξαι τὸ βιβλίον,
3 καὶ λῦσαι τὰς σφραγῖδας αὐτοῦ; Καὶ οὐδεὶς
ἠδύνατο ἐν τῷ οὐρανῷ, οὐδὲ ἐπὶ τῆς γῆς,
οὐδὲ ὑποκάτω τῆς γῆς, ἀνοῖξαι τὸ βιβλίον,
4 οὐδὲ βλέπειν αὐτό. Καὶ ἐγὼ ἔκλαιον ^eπολύ,¹
ὅτι οὐδεὶς ἄξιος εὑρέθη ἀνοῖξαι ^f¹ τὸ βιβλίον,
5 οὔτε βλέπειν αὐτό. καὶ εἷς ἐκ τῶν πρεσβυτέρων
λέγει μοι· Μὴ κλαῖε· ἰδοὺ ἐνίκησεν ὁ λέων ὁ^g¹
ἐκ τῆς φυλῆς Ἰούδα, ἡ ῥίζα ^hΔαυὶδ¹ ἀνοῖξαι τὸ
βιβλίον, καὶ ⁱ¹ τὰς ἑπτὰ σφραγῖδας αὐτοῦ.

6 Καὶ εἶδον, ^k¹ ἐν μέσῳ τοῦ θρόνου καὶ τῶν τεσ-

---

^a [εἰσι.]	^b ~ ἔξωθεν.	^c Rec. –
	^g + [ὧν.]	^h [Δαβὶδ.]

11. τὰ πάντα) — τὰ a 9. β 4.
    τὸ θέλημα) θελήματι A.
    *εἰσι) ἦσαν A.B. a 17. β 4. γ 3.   Vulg. Copt. Arr. Slav. MS. Georg.
    καὶ ἐκτίσθησαν) — A.

1. ὄπισθεν) [So A. 12. 14. 92 vdtr.] ἔξωθεν a 26. β 6. γ 2. Compl.
    Vulg. Copt. Æth. Arm. Arr. Slav. ed. [but it is very doubtful
    if those versions have not given the supposed sense of ὄπισθεν.]
2. *φωνῇ) ἐν φω. A. a 20. β 5. γ 2.
    *ἐστιν) — A. 10. 12. 13. 36. 37. 38. 49. 91. Compl.   After ἄξιος
    a 14. β 5.
3. οὐρανῷ) + ἄνω a 18. β 5.   Copt. Syr. Ar. P.
    οὐδὲ [bis vel ter] οὔτε a 15. β 4.
    οὐδὲ ὑποκ.) καὶ ὑποκ. Er.

all things, and for thy pleasure they were and have
been created.

V. And I saw in the right hand of him that
sat on the throne a book written within and on
the backside, sealed up with seven seals. And I 2
saw a strong angel proclaiming with a loud voice,
Who *is* worthy to open the book, and to loose
the seals thereof? And no one in heaven, nor 3
on the earth, neither under the earth, was able
to open the book, neither to look thereon. And 4
I wept much, because no man was found worthy
to open the book, neither to look thereon. And 5
one of the elders saith unto me, Weep not: behold,
the Lion of the tribe of Juda, the Root of David,
hath prevailed to open the book, and the seven
seals thereof.

And I saw in the midst of the throne and of the 6

---

^{d} + [ἐστιν.] ^{e} [πολλά.] ^{f} + [καὶ ἀναγνῶναι.]
^{i} + [λῦσαι.] ^{k} + [καὶ ἰδού]

---

3. οὐδὲ βλεπ.) οὔτε βλ. A. 16.
4. the whole verse — A.
   ἐγὼ) — 12. 36. Er.   Copt. Æth. Arm.
   *πολλὰ) πολὺ a 28. β 7. γ 3. Compl.
   *καὶ ἀναγνῶναι) — B. a 23. β 6.   Vulg. Copt. Æth. Syr. Arr.
5. ἐκ) — Er.
   *ὧν) — A. a 28. β 7. γ 3. Compl.   Vulg.
   ἀνοῖξαι) ὁ ἀνοίγων B. a 18. β 4.
   *λῦσαι) — A. B. a 27. β 8. γ 3. Compl.   Verss. exc. Vulg. ed.
      and Slav. MS.
6. καὶ εἶδον) — A.
   *καὶ ἰδού) — a 26. β 8. Copt. Æth. Syr. Arm. Arr. Slav. MSS.
      + καὶ A.
   ἐν μέσῳ) ἐμμέσῳ A.

σάρων ζώων, καὶ ἐν μέσῳ τῶν πρεσβυτέρων,
ἀρνίον ἑστηκὸς ὡς ἐσφαγμένον, ἔχον κέρατα
ἑπτὰ καὶ ὀφθαλμοὺς ἑπτά, οἵ εἰσι τὰ [ἑπτὰ]
^aπνεύματα τοῦ Θεοῦ | ^bἀπεσταλμένοι | εἰς
7 πᾶσαν τὴν γῆν. καὶ ἦλθε, καὶ εἴληφε ^c| ἐκ τῆς
δεξιᾶς τοῦ καθημένου ἐπὶ τοῦ θρόνου.

8 Καὶ ὅτε ἔλαβε τὸ βιβλίον, τὰ τέσσαρα ζῶα
καὶ οἱ εἰκοσιτέσσαρες πρεσβύτεροι ^dἔπεσαν |
ἐνώπιον τοῦ ἀρνίου, ἔχοντες ἕκαστος ^eκιθάραν, |
καὶ φιάλας χρυσᾶς γεμούσας θυμιαμάτων, αἵ
9 εἰσιν αἱ προσευχαὶ τῶν ἁγίων· καὶ ᾄδουσιν
ᾠδὴν καινὴν, λέγοντες·

Ἄξιος εἶ λαβεῖν τὸ βιβλίον, καὶ ἀνοῖξαι τὰς
σφραγῖδας αὐτοῦ· ὅτι ἐσφάγης, καὶ ἠγόρασας
τῷ Θεῷ ἡμᾶς ἐν τῷ αἵματί σου, ἐκ πάσης
10 φυλῆς καὶ γλώσσης καὶ λαοῦ καὶ ἔθνους· Καὶ
ἐποίησας ^fαὐτοὺς | τῷ Θεῷ ἡμῶν βασιλεῖς καὶ
ἱερεῖς· καὶ ^gβασιλεύουσιν | ἐπὶ τῆς γῆς.

---

^a [τοῦ θεοῦ πνεύματα.]   ^b [τὰ ἀπεσταλμένα] ∽ ἀποστελλόμενα.
^g ∽ βασιλεύσουσιν.   [βασιλεύσομεν.]

6. ἐν μέσῳ) ἐμμέσῳ A.
ἐσφαγμένον) ἐσφαγισμένον Compl.
ἔχον) ἔχων A.
οἵ) ἅ. a 23. β 8. γ 3. Compl. Slav. ed.
τὰ ἑπτὰ) — ἑπτὰ A. 12. Er. Am.* Harl.* Æth.
*τοῦ θεοῦ πνεύματα) πνευ. τ. θεοῦ A. a 19. β 8. Compl. Vulg.
  Syr. Arr. Arm.
*τὰ ἀπεσταλμένα) ἀπεσταλμένοι A. ἀπεσταλμένα 38. 49. ἀποστελ-
  λόμενα a 20. β 5. Compl. τὰ ἀποστελλόμενα 6. 7. 8. 9. 13. 16.
7. *τὸ βιβλίον) — A. a 24. β 6. γ 2. Harl.* Am.* Æth. Arm
  After θρόνου 38. Compl. Vulg. ed. — τὸ Compl.
8. οἱ) — 30. Compl.

four living creatures, and in the midst of the elders,
a Lamb, standing, as it had been slain, having seven
horns and seven eyes, which are the [seven] Spirits
of God sent forth into all the earth.   And he came 7
and took *the book* out of the right hand of him
that sat upon the throne.

And when he took the book, the four living 8
creatures and twenty-four elders fell down before
the Lamb, having every one of them a harp and
golden cups full of odours, which are the prayers
of the saints.   And they sing a new song, saying,

Thou art worthy to take the book, and to open 9
the seals thereof: for thou wast slain, and hast redeemed us to God by thy blood out of every kindred,
and tongue, and people, and nation ; and thou hast 10
made them unto our God kings and priests : and
i they reign over the earth.

---

c + [τὸ βιβλίον.]   d [ἔπεσον.]   e [κιθάρας.]   f [ἡμᾶς.]
i ∼ [they will reign.]

8. *ἔπεσον) ἔπεσαν A. 7. 9. 26. 27. 42. Er.
   *κιθάρας) κιθάραν A. a 19. β 5. γ 2.   Æth. Syr. Arm. Erp.

9. ᾄδουσιν) ᾄδωσιν A.
   τῷ θεῷ) — Er.   Harl.*
   ἡμᾶς) — A.   Æth.

10. *ἡμᾶς) αὐτοὺς A. B. a 27.   β 8. γ 5. Compl.   Vulg. MS. Am.
    Copt. Æth. Syr. Ar. P. Slav. MS.
    τῷ θεῷ ἡμῶν) — A.   Æth.
    βασιλεῖς) βασιλείαν A.   Vulg. Copt.
    *βασιλεύσομεν) βασιλεύουσιν A. a 9. β 4. γ 2. Compl.   Syr.
    Copt. Ar. P. Slav MS.   βασιλεύσουσιν a 12. β 4. γ 2.   Am.
    Harl.

11 Καὶ εἶδον, καὶ ἤκουσα φωνὴν ἀγγέλων πολ-
λῶν ᵃκύκλῳ| τοῦ θρόνου καὶ τῶν ζώων καὶ τῶν
πρεσβυτέρων· καὶ ἦν ὁ ἀριθμὸς αὐτῶν μυριάδες
12 μυριάδων καὶ χιλιάδες χιλιάδων, λέγοντες φωνῇ
μεγάλῃ· Ἄξιόν ἐστι τὸ ἀρνίον τὸ ἐσφαγμένον
λαβεῖν τὴν δύναμιν καὶ πλοῦτον καὶ σοφίαν καὶ
13 ἰσχὺν καὶ τιμὴν καὶ δόξαν καὶ εὐλογίαν. Καὶ
πᾶν κτίσμα ὃ ᵇ| ἐν τῷ οὐρανῷ, καὶ ᶜἐπὶ τῆς γῆς,|
καὶ ὑποκάτω τῆς γῆς, καὶ ἐπὶ τῆς θαλάσσης ᵈ|
ἐστι, καὶ τὰ ἐν αὐτοῖς πάντα, ἤκουσα λέγοντας·
Τῷ καθημένῳ ἐπὶ ᵉτῷ θρόνῳ| καὶ τῷ ἀρνίῳ ἡ
εὐλογία καὶ ἡ τιμὴ καὶ ἡ δόξα καὶ τὸ κράτος εἰς
14 τοὺς αἰῶνας τῶν αἰώνων. Καὶ τὰ τέσσαρα ζῶα
ἔλεγον· Ἀμήν. καὶ οἱ ᶠ| πρεσβύτεροι ἔπεσαν,
καὶ προσεκύνησανᵍ|.

VI. Καὶ εἶδον ὅτε ἤνοιξε τὸ ἀρνίον μίαν ἐκ
τῶν ʰἑπτὰ| σφραγίδων, καὶ ἤκουσα ἑνὸς ἐκ τῶν

ᵃ [κυκλόθεν.]   ᵇ + [ἐστιν.]   ᶜ [ἐν τῇ γῇ.]   ᵈ + [ἄ.]   ᵉ [τοῦ θρόνου.]

11. ἤκουσα) + ὡς a 22. β 6. Compl.   Syr.
*κυκλόθεν) κύκλῳ A. a 24. β 9. γ 4. Compl.
τῶν πρεσβ.) —τῶν Er.
καὶ ἦν . . . . μυριάδων) —Er.
12. ἄξιον) ἄξιος A. Er.   τὸ ἀρν.) —τὸ Er.
πλοῦτον) τὸν πλοῦτον a 19. β 6.
13. *ἐστιν) —A. a 18. β 5.   Vulg. M.S. Tol. Copt. Arr.
*ἐν τῇ γῇ) ἐπὶ τῆς γῆς A. a 27. β 7. Compl.   Vulg.   ἐπὶ γῆς 16. 28.
*ἄ) —A. a 20. β 5.   Vulg. Copt.
πάντα) πάντας a 16. β 3. Compl.
λέγοντας) λέγοντα A. 12.   Copt. Syr.   -τες Er.
*τοῦ θρόνου) τῷ θρόνῳ A. a 15. β 3.
καὶ τῷ) —καὶ A. Slav. MS.

And I saw, and I heard the voice of many angels 11
round about the throne and the living creatures
and the elders : and the number of them was
myriads of myriads, and thousands of thousands ;
saying with a loud voice, Worthy is the Lamb 12
that was slain to receive power, and riches, and
wisdom, and strength, and honour, and glory, and
blessing.   And every creature which is in heaven, 13
and on the earth, and under the earth, and in the
sea, and all things that are in them, heard I saying; Unto him that sitteth upon the throne, and unto
the Lamb, *be* blessing, and honour, and glory, and
power, for ever and ever.   And the four living 14
creatures said, Amen.   And the elders fell down
and worshipped.

VI. And I saw when the Lamb opened one of
the seven seals, and I heard, one of the four living

---

f + [εἴκοσι τέσσαρες.]   *g* + [ζῶντι εἰς τοὺς αἰῶνας τῶν αἰώνων.]   *h* Rec. —

---

13. αἰώνων) + ἀμὴν a 24. β 8. Compl.   Æth. Slav. MSS.
14. ἔλεγον) λέγοντα a 20. β 4. Compl.
    ἀμὴν) τὸ ἀμ. a 24. β 6 γ 2.
    *εἴκοσι τέσσαρες) — A. B. a 28. β 8. γ 3. Compl.   Vulg. MS. *Am.*
        Tol. Copt. Æth. Syr. Ar. P. Slav. MS.
    ἔπεσαν) ἔπεσον a 11. β 4. γ 2. Compl.
    *ζῶντι εἰς τοὺς αἰῶνας τῶν αἰώνων) — A.B.C. a 27. β 8. γ 3. Compl.
        Vulg. MS. *Am. Tol. Harl.* Copt. Syr. (Arm.) Ar. P. Slav. MS.

1. ὅτε) ὅτι a 21. β 3. Compl.
    μίαν) ἐν Er.
    *σφραγίδων) ἑπτὰ σφραγ. A.B.C. a 25. β 3. Compl.   Vulg. Æth.
        Syr. Ar. P. Slav.

τεσσάρων ζώων λέγοντος, ὡς ᵃφωνῇ¹ βροντῆς·
2 "Ερχου ᵇ¹. [Καὶ εἶδον,] καὶ ἰδοὺ ἵππος λευκὸς,
καὶ ὁ καθήμενος ἐπ' ᶜαὐτὸν¹ ἔχων τόξον· καὶ
ἐδόθη αὐτῷ στέφανος, καὶ ἐξῆλθε νικῶν, καὶ
ἵνα νικήσῃ.
3 Καὶ ὅτε ἤνοιξε τὴν ᵈσφραγῖδα τὴν δευτέραν,¹
ἤκουσα τοῦ δευτέρου ζώου λέγοντος· "Ερχου ᵉ¹.
4 Καὶ ἐξῆλθεν ἄλλος ἵππος πυῤῥός· καὶ τῷ
καθημένῳ ἐπ' ᶠαὐτὸν¹ ἐδόθη αὐτῷ λαβεῖν τὴν
εἰρήνην ᵍἐκ¹ τῆς γῆς, καὶ ἵνα ἀλλήλους ʰσφά-
ξουσι·¹ καὶ ἐδόθη αὐτῷ μάχαιρα μεγάλη.
5 Καὶ ὅτε ἤνοιξε τὴν ⁱσφραγῖδα τὴν τρίτην,¹
ἤκουσα τοῦ τρίτου ζώου λέγοντος· "Ερχου ᵏ¹.
[Καὶ εἶδον], καὶ ἰδοὺ ἵππος μέλας, καὶ ὁ καθήμενος ἐπ' ˡαὐτὸν¹ ἔχων ζυγὸν ἐν τῇ χειρὶ αὐτοῦ.
6 καὶ ἤκουσα ᵐ[ὡς]¹ φωνὴν ἐν μέσῳ τῶν τεσσάρων
ζώων λέγουσαν· Χοῖνιξ σίτου δηναρίου, καὶ

ᵃ [φωνῆς.]   ᵇ [καὶ βλέπε.]   ᶜ [αὐτῷ.]   ᵈ [δευτέραν σφραγῖδα.]
ᵏ + [καὶ βλέπε.]

---

1. *φωνῆς) φωνῇ A. C. a 25. β 7. Compl.   (Syr. Arr.)
   βροντῆς) + λέγοντος A.   Slav. MS.
   *καὶ βλέπε) — A. C. a 9. β 2. Compl.   Vulg. MS. Am. Erp.   καὶ
   ἴδε a 17. β 7.

2. καὶ εἶδον) — a 18. β 4. γ 2.   Vulg. MS. Harl.* Tol. Slav. MSS.
   *αὐτῷ 1st) αὐτὸν A. C. a 24. β 7. γ 4. Compl.
   ἐξῆλθε) + ὁ A.

3. *δευτέραν σφαγῖδα) σφραγ. τὴν δευτ. A.C. 6. 12. 34. 35. 49.   Er.
   *καὶ βλέπε) — A.B.C. a 25. β 7. γ 2. Compl.   Vulg. MS. Am. Syr.
   Arm. (Erp.)   καὶ ἴδε 34. 35. 39. 40. 43.

4. πυῤῥός) πυρὸς A. a 19. β 5. γ 2.   Erp.
   καὶ τῷ) κ. ἐν. τ. A.
   *αὐτῷ 1st) αὐτὸν A. C. a 24. β 6. γ 4. Compl.

creatures saying, as it were with a voice of thunder, Come. ⌈And I saw,⌉ and behold a white horse : 2 and he that sat on him had a bow ; and a crown was given unto him : and he went forth conquering, and to conquer.

And when he opened the second seal, I heard the 3 second living creature saying, Come. And there 4 went out another horse *that was* red : and *power* was given to him that sat on him to take peace from the earth, and that they should slay one another : and there was given unto him a great sword.

And when he opened the third seal, I heard the 5 third living creature saying, Come. ⌈And I saw,⌉ and behold a black horse ; and he that sat on him had a pair of balances in his hand. And I heard 6 ⌈as it were⌉ a voice in the midst of the four living creatures, saying, A measure of wheat for a penny,

---

ᵉ + [καὶ βλέπε.]   ᶠ [αὐτῷ.]   ᵍ [ἀπὸ.]   ʰ [σφάξωσι.]   ⁱ [τρίτην σφραγῖδα.]
ˡ [αὐτῷ.]   ᵐ Rec.—

4. αὐτῷ 2nd) — A.
   *ἀπὸ) ἐκ C. a 26. β 6. Compl. — A. 7. 16. 39. 46.
   καὶ ἵνα) —καὶ a 22. β 5. γ 2. Compl. Copt. Arm. Arr. Slav. MSS.
   *σφάξωσι) - ουσιν A. C.
   μάχαιρα μεγάλη) μεγ. μάχ. A.

5. *τρίτην σφραγῖδα) σφρ. τὴν τρ. A. C. a 18. β 5. Compl.
   *καὶ βλέπε) — A. C. a 11. β 2. (& 80.) Compl. Am. Arm. Erp.
      καὶ ἴδε a 15. β 6.
   καὶ εἶδον) — those MSS. which read κ. ἴδε (exc. two) also 26. 27
      38. 80. Vulg. Æth. Slav. MSS.
   *αὐτῷ) αὐτὸν A. C. a 18. β 6. γ 2. Compl.

6. *ἤκουσα) + ὡς A. C. 6. 12. 17. Vulg. Slav. MS.
   ἐν μέσῳ) ἐμμέσῳ A. C.

τρεῖς χοίνικες ^aκριθῶν¹ δηναρίου· καὶ τὸ ἔλαιον καὶ τὸν οἶνον μὴ ἀδικήσῃς.

7 Καὶ ὅτε ἤνοιξε τὴν σφραγῖδα τὴν τετάρτην, ἤκουσα φωνὴν τοῦ τετάρτου ζώου ^bλέγοντος·¹ 8 Ἔρχου^{c1}. [Καὶ εἶδον,] καὶ ἰδοὺ ἵππος χλωρὸς, καὶ ὁ καθήμενος ἐπάνω αὐτοῦ, ὄνομα αὐτῷ ὁ Θάνατος, καὶ ὁ ἄδης ^dἠκολούθει¹ μετ᾽ αὐτοῦ· καὶ ἐδόθη ^eαὐτῷ¹ ἐξουσία ^fἐπὶ τὸ τέταρτον τῆς γῆς, ἀποκτεῖναι¹ ἐν ῥομφαίᾳ, καὶ ἐν λιμῷ καὶ ἐν θανάτῳ, καὶ ὑπὸ τῶν θηρίων τῆς γῆς.

9 Καὶ ὅτε ἤνοιξε τὴν πέμπτην σφραγῖδα, εἶδον ὑποκάτω τοῦ θυσιαστηρίου τὰς ψυχὰς τῶν ἐσφαγμένων διὰ τὸν λόγον τοῦ Θεοῦ, καὶ διὰ 10 τὴν μαρτυρίαν ἣν εἶχον· καὶ ^gἔκραξαν¹ φωνῇ μεγάλῃ, λέγοντες· Ἕως πότε, ὁ Δεσπότης ὁ ἅγιος καὶ ^{h1} ἀληθινὸς, οὐ κρίνεις καὶ ἐκδικεῖς τὸ αἷμα ἡμῶν ⁱἐκ¹ τῶν κατοικούντων ἐπὶ τῆς γῆς;

---

^a ∾ [κριθῆς.]   ^b [λέγουσαν.]   ^c + [καὶ βλέπε.]   ^d [ἀκουλουθεῖ.]   ^e ∾ [αὐτοῖς.]

6. *κριθῆς) κριθῶν A. C. 12.   Syr.   + τοῦ A.

7. σφραγῖδα τὴν τετ.) τετ. σφραγ. 38. Compl.
   φωνὴν) — C. a 20. β 4.   Copt. Syr. Arr. Slav. MSS.
   τοῦ τετάρτου ξώου) τὸ τέταρτον ζώον C.
   *λέγουσαν) λέγοντος A.C. a 20. β 6. γ 3. Compl.   Vulg. Copt. Syr.
       Arr. Slav. MSS.
   *καὶ βλέπε) — A.C. a 8. β 4. Compl.   Am. Erp.   καὶ ἴδε a 18. β 4.

8. καὶ εἶδον) — the MSS. which read κ. ἴδε (exc. three) also 13. 38.
       Vulg.   — καὶ C.
   ὁ καθ.) — ὁ C.
   αὐτοῦ) — C. 12. Er.   Harl.
   ὁ θάν.) — ὁ C. 16*. 37. 49. 91. Compl.   ὁ ἀθάνατος A.
   *ἀκουλουθεῖ) ἠκολούθει B. C. a 20. β 7. γ 2.   Vulg. Æth. Arr. Slav.
   μετ᾽ αὐτοῦ) αὐτῷ B. a 20. β 5. γ 2.

and three measures of barley for a penny ; and *see* thou hurt not the oil and the wine.

And when he opened the fourth seal, I heard the 7 voice of the fourth living creature saying, Come. [And I saw,] and behold a pale horse : and his 8 name that sat on him was Death, and Hades followed with him. And power was given unto [k] him over the fourth part of the earth, to kill with sword,' and with hunger, and with death, and by the beasts of the earth.

And when he opened the fifth seal, I saw under 9 the altar the souls of those that were slain because of the word of God, and because of the testimony which they held : and they cried with a loud voice, 10 saying, How long, O Master, holy and true, dost thou not judge and avenge our blood of those that dwell on the earth ? And a white robe was given

---

f [ἀποκτεῖναι ἐπὶ τὸ τέταρτον τῆς γῆς.]   g [ἔκραζον.]   h + [ὁ.]   i [ἀπὸ.]   k ∾ them.

8. *αὐτοῖς) αὐτῷ B. a 25. β 6. γ 3. Compl.   Vulg. Copt. Æth. Syr. Arm. Arr. Slav.
  *ἀποκτεῖναι ἐπὶ τὸ τέταρτον τῆς γῆς) ἐπὶ τ. τετ. τ. γῆς ἀποκτ. A.B.C. a 28. β 8. γ 3. Compl.
  καὶ ὑπὸ) — καὶ Er.   καὶ τὸ τέταρτον A.
9. εἶδον) + καὶ C.
  ψυχὰς) + τῶν ἀνθρώπων 10. 12. 17. 36. 37. 46. 49. 91. Compl. Æth. Arm.
  ἐσφαγμένων) ἐσφαγισμένων Compl.
  διὰ τὴν) — διὰ A.
  μαρτυρίαν) + τοῦ ἀρνίου B. a 24. β 6. γ 2. Compl.   Syr. Ar. P.
10. *ἔκραζον) ἔκραξαν A.B.C. a 25. β 5. Compl.
  φωνῇ μεγάλῃ) φωνὴν μεγάλην a 17. β 3.
  *ὁ ἀληθ.) – ὁ A.C. a 17. β 6. Compl.
  *ἀπὸ) ἐκ A.C. a 26. β 4. Compl.

11 Καὶ ^aἐδόθη |^b αὐτοῖς [ἑκάστω]|^c στολὴ λευκὴ,| καὶ
ἐρρέθη αὐτοῖς ἵνα ἀναπαύσωνται ἔτι χρόνον
⌈μικρὸν⌉ ἕως ^d| ^eπληρωθῶσι| καὶ οἱ σύνδουλοι
αὐτῶν καὶ οἱ ἀδελφοὶ αὐτῶν, οἱ μέλλοντες
^fἀποκτέννεσθαι| ὡς καὶ αὐτοί.

12 Καὶ εἶδον ὅτε ἤνοιξε τὴν σφραγῖδα τὴν ἕκτην·
καὶ ^g| σεισμὸς μέγας ἐγένετο, καὶ ὁ ἥλιος ἐγένετο
μέλας ὡς σάκκος τρίχινος, καὶ ἡ σελήνη ^hὅλη|
13 ἐγένετο ὡς αἷμα, καὶ οἱ ἀστέρες τοῦ οὐρανοῦ
ἔπεσαν εἰς τὴν γῆν, ὡς συκῆ βάλλει τοὺς
ὀλύνθους αὐτῆς, ὑπὸ ⁱἀνέμου μεγάλου| σειο-
14 μένη· καὶ ^kὁ| οὐρανὸς ἀπεχωρίσθη ὡς βιβλίον
^lἑλισσόμενον|, καὶ πᾶν ὄρος καὶ νῆσος ἐκ τῶν
15 τόπων αὐτῶν ἐκινήθησαν· καὶ οἱ βασιλεῖς τῆς
γῆς, καὶ οἱ μεγιστᾶνες, καὶ οἱ ^mχιλίαρχοι καὶ οἱ
πλούσιοι,| καὶ οἱ ⁿἰσχυροὶ,| καὶ πᾶς δοῦλος καὶ^o|

---

^a [ἐδόθησαν.]   ^b [ἑκάστοις.]   ^c [στολαὶ λευκαὶ.]   ^d [οὗ.]   ^e ∾ πληρώσωσι.
        ^k Rec.—   ^l [εἰλισσόμενον.]   ^m [πλούσιοι καὶ

11. *ἐδόθησαν) ἐδόθη Α.Β.C. a 28. β 7. γ 3. Compl.   Syr. Arm. Erp.
    *ἑκάστοις) αὐτοῖς ἑκάστῳ Α.C. a 11. β 4. γ 3. (Vulg.) αὐτοῖς.Β. a 14.
    β 3. (& 31) Compl.   Arm.   ἑκάστῳ 2.4.11.12.19. ἑκάσταις Er.
    *στολαὶ λευκαὶ) στολὴ λευκὴ the same as those which read ἐδόθη
        (also 39.)   — στολαὶ λευκαὶ καὶ ἐρρέθη αὐτοῖς Compl.
    ἀναπαύσωνται) - σονται Α. 13. 28. 30.* 32. 36.
    ἔτι χρόν.) χρόν. ἔτι Α.
    μικρὸν) —Β. a 25. β 6. β 2. Compl.   Æth. Ar. P.
    *οὗ) —A.B.C. a 16. β 5.
    *πληρώσονται) πληρωθῶσι Α. C. 29. Compl.   Vulg. Copt. Æth.
        Syr.   -σωσι Β. a 28. β 5.   Erp.
    οἱ μελλ.) καὶ οἱ μ. a 15. β 6.
    *ἀποκτείνεσθαι) ἀποκτέννεσθαι Α.C. a 8.   ἀποκτένεσθαι. a 7. β 4.
12. εἶδον) + καὶ a 7. β 3. Compl.
    ἰδοὺ) — C. a 26. β 8. γ 2. Compl.   Vulg. MS. Am. Tol. Harl.
        Copt. Æth. Syr. Arr. Slav. MS.
    μέγας ἐγέν) ἐγέν-μέγ. Α.

unto [each of] them ; and it was said unto them, 11
that they should rest yet for a ⸢little⸣ season, until
both their fellow-servants and their brethren, that
should be killed as they *were*, shall have been completed.

And I saw when he opened the sixth seal, and 12
there was a great earthquake ; and the sun became
black as sackcloth of hair, and the whole of the
moon became as blood ; and the stars of heaven fell 13
unto the earth, even as a fig-tree casteth its untimely
figs, when it is shaken of a mighty wind.   And the 14
heaven departed as a scroll when it is rolled together;
and every mountain and island were moved out of
their places.   And the kings of the earth, and the 15
great men, and the chief captains, and the rich men,
and the mighty men, and every bondman, and free-

[πληρώσονται.]   *ᶠ* [ἀποκτείνεσθαι.]   *ᵍ* + [ἰδού.]   *ʰ* Rec.—   *ⁱ* [μεγάλου ἀνέμου.]
οἱ χιλίαρχοι.]   *ⁿ* [δυνατοὶ]   *ᵒ* + [πᾶς.]

12. ἐγένετο μέλας) μ. ἐγέν. a 14. β 4. Compl.   μέλας) μέγας A.
    *σελήνη) + ὅλη A. B. C. a 17. β 8. γ 2.   Vulg. Copt. Æth. Syr.
        Arm. Arr. Slav. MS.
13. οὐρανοῦ) Θεοῦ A.   Vulg. MS.
    ἔπεσαν) -σον a 13. β 4. Compl.
    βάλλει) βαλοῦσα a 17. β 4. γ 2. Syr. Slav. MSS. βαλλοῦσα a 4. (& 39.)
    *μεγάλου ἀνέμου) ἀνεμ. μεγ. A. C. a 15. β 5.
    σειομένη) σαλευομένη A. 12.
14. *οὐραν.) ὁ οὐραν. A. C. a 18. β 7. Compl.
    *εἰλισσόμενον) ἑλισσ. or ἑλισσόμενον A. C. a 12. Compl.   εἱλισσό-
        μενος. a 12. β 2. γ 3.
    ἐκινήθησαν) ἀπεκίνησαν A.
15. *πλούσιοι καὶ οἱ χιλ.) χιλ. κ. οἱ πλ. A. C. a 22. β 7. Compl.   Vulg.
        Copt. Æth. Syr. Arm. Arr. Slav. MS.
    *δυνατοὶ) ἰσχυροὶ A. C. a 27. β 7. Compl.   —12. 36.
    *καὶ πᾶς ἐλ.) —κ. π. A.   —π. A. C. a 19. β 7.   Vulg. Æth. Syr.
        Arr. Slav. MS.

ἐλεύθερος ἔκρυψαν ἑαυτοὺς εἰς τὰ σπήλαια
16 καὶ εἰς τὰς πέτρας τῶν ὀρέων. καὶ λέγουσι τοῖς
ὄρεσι καὶ ταῖς πέτραις· Πέσετε ἐφ᾽ ἡμᾶς, καὶ
κρύψατε ἡμᾶς ἀπὸ προσώπου τοῦ καθημένου ἐπὶ
τοῦ θρόνου, καὶ ἀπὸ τῆς ὀργῆς τοῦ ἀρνίου·
17 ὅτι ἦλθεν ἡ ἡμέρα ἡ μεγάλη τῆς ὀργῆς ᵃαὐτοῦ,|
καὶ τίς δύναται σταθῆναι ;

VII. ᵇ|Μετὰ ᶜτοῦτο| εἶδον τέσσαρας ἀγγέλους
ἑστῶτας ἐπὶ τὰς τέσσαρας γωνίας τῆς γῆς,
κρατοῦντας τοὺς τέσσαρας ἀνέμους τῆς γῆς, ἵνα
μὴ πνέῃ ἄνεμος ἐπὶ τῆς γῆς, μήτε ἐπὶ τῆς θα-
λάσσης, μήτε ἐπί ᵈτι| δένδρον.
2 Καὶ εἶδον ἄλλον ἄγγελον ᵉἀναβαίνοντα| ἀπὸ
ἀνατολῆς ἡλίου, ἔχοντα σφραγῖδα Θεοῦ ζῶντος·
καὶ ἔκραξε φωνῇ μεγάλῃ τοῖς τέσσαρσιν ἀγγέλοις, οἷς ἐδόθη αὐτοῖς ἀδικῆσαι τὴν γῆν καὶ τὴν
3 θάλασσαν, λέγων· Μὴ ἀδικήσητε τὴν γῆν, μήτε
τὴν θάλασσαν, μήτε τὰ δένδρα, ᶠἄχρι| σφρα-
γίσωμεν τοὺς δούλους τοῦ Θεοῦ ἡμῶν ἐπὶ τῶν
μετώπων αὐτῶν.

ᵃ ∾ αὐτῶν.   ᵇ + [καὶ.]   ᶜ [ταῦτα.]

16. πέσετε) πέσατε Α. 7. 28.
   τοῦ θρόνου) τῷ θρόνῳ. a 15. β 5.
17. αὐτοῦ) αὐτῶν C. 38.   Vulg. Syr.

1. *καὶ) — A.C.   Vulg. Copt.
   *ταῦτα) τοῦτο Α.C. a 22. β 6. γ 2. Compl.
   ὁ ἄνεμ.) — ὁ C.
   τῆς γῆς 2nd) —38. Vulg. MS. Copt. Erp.
   ἐπὶ τῆς γῆς) —A.

man, hid themselves in the caves and in the
rocks of the mountains ; and said to the moun- 16
tains and rocks, Fall on us, and hide us from
the face of him that sitteth on the throne, and
from the wrath of the Lamb : for the great 17
day of ⁸ his wrath is come; and who is able
to stand ?

VII. After this I saw four angels standing
on the four corners of the earth, holding the
four winds of the earth, that the wind should
not blow on the earth, nor on the sea, nor on
any tree.

And I saw another angel ascending from the 2
sun-rising, having the seal of the living God :
and he cried with a loud voice to the four
angels, to whom it was given to hurt the earth
and the sea, saying, Hurt not the earth, nor 3
the sea, nor the trees, till we have sealed the
servants of our God upon their foreheads.

ᵈ [πᾶν.]   ᵉ [ἀναβάντα.]   ᶠ [ἄχρις οὗ.]   ᵍ ∾ [their.]

---

1. τῆς θαλ.) — τῆς A.
   μήτε 2nd) μὴ C.
   *πᾶν δένδρον) τι δένδρον C. a 22. β 6.   Vulg. Ar. Copt.   δένδρου A.
2. *ἀναβάντα) ἀναβαίνοντα A. C. a 27. β 7. Compl.
   ἀνατολῆς) ἀνατολῶν A. 90.   ἔκραξε) ἔκραζεν A.
3. μήτε 1st) καὶ A.
   *ἄχρις οὗ) — οὗ A. C. 12. Er.
   σφραγίσωμεν) -ζωμεν Er.

4 Καὶ ἤκουσα τὸν ἀριθμὸν τῶν ἐσφραγισμένων·
ᵃἑκατὸν καὶ τεσσαράκοντα τέσσαρες| χιλιάδες
ἐσφραγισμένοι, ἐκ πάσης φυλῆς υἱῶν Ἰσραήλ·
5 ἐκ φυλῆς Ἰούδα, ᵇδώδεκα| χιλιάδες ἐσφραγι-
σμένοι· ἐκ φυλῆς Ῥουβὴν, ᵇδώδεκα| χιλιάδες
[ἐσφραγισμενοι·] ἐκ φυλῆς Γὰδ, ᵇδώδεκα| χιλι-
6 άδες [ἐσφραγισμένοι·] ἐκ φυλῆς Ἀσὴρ, ᵇδώδεκα|
χιλιάδες [ἐσφραγισμενοι·] ἐκ φυλῆς Νεφθαλεὶμ,
ᵇδώδεκα| χιλιάδες [ἐσφραγισμένοι·] ἐκ φυλῆς
Μανασσῆ, ᵇδώδεκα| χιλιάδες [ἐσφραγισμένοι·]
7 ἐκ φυλῆς Συμεὼν, ᵇδώδεκα| χιλιάδες [ἐσφραγι-
σμένοι·] ἐκ φυλῆς Λευῒ, ᵇδώδεκα| χιλιάδες
[ἐσφραγισμένοι·] ἐκ φυλῆς Ἰσαχὰρ, ᵇδώδεκα|
8 χιλιάδες [ἐσφραγισμένοι·] ἐκ φυλῆς Ζαβουλὼν,
ᵇδώδεκα| χιλιάδες [ἐσφραγισμένοι·] ἐκ φυλῆς
Ἰωσὴφ, ᵇδώδεκα| χιλιάδες [ἐσφραγισμένοι·] ἐκ φυ-
λῆς Βενιαμὶν, ᵇδώδεκα| χιλιάδες ἐσφραγισμένοι.
9 Μετὰ ταῦτα εἶδον, καὶ [ἰδοὺ] ὄχλος πολὺς, ὃν
ἀριθμῆσαι αὐτὸν οὐδεὶς ᶜἐδύνατο,| ἐκ παντὸς
ἔθνους καὶ φυλῶν καὶ λαῶν καὶ γλωσσῶν,
ἑστῶτες ἐνώπιον τοῦ θρόνου καὶ ἐνώπιον τοῦ

ᵃ ρμδ´.　　　　ᵇ [ιβ´.]

---

4. καὶ ἤκου. τ. ἀρ. τ. ἐσφραγισμένων) — A.　τὸν ἀριθμὸν) τῶν ἀριθμῶν
Compl.
*ρμδ´). So Rec.　ἑκατὸν) + καὶ C. α 7. Compl.
ἐσφραγισμένοι) -μένων α 13. β 3.
5. &c.) *ιβ´) δώδεκα A. C.　Many MSS. [92.]
ἐσφραγισμένοι) -μέναι α 12. β 4. γ 2.
5—8. ἐσφραγισμένοι) — 10 times (all except first and last) A. C.
α 22. β 6. γ 3. Compl.　Vulg. M.S. Harl.* Copt. Æth. Syr. Erp.

And I heard the number of those who were 4
sealed : an hundred and forty-four thousand *were*
sealed, *they were* from every tribe of the children
of Israel.   Of the tribe of Juda, twelve thousand 5
were sealed.   Of the tribe of Reuben, twelve thousand [*were* sealed.]   Of the tribe of Gad, twelve
thousand [*were* sealed.]   Of the tribe of Aser, 6
twelve thousand [*were* sealed.]   Of the tribe of
Nepthalim, twelve thousand [*were* sealed.]   Of the
tribe of Manasses, twelve thousand [*were* sealed.]
Of the tribe of Simeon, twelve thousand [*were* 7
sealed.]   Of the tribe of Levi, twelve thousand [*were*
sealed.]   Of the tribe of Issachar, twelve thousand
[*were* sealed.]   Of the tribe of Zebulon, twelve 8
thousand [*were* sealed.]   Of the tribe of Joseph,
twelve thousand [*were* sealed.]   Of the tribe of
Benjamin, twelve thousand *were* sealed.

After these things I saw, and, behold, a great 9
multitude, which no man could number, of all
nations, and kindreds, and peoples, and tongues,
stood before the throne, and before the Lamb,

---

^c [ἠδύνατο.]

---

8. ἐσφραγισμένοι last) -μέναι a 12. β 4.
9. καὶ ἰδοὺ ὄχλος πολὺς ὂν) ὄχλον πολὺν καὶ A.   — ἴδου C.   Vulg.
   Copt. Æth.
   αὐτὸν) — a 16. . β .
   *ἠδύνατο) ἐδυ. A. C. a 10. β 4. Compl.
   καὶ φυλῶν) — Er.
   ἑστῶτες) -τας. a 14 β 4.   -τῶν C.
   ἐνώπιον) ἐπὶ A.

ἀρνίου, ᵃπεριβεβλημένους¹ στολὰς λευκὰς, καὶ
10 φοίνικες ἐν ταῖς χερσὶν αὐτῶν· καὶ ᵇκράζουσι¹
φωνῇ μεγάλῃ, λέγοντες· Ἡ σωτηρία τῷ Θεῷ
ἡμῶν τῷ καθημένῳ ἐπὶ ᶜτῷ θρόνῳ,¹ καὶ τῷ
11 ἀρνίῳ. Καὶ πάντες οἱ ἄγγελοι ᵈἑστήκεισαν¹
κύκλῳ τοῦ θρόνου καὶ τῶν πρεσβυτέρων καὶ τῶν
τεσσάρων ζώων, καὶ ᵉἔπεσαν¹ ἐνώπιον τοῦ
θρόνου ἐπὶ ᶠτὰ πρόσωπα¹ αὐτῶν, καὶ προσεκύ-
12 νησαν τῷ Θεῷ, λέγοντες· Ἀμήν· ἡ εὐλογία καὶ
ἡ δόξα καὶ ἡ σοφία καὶ ἡ εὐχαριστία καὶ ἡ τιμὴ
καὶ ἡ δύναμις καὶ ἡ ἰσχὺς τῷ Θεῷ ἡμῶν εἰς τοὺς
αἰῶνας τῶν αἰώνων· [ἀμήν.]
13 Καὶ ἀπεκρίθη εἷς ἐκ τῶν πρεσβυτέρων, λέγων
μοι· Οὗτοι οἱ περιβεβλημένοι τὰς στολὰς τὰς
14 λευκὰς, τίνες εἰσὶ, καὶ πόθεν ἦλθον; καὶ εἴρηκα
αὐτῷ· Κύριέ ᵍμου,¹ σὺ οἶδας. Καὶ εἶπέ μοι·
Οὗτοί εἰσιν οἱ ἐρχόμενοι ἐκ τῆς θλίψεως τῆς
μεγάλης, καὶ ἔπλυναν τὰς στολὰς αὐτῶν, καὶ
ἐλεύκαναν [ʰαὐτὰς¹] ἐν τῷ αἵματι τοῦ ἀρνίου.

ᵃ [περιβεβλημένοι.]   ᵇ [κράζοντες.]   ᶜ [τοῦ θρόνου.]   ᵈ [ἑστήκεσαν.]

9. *περιβεβλημένοι) -μένους A. C. a 21. β 5.
   φοίνικες) -κας a 22. β 4.
10. *κράζοντες) κράζουσι A. C. a 27. β 7. γ 4. Compl.   Vulg. Æth.
    Arm. Arr. Slav.
    τῷ θεῷ) τοῦ θεοῦ A.
    τῷ Θ. ἡ. τῷ καθ. ἐπὶ τοῦ θρ.) τ. καθ. ἐπὶ τ. θρόνου τοῦ Θ. ἡ. Er.
    *τοῦ θρόνου) τῷ θρόνῳ A. C. a 16. β 4. γ 2.
11 *ἑστήκεσαν) -κεισαν A. C. a 9. β 3.   εἱστήκεισαν 14. 47. 48. 49.
    50. 90. Compl.
    *ἔπεσον) -σαν A. C. a 5. β 3. Er.
    θρόνου) + αὐτοῦ a 17. β 5.   Syr. Ar. P.
    *πρόσωπον) τὰ πρόσωπα A. C. a 27. β 7. γ 2. Compl.   Vulg. Syr.
    Arm. Arr.

clothed with white robes, and palms in their hands ;
and they cry with a loud voice, saying, Salvation 10
to our God who sitteth upon the throne, and
unto the Lamb.   And all the angels stood round 11
about the throne, and *about* the elders and the
four living creatures, and they fell before the
throne on their faces, and worshipped God,
saying, Amen : Blessing, and glory, and wis- 12
dom, and thanksgiving, and honour, and power,
and might, *be* unto our God for ever and ever.
[Amen.]

And one of the elders answered, saying unto 13
me, What are these which are arrayed in white
robes ? and whence came they ?   And I said 14
unto him, my lord, thou knowest.   And he said
to me, These are those who come out of the
great tribulation, and have washed their robes,
and made [them] white in the blood of the Lamb.

ͤ [ἔπεσον.]   ᶠ [πρόσωπον.]   ᵍ Rec.—   ʰ [στολὰς αὐτῶν.]

12. καὶ ἡ σοφία) — A.
    ἀμήν.) — C. 28. 36.
    ἡ ἰσχ.) — ἡ Compl.

13. εἰσὶ) — 12 Er.

14. εἴρηκα) εἶπον a 25. β 5. Compl.
    *κύριε) + μου C. a 26. β 6. γ 2. Compl.   Vulg. Copt. Syr. Ar. P.
        Slav. MSS.
    ἐκ τῆς θλίψεως τῆς) ἀπὸ θλίψ. A.
    ἔπλυναν) ἐπλάτυναν a 6. β 2. Er.
    *στολὰς αὐτῶν) αὐτὰς A. 10. 12. 19. 37. 46. 49. 91. Compl.   Vulg·
        Copt. Syr. Ar. P. Slav. MS.   τὰς στ. αὐτ. B.   — a 19. β 6.
        Æth. Arm. Erp.

15 διὰ τοῦτό εἰσιν ἐνώπιον τοῦ θρόνου τοῦ Θεοῦ,
καὶ λατρεύουσιν αὐτῷ ἡμέρας καὶ νυκτὸς ἐν τῷ
ναῷ αὐτοῦ· καὶ ὁ καθήμενος ἐπὶ τοῦ θρόνου,
16 σκηνώσει ἐπ᾽ αὐτούς. οὐ πεινάσουσιν ἔτι, οὐδὲ
διψήσουσιν ἔτι, οὐδὲ μὴ πέσῃ ἐπ᾽ αὐτοὺς ὁ ἥλιος,
17 οὐδὲ πᾶν καῦμα· ὅτι τὸ ἀρνίον τὸ ἀνὰ μέσον
τοῦ θρόνου ποιμανεῖ αὐτούς, καὶ ὁδηγήσει
αὐτοὺς ἐπὶ ᵃζωῆς¹ πηγὰς ὑδάτων, καὶ ἐξαλείψει
ὁ Θεὸς πᾶν δάκρυον ᵇἐκ¹ τῶν ὀφθαλμῶν αὐτῶν.

VIII. Καὶ ᶜὅταν¹ ἤνοιξε τὴν σφραγῖδα τὴν ἑβ-
δόμην, ἐγένετο σιγὴ ἐν τῷ οὐρανῷ ὡς ᵈἡμίωρον.¹
2 Καὶ εἶδον τοὺς ἑπτὰ ἀγγέλους, οἳ ἐνώπιον
τοῦ Θεοῦ ἑστήκασι, καὶ ἐδόθησαν αὐτοῖς ἑπτὰ
3 σάλπιγγες. καὶ ἄλλος ἄγγελος ἦλθε, καὶ ἐστάθη
ἐπὶ ᵉτὸ θυσιαστήριον,¹ ἔχων λιβανωτὸν χρυσοῦν·
καὶ ἐδόθη αὐτῷ θυμιάματα πολλὰ ἵνα δώσῃ ταῖς
προσευχαῖς τῶν ἁγίων πάντων ἐπὶ τὸ θυσια-
4 στήριον τὸ χρυσοῦν τὸ ἐνώπιον τοῦ θρόνου. καὶ
ἀνέβη ὁ καπνὸς τῶν θυμιαμάτων ταῖς προσευχαῖς τῶν ἁγίων, ἐκ χειρὸς τοῦ ἀγγέλου,

---

ᵃ [ζώσας.]   ᵇ [ἀπὸ.]   ᶜ [ὅτε.]

---

15. ἐπὶ τοῦ θρόνου) ἐ. τῷ θρόνῳ a 15. β 4. Compl.

16. οὐδὲ 1st) + μὴ A. 92.
ἔτι 2nd) 34. 35. 36. 38. 40. Er.   Æth. Arm. Ar. P. Slav.
οὐδὲ) οὐδ᾽ οὐ a 23. β 4. Compl.

17. ποιμανεῖ . . . . ὁδηγήσει) ποιμαίνει . . . . ὁδηγεῖ a 18. β 3.
*ζώσας) ζωῆς A. a 25. β 7. γ 2. Compl.   Vulg. Æth. Arm. Erp.
καὶ ἐξαλείψει . . . . αὐτῶν) — 38. Er.
*ἀπὸ) ἐκ A. C. a 14. β 5.

Therefore are they before the throne of God, and 15
serve him day and night in his temple : and he that
sitteth on the throne shall be the covert over them.
They shall hunger no more, neither thirst any more ; 16
neither shall the sun light on them, nor any heat.
For the Lamb which is in the midst of the throne 17
shall be their shepherd, and he shall lead them unto
fountains of living waters : and God shall wipe away
all tears from their eyes.

VIII.   And when he opened the seventh seal, there
was silence in heaven about the space of half an hour.
And I saw the seven angels who stood before 2
God ; and to them were given seven trumpets.
And another angel came and stood at the altar, 3
having a censer of gold ; and there was given
unto him much incense, that he should put
it to the prayers of all saints upon the altar of
gold which was before the throne.   And the 4
smoke of the incense, went up with the prayers
of the saints, out of the angel's hand before God.

---

^d [ἡμιώριον.]   ^e ∾ τοῦ θυσιαστηρίου.᠁

---

1. *ὅτε) ὅταν A. C.
   *ἡμιώριον) ἡμίωρον A. C.

2. τοὺς ἑπτὰ) — 26 Er.
   ἐδόθησαν) ἐδόθη A.

3. τὸ θυσιαστήριον) τοῦ θυσιαστηρίου a 23. β 5. γ 2. Compl.   τοῦ
      θυσιαστηρίον C.
   λιβανωτὸν) λίβανον τὸ C.
   δώσῃ) δώσει. A. a 8. β 2.

5 ἐνώπιον τοῦ Θεοῦ. καὶ εἴληφεν ὁ ἄγγελος τὸν λιβανωτὸν, καὶ ἐγέμισεν αὐτὸν ἐκ τοῦ πυρὸς τοῦ θυσιαστηρίου, καὶ ἔβαλεν εἰς τὴν γῆν· καὶ ἐγένοντο ᵃβρονταὶ καὶ ἀστραπαὶ καὶ φωναὶ¹ καὶ σεισμός.

6 Καὶ οἱ ἑπτὰ ἄγγελοι ᵇοἱ¹ ἔχοντες τὰς ἑπτὰ σάλπιγγας, ἡτοίμασαν ἑαυτοὺς ἵνα σαλπίσωσι.

7 Καὶ ὁ πρῶτος ᶜ¹ ἐσάλπισε, καὶ ἐγένετο χάλαζα καὶ πῦρ μεμιγμένα ᵈἐν¹ αἵματι, καὶ ἐβλήθη εἰς τὴν γῆν· ᵉκαὶ τὸ τρίτον τῆς γῆς κατεκάη,¹ καὶ τὸ τρίτον τῶν δένδρων κατεκάη, καὶ πᾶς χόρτος χλωρὸς κατεκάη.

8 Καὶ ὁ δεύτερος ἄγγελος ἐσάλπισε, καὶ ὡς ὄρος μέγα πυρὶ καιόμενον ἐβλήθη εἰς τὴν θάλασσαν· καὶ ἐγένετο τὸ τρίτον τῆς θαλάσσης 9 αἷμα· καὶ ἀπέθανε τὸ τρίτον τῶν κτισμάτων τῶν ἐν τῇ θαλάσσῃ, τὰ ἔχοντα ψυχὰς, καὶ τὸ τρίτον τῶν πλοίων ᶠδιεφθάρησαν.¹

10 Καὶ ὁ τρίτος ἄγγελος ἐσάλπισε, καὶ ἔπεσεν ἐκ τοῦ οὐρανοῦ ἀστὴρ μέγας καιόμενος ὡς λαμπὰς, καὶ ἔπεσεν ἐπὶ τὸ τρίτον τῶν ποταμῶν, καὶ

ᵃ [φωναὶ καὶ βρονταὶ καὶ ἀστραπαὶ.]   ᵇ Rec.−   ᶜ + [ἄγγελος.]

5. τὸ . . . . . αὐτὸ) 33. 34. Er.
ἔβαλεν) ἔλαβον A.
*φωναὶ καὶ βρονταὶ καὶ ἀστραπαὶ) βρ. κ. ἀστρ. κ. φω. A. 16. 38. Copt. Syr. βρ. κ. φω. κ. ἀστρ. a 15. β 5. Vulg. Arm. Erp.
6 οἱ ἑπτὰ) — οἱ Er.
*ἔχον.) οἱ ἔχον. A. a 20. β 4. Compl.
7. *ἄγγελος) — A. a 27. β 5. Compl. Vulg. MS. Harl.* Tol. Syr. Ar. P.
*αἵματι) ἐν αἵμ. A. a 24. β 4. γ 3. Compl.

And the angel took the censer, and filled it with 5 the fire of the altar, and cast *it* into the earth : and there were thunderings, and lightnings, and voices, and an earthquake.

And the seven angels who had the seven trum- 6 pets prepared themselves to sound.

And the first sounded, and there was hail and 7 fire mingled with blood, and they were cast upon the earth : and the third part of the earth was burned up, and the third part of trees was burned up, and all green grass was burned up.

And the second angel sounded, and as it were a 8 great mountain burning with fire was cast into the sea : and the third part of the sea became blood ; and the third part of the creatures which were in 9 the sea, which had life, died ; and the third part of the ships were destroyed.

And the third angel sounded, and there fell a 10 great star from heaven, burning as it were a lamp, and it fell upon the third part of the rivers, and

---

^d Rec. —   ^e Rec. —   ^f [διεφθάρη.]

7. *γῆν) + καὶ τὸ τρίτον τῆς γῆς κατεκάη. A. a 26. β 7. γ 5. Compl.
    Vulg. Æth. Syr. Arm. Ar. P. Slav. MSS.
    καὶ τὸ τρ. τ. δένδρων κατεκάη) — 10. 14. 30. 32. 33. 90. Compl.
8. πυρὶ) — B. a 24. β 5. Compl.
9. τῶν ἐν) — τῶν a 14. β 5. Compl. Er.
    ἐν τῇ θαλάσσῃ) — 12 Er.   *Harl.* Arm. Slav. MS.
    *διεφθάρη) -ρησαν A. a 5. β 2. Compl.   -ρησεν Er.
10. κ. ἐπὶ τ. π. ὑδάτων) — A.

11 ἐπὶ τὰς πηγὰς ὑδάτων. καὶ τὸ ὄνομα τοῦ
ἀστέρος λέγεται ᵃὁ Ἄψινθος· καὶ ᵇἐγένετο τὸ
τρίτον τῶν ὑδάτων εἰς ἄψινθον, καὶ πολλοὶ
ᶜτῶν ἀνθρώπων ἀπέθανον ἐκ τῶν ὑδάτων, ὅτι
ἐπικράνθησαν.

12 Καὶ ὁ τέταρτος ἄγγελος ἐσάλπισε, καὶ ἐπλήγη
τὸ τρίτον τοῦ ἡλίου καὶ τὸ τρίτον τῆς σελήνης
καὶ τὸ τρίτον τῶν ἀστέρων· ἵνα σκοτισθῇ τὸ
τρίτον αὐτῶν, καὶ ἡ ἡμέρα μὴ ᵈφανῇ τὸ τρίτον
αὐτῆς, καὶ ἡ νὺξ ὁμοίως.

13 Καὶ εἶδον, καὶ ἤκουσα ἑνὸς ᵉἀετοῦ ᶠπετο-
μένου ἐν μεσουρανήματι, λέγοντος φωνῇ μεγάλῃ.
Οὐαὶ, οὐαὶ, οὐαὶ ᵍτοῖς κατοικοῦσιν ἐπὶ τῆς γῆς,
ἐκ τῶν λοιπῶν φωνῶν τῆς σάλπιγγος τῶν τριῶν
ἀγγέλων τῶν μελλόντων σαλπίζειν.

IX. Καὶ ὁ πέμπτος ἄγγελος ἐσάλπισε, καὶ
εἶδον ἀστέρα ἐκ τοῦ οὐρανοῦ πεπτωκότα εἰς τὴν
γῆν, καὶ ἐδόθη αὐτῷ ἡ κλεὶς τοῦ φρέατος τῆς
2 ἀβύσσου· [καὶ ἤνοιξε τὸ φρέαρ τῆς ἀβύσσου.]

ᵃ Rec.— ᵇ [γίνεται.] ᶜ Rec.— ᵈ [φαίνῃ.]

10. ὑδάτων) τῶν ὑδ. a 18. β 6. Compl.
11. *ἄψινθος) ὁ ἀψ. A. a 23. β 4. γ 3. Compl.
*γίνεται) ἐγένετο. A. a 26. β 6. γ 2. Compl.
τῶν ὑδάτων) — Er.
*ἀνθρώπων) τῶν ἀνθρ. A. a 19. β 6. Compl.
ἐκ τῶν) ἐπὶ τῶν A.
12. ἡ ἡμέρα .... αὐτῆς καὶ) τὸ τρίτον αὐτῆς (αὐτῶν 4 MSS. Copt.)
μὴ φανῇ· ἡ ἡμέρα καὶ B. a 18. β 4. γ 3. Vulg. Copt.
*φαίνῃ) φανῇ A. a 20. β 4. γ 4.
τρίτον last) τετάρτον A.

upon the fountains of waters ; and the name of the 11
star is called Wormwood : and the third part of the
waters became wormwood ; and many men died of
the waters, because they were made bitter.

And the fourth angel sounded, and the third part 12
of the sun was smitten, and the third part of the
moon, and the third part of the stars ; so that the
third part of them was darkened, and the day shone
not for a third part of it, and the night likewise.

And I saw, and heard an eagle flying in the mid- 13
heaven, saying with a loud voice, Woe, woe, woe,
to those who dwell upon the earth by reason of the
other voices of the trumpet of the three angels,
which are about to sound!

IX. And the fifth angel sounded, and I saw
a star fallen from heaven unto the earth : and to
him was given the key of the bottomless pit.
[And he opened the bottomless pit,] and there 2

---

e [ἀγγέλου.]   f [πετωμένου.]   g ∼ τοὺς κατοικοῦντας.

13. *ἀγγέλου) ἀετοῦ A. B. a 23. β 3. Compl.   Vulg. Copt. Æth. Syr.
    Arm. ed. in m.
    *πετωμένου) πετομ. A. a 13. β 5. Compl.
    μεσουρανήματι) -νίσματι Er.
    μεγάλῃ) + τρὶς 5. 7. 10. 28. 37. 49. 91. Compl.
    οὐαὶ) — Er.
    τοῖς κατοικοῦσιν) τοὺς κατοικοῦντας B. a 18. β 5.

 2. καὶ ἤνοιξε τ. φρ. τ. ἀβύσ.) — a 15. β 5. γ 3.   Am. Harl.* Tol.
    Copt. Æth. Arm. ed. Ven.

καὶ ἀνέβη καπνὸς ἐκ τοῦ φρέατος ὡς καπνὸς
καμίνου μεγάλης· καὶ ἐσκοτίσθη ὁ ἥλιος καὶ ὁ
3 ἀὴρ ἐκ τοῦ καπνοῦ τοῦ φρέατος. καὶ ἐκ τοῦ
καπνοῦ ἐξῆλθον ἀκρίδες εἰς τὴν γῆν, καὶ ἐδόθη
αὐταῖς ἐξουσία, ὡς ἔχουσιν ἐξουσίαν οἱ σκορ-
4 πίοι τῆς γῆς· καὶ ἐρρέθη αὐταῖς ἵνα μὴ ἀδικήσωσι τὸν χόρτον τῆς γῆς, οὐδὲ πᾶν χλωρὸν, οὐδὲ
πᾶν δένδρον, εἰ μὴ τοὺς ἀνθρώπους ᵃ| οἵτινες
οὐκ ἔχουσι τὴν σφραγῖδα τοῦ Θεοῦ ἐπὶ τῶν με-
5 τώπων [αὐτῶν.] καὶ ἐδόθη αὐταῖς ἵνα μὴ ἀπο-
κτείνωσιν αὐτοὺς, ἀλλ' ἵνα ᵇβασανισθήσονται|
μῆνας πέντε· καὶ ὁ βασανισμὸς αὐτῶν ὡς βασα-
6 νισμὸς σκορπίου, ὅταν παίσῃ ἄνθρωπον. καὶ ἐν
ταῖς ἡμέραις ἐκείναις ζητήσουσιν οἱ ἄνθρωποι τὸν
θάνατον, καὶ ᶜοὐ μὴ| ᵈεὕρωσιν| αὐτόν· καὶ ἐπιθυ-
μήσουσιν ἀποθανεῖν, καὶ ᶜφεύγει| ὁ θάνατος
ἀπ' αὐτῶν.

7 Καὶ τὰ ὁμοιώματα τῶν ἀκρίδων ὅμοια ἵπποις
ἡτοιμασμένοις εἰς πόλεμον, καὶ ἐπὶ τὰς κεφαλὰς
αὐτῶν ὡς στέφανοι ᶠὅμοιοι χρυσῷ| καὶ τὰ πρόσ-

ᵃ + [μόνους.]   ᵇ [βασανισθῶσι.]   ᶜ [οὐχ.]   ᵈ [εὑρήσουσιν.]

2. ἐκ τ. φρ. ὡς καπ.) — 35. 41. Er.   ὡς — A.
μεγάλης) καιομένης a 23. β 5. Compl.   Syr. Ar. P. Slav. MS.
καιομ. μεγ. 37. 38. 40. 41. 42.   Slav. MSS.
ἐσκοτίσθη) ἐσκοτώθη A. 12. 14. 92.
4. ἀδικήσωσι) -σουσιν A. 36.
*μόνους) — A. a 24. β 6. Er.   Copt. Syr. Arr.
οὐκ) — Er.
τοῦ θεοῦ) — 12. 17. 47. Er.   Harl.* Arm.
αὐτῶν) — A. 12. 28. Er.   Am. Harl.* Tol.
5. αὐταῖς) αὐτοῖς A. 12. Er.

arose a smoke out of the pit, as the smoke of a
great furnace; and the sun and the air were
darkened by reason of the smoke of the pit.   And 3
there came out of the smoke locusts upon the
earth: and unto them was given power, as the
scorpions of the earth have power.   And it was 4
commanded them that they should not hurt the
grass of the earth, neither any green thing, neither
any tree; but those men which have not the seal
of God in [their] foreheads.   And to them it 5
was given that they should not kill them, but that
they should be tormented five months : and their torment *was* as the torment of a scorpion, when he
striketh a man.   And in those days shall men seek 6
death, and not find it; and shall desire to die, and
death shall flee from them.

And the likenesses of the locusts *were* like unto 7
horses prepared for war; and on their heads *were*
as it were crowns *ᵍ* like unto gold, and. their faces

| *e* [φεύξεται.] | *f* ∽ χρυσοῖ. | *g* ∽ of gold. |

5. *βασανισθῶσι) - σθήσονται A. 12. 36. 38.   - σωσι 7. Compl.
     -σθήσωνται Er.
   παίσῃ) πλήξῃ a 5. β 2. Compl.
6. ζητήσουσιν) ζητοῦσιν a 8. Compl.
   *οὐχ) οὐ μὴ A. a 26. β 6. Compl.
   *εὑρήσουσιν) εὕρωσιν A. 12. 17. 28. 34. 35. 46. 49. 92.
   *φεύξεται) φεύγει A. 12. 17. 36. 38. Er.
   ὁ θάν. ἀπ' αὐτ.) ἀπ' αὐτ. ὁ θάν. a 18. β 4. Compl.
7. ὅμοια) ὁμοιώματα A.
   ἡτοιμασμένοις) -μενα. Compl.
   ὅμοιοι χρυσῷ) χρυσοῖ a 25. β 5. γ 3. Compl.   Ar. P. Slav. MS.

8 ωπα αὐτῶν ὡς πρόσωπα ἀνθρώπων· καὶ εἶχον
τρίχας ὡς τρίχας γυναικῶν· καὶ οἱ ὀδόντες
9 αὐτῶν ὡς λεόντων ἦσαν· καὶ εἶχον θώρακας
ὡς θώρακας σιδηροῦς· καὶ ἡ φωνὴ τῶν πτε-
ρύγων αὐτῶν ὡς φωνὴ ἁρμάτων ἵππων πολ-
10 λῶν τρεχόντων εἰς πόλεμον. καὶ ἔχουσιν οὐρὰς
ὁμοίας σκορπίοις, καὶ κέντρα· ᵃκαὶ| ἐν ταῖς
οὐραῖς αὐτῶν ᵇ| ἡ ἐξουσία αὐτῶν ἀδικῆσαι
11 τοὺς ἀνθρώπους μῆνας πέντε. ᶜ| ᵈἔχουσιν|
ᵉἐπ᾽ αὐτῶν| βασιλέα τὸν ἄγγελον τῆς ἀβύσσου,
ὄνομα αὐτῷ Ἑβραϊστὶ Ἀβαδδὼν, καὶ ἐν τῇ Ἑλ-
ληνικῇ ὄνομα ἔχει Ἀπολλύων.
12 Ἡ οὐαὶ ἡ μία ἀπῆλθεν· ἰδοὺ ᶠἔρχεται| ἔτι δύο
οὐαὶ μετὰ ταῦτα.
13 Καὶ ὁ ἕκτος ἄγγελος ἐσάλπισε, καὶ ἤκουσα
φωνὴν μίαν ἐκ τῶν [τεσσάρων] κεράτων τοῦ
θυσιαστηρίου τοῦ χρυσοῦ τοῦ ἐνώπιον τοῦ Θεοῦ,
14 ᵍλέγουσαν| τῷ ἕκτῳ ἀγγέλῳ ʰὁ ἔχων| τὴν σάλ-
πιγγα· Λῦσον τοὺς τέσσαρας ἀγγέλους τοὺς
δεδεμένους ἐπὶ τῷ ποταμῷ τῷ μεγάλῳ Εὐφράτῃ.

ᵃ [ἦν.]   ᵇ + [καὶ.]   ᶜ + [καὶ.]   ᵈ ∾ἔχουσαι.

8. εἶχον) εἶχαν A:
10. ὁμοίας) — οις A.
  *κέντρα ἦν ἐν ταῖς οὐραῖς αὐτῶν· καὶ ἡ ἐξουσία αὐτῶν) καὶ in place of
  ἦν, and the following καὶ omitted, A. 17.   Vulg. MS. Syr.
  Erp. (καὶ a 4. β 2.) κεν.· καὶ ἐν τ. οὐρ. αὐτ. ἐξουσίαν ἔχουσι (τοῦ)
  B. a 21. β 5.   Compl.
11. *καὶ 1st) — A. a 23. β 7. γ 2. Compl.   Copt. Ar. Slav. MS.
  ἔχουσιν) ἔχουσαι a 21. β 3. Compl.
  *ἐφ᾽ αὐτ. βασ.) ἐπ᾽ αὐτ. βασ. A. 14. Er.   βασ. ἐπ᾽ αὐτ. a 16.
  β 3. Compl.

were as the faces of men.   And they had hair as the 8
hair of women, and their teeth were as *the teeth* of
lions.   And they had breastplates, as it were breast- 9
plates of iron; and the sound of their wings *was* as
the sound of chariots of many horses rushing to
battle.   And they have tails like unto scorpions, 10
and stings; and their power *was* in their tails, to
hurt men five months.   They have a king over them, 11
the angel of the bottomless pit, whose name in the
Hebrew tongue *is* Abaddon, and in the Greek tongue
he hath *his* name Apollyon.

One woe is past; behold, there come two woes 12
more hereafter.

And the sixth angel sounded, and I heard 13
a voice from the [four] horns of the golden altar
which is before God, saying to the sixth angel 14
which had the trumpet, Loose the four angels
which are bound at the great river Euphrates.

ᵉ [ἐφ' αὐτῶν.]   *ᶠ* [ἔρχονται.]   *ᵍ* ∾ λέγοντος   *ʰ* [ὃς εἶχε.]

---

11. ἄγγελον τῆς ἀβύσσου) ἄρχοντα τῆς ἀβύσ. τ. ἀγγ. A.
καὶ ἐν) ἐν δὲ a 20. β 3. γ 2. Compl.
'Απο=λλ.) ὁ 'Απ. Compl.
12. *ἔρχονται) -εται A. a 16. β 5. Compl.   Copt.
ἔτι) — 49. Er.
13. τεσσάρων) — A. 28.   Vulg. MS. *Am. Harl. Tol.* Æth. Syr. Arr.
τοῦ ἐνώ.) — τοῦ Er.
14. λέγουσαν) -οντος B. a 15. β 4.   -οντα A.
ἕκτῳ) — A.
*ὃς εἶχε) ὁ ἔχων A. B. a 27. β 6. γ 3. Compl.

15 Καὶ ἐλύθησαν οἱ τέσσαρες ἄγγελοι οἱ ἡτοιμα-
σμένοι εἰς τὴν ὥραν καὶ ἡμέραν καὶ μῆνα καὶ
ἐνιαυτὸν, ἵνα ἀποκτείνωσι τὸ τρίτον τῶν ἀνθρώ-
16 πων. καὶ ὁ ἀριθμὸς ^aτῶν[|] στρατευμάτων τοῦ
ἱππικοῦ ^bδυσμυριάδες[|] μυριάδων· (^{c|} ἤκουσα
17 τὸν ἀριθμὸν αὐτῶν.) καὶ οὕτως εἶδον τοὺς
ἵππους ἐν τῇ ὁράσει, καὶ τοὺς καθημένους ἐπ'
αὐτῶν, ἔχοντας θώρακας πυρίνους καὶ ὑακιν-
θίνους καὶ θειώδεις· καὶ αἱ κεφαλαὶ τῶν ἵππων
ὡς κεφαλαὶ λεόντων, καὶ ἐκ τῶν στομάτων αὐτῶν
18 ἐκπορεύεται πῦρ καὶ καπνὸς καὶ θεῖον. ^dἀπὸ[|]
τῶν τριῶν ^eπληγῶν[|] τούτων ἀπεκτάνθησαν τὸ
τρίτον τῶν ἀνθρώπων, ἐκ τοῦ πυρὸς καὶ ^{f|} τοῦ
καπνοῦ καὶ ^{g|} τοῦ θείου, τοῦ ἐκπορευομένου ἐκ
19 τῶν στομάτων αὐτῶν. ^hἡ γὰρ ἐξουσία τῶν
ἵππων[|] ἐν τῷ στόματι αὐτῶν ⁱἐστι,[|] ^kκαὶ ἐν ταῖς
οὐραῖς αὐτῶν.[|] αἱ γὰρ οὐραὶ αὐτῶν ὅμοιαι ὄφε-
σιν, ἔχουσαι κεφαλὰς, καὶ ἐν αὐταῖς ἀδικοῦσι.
20 Καὶ οἱ λοιποὶ τῶν ἀνθρώπων οἳ οὐκ ἀπεκτάν-
θησαν ἐν ταῖς πληγαῖς ταύταις, ^lοὐ[|] μετενόησαν

---

^a Rec.— ^b [δύο μυριάδες.] ∾ μυριάδες. ^c + [καὶ.] ^d [ὑπὸ.] ^e Rec.—

15. ἐλύθησαν) ἐλυπήθησαν Α.
καὶ ἡμέραν) — Compl.
16. *ἀριθμὸς) +τῶν Α. α 23. β 6. Compl.
ἱππικοῦ) ἵππου α 22. β 3. Compl.
*δύο μυριάδες) δυσμυριάδες Α. 11. 12. (δισμυριάδες 36.) — δύο
α 25. β 4. γ 2. Compl. Ar. P. Slav. MSS.
*καὶ ἤκου.) — καὶ Α. α 25. β 4. Compl.
18. *ὑπὸ) ἀπὸ Α. C. α 27. β 6. γ 3. Compl.
τῶν τρ.) — τῶν C.

And the four angels were loosed, that were 15
prepared for the hour, and day, and month, and
year, to slay the third part of men.   And the 16
number of the armies of the horsemen *was* two
myriads of myriads : (I heard the number of them).
And thus I saw the horses in the vision, and those 17
that sat on them, having breastplates of fire, and
of jacinth, and like unto brimstone : and the heads
of the horses *were* as the heads of lions ; and out of
their mouths issued fire and smoke and brimstone.
By these three plagues was the third part of men 18
killed, by reason of the fire, and the smoke, and
the brimstone, which issued out of their mouths.
For the power of the horses is in their mouth, 19
and in their tails : for their tails *were* like unto
serpents, and had heads, and with them they do
hurt.

And the rest of the men who were not killed 20
by these plagues, repented not of the works of their

---

f + [ἐκ.]   *g* + [ἐκ.]   *h* [αἱ γὰρ ἐξουσίαι αὐτῶν.]   *i* [εἰσιν.]   *k* Rec.—   *l* [οὔτε.]

18. *τριῶν) + πληγῶν A. C. a 22. β 7. Compl.   Vulg. Copt. Æth. Syr.
    Erp. Arm. Slav.
    ἐκ 1st) ἀπὸ a 21. β 4.
    *ἐκ 2nd and 3rd) — A. a 25. β 7. Compl.
    ἐκ 3rd) — C.
19. *αἱ γὰρ ἐξουσίαι αὐτῶν) ἡ γὰρ ἐξουσία τῶν ἵππων (A.) B. C. a 27. β 7.
    Compl. (τοπῶν A.)   Vulg. Copt. Æth. Syr. Arr. Slav.
    *εἰσιν) ἐστι, καὶ ἐν ταῖς οὐραῖς αὐτῶν. The MSS. &c. just cited (exc. 2.)
    ὄφεσιν) ὄφεων a 17. β 4.
20. *οὔτε) οὐ C. a 20. β 4. Compl.

ἐκ τῶν ἔργων τῶν χειρῶν αὐτῶν, ἵνα μὴ "προσκυνήσουσι¹ τὰ δαιμόνια, καὶ ᵇτὰ¹ εἴδωλα τὰ χρυσᾶ καὶ τὰ ἀργυρᾶ καὶ τὰ χαλκᾶ καὶ τὰ λίθινα καὶ τὰ ξύλινα, ἃ οὔτε βλέπειν δύναται, 21 οὔτε ἀκούειν, οὔτε περιπατεῖν· καὶ οὐ μετενόησαν ἐκ τῶν φόνων αὐτῶν, οὔτε ἐκ τῶν φαρμακειῶν αὐτῶν, οὔτε ἐκ τῆς πορνείας αὐτῶν, οὔτε ἐκ τῶν κλεμμάτων αὐτῶν.

Χ. Καὶ εἶδον ἄλλον ἄγγελον ἰσχυρὸν καταβαίνοντα ἐκ τοῦ οὐρανοῦ, περιβεβλημένον νεφέλην, καὶ ᶜἡ¹ ἶρις ἐπὶ ᵈτὴν κεφαλὴν¹ ᵉαὐτοῦ,¹ καὶ τὸ πρόσωπον αὐτοῦ ὡς ὁ ἥλιος, καὶ οἱ πόδες 2 αὐτοῦ ὡς στύλοι πυρός· καὶ ᶠἔχων¹ ἐν τῇ χειρὶ αὐτοῦ ᵍβιβλάριδιον¹ ʰἠνεῳγμένον·¹ καὶ ἔθηκε τὸν πόδα αὐτοῦ τὸν δεξιὸν ἐπὶ ⁱτῆς θαλάσσης,¹ 3 τὸν δὲ εὐώνυμον ἐπὶ ᵏτῆς γῆς,¹ καὶ ἔκραξε φωνῇ μεγάλῃ ὥσπερ λέων μυκᾶται· καὶ ὅτε ἔκραξεν, ἐλάλησαν αἱ ἑπτὰ βρονταὶ τὰς ἑαυτῶν φωνάς· 4 καὶ ὅτε ἐλάλησαν αἱ ἑπτὰ βρονταὶ ˡ¹ ᵐἤμελλον¹

ᵃ [προσκυνήσωσι.]   ᵇ Rec.—   ᶜ Rec.—   ᵈ [τῆς κεφαλῆς.]
ⁱ [τὴν θάλασσαν.]   ᵏ [τὴν γῆν.]

20. *προσκυνήσωσι) -σουσι A. C. 7. 36. 42.
   *εἴδωλα) τὰ εἴδ. A. C. a 18. β 6. Compl. Er.
   καὶ τὰ χαλκᾶ) — a 18. β 5.   Æth. Arr
   δύναται) -ανται A. a 7.
21. φαρμακειῶν) -κων C. a 12. β 5.
   πορνείας) πονηρίας A.

1. ἄλλον) — a 23. β 5. Compl.   Slav. MSS.
   *ἶρις) ἡ ἶρις A. B. C. a 22. β 4. γ 2. Compl.
   *τῆς κεφαλῆς) τὴν κεφαλὴν A. C. 8. 9. 12.   + αὐτοῦ A. B. C. a 27.
   β 6. γ 2. Compl.   Vulg. Copt. Syr. Arm. Arr. Slav.

hands, that they should not worship demons, and idols of gold, and silver, and brass, and stone, and wood: which can neither see, nor hear, nor walk : neither repented they of their murders, nor 21 of their sorceries, nor of their fornication, nor of their thefts.

X. And I saw another mighty angel coming down from heaven, clothed with a cloud: and the rainbow *was* upon his head, and his face *was* as it were the sun, and his feet as pillars of fire : and he 2 had in his hand a little book open : and he set his right foot upon the sea, and *his* left *foot* on the earth, and cried with a loud voice, as *when* a 3 lion roareth : and when he had cried, the seven thunders uttered their voices. And when the 4 seven thunders had spoken, I was about to write:

---

^{e} Rec. — ^{f} [εἶχεν.] ^{g} ∾ βιβλιδάριον. ^{h} [ἀνεῳγμένον.]
        ^{i} + [τὰς φωνὰς ἑαυτῶν.] ^{m} [ἔμελλον.]

---

2. *εἶχεν) ἔχων A. B. C. a 16. β 5.
    βιβλαρίδιον) βιβλιδάριον C*. a 9. β 3. Compl.   βιβλίον B. a 18.
    β 4. γ 2.
    *ἀνεῳγμένον) — A. Copt.   ἠνεῳγ. C. 7. 33. 34. 35. Er.
    τὸν δεξιὸν) — C.
    *τὴν θάλασσαν . . . . τὴν γῆν) τῆς θαλάσσης . . . . τῆς γῆς A.B.C.
    a 28. β 7. γ 4. Compl.
3. & 4. αἱ) — 4. 7. 18. Er.
4. *τὰς φωνὰς ἑαυτῶν) — A. B. C. a 28. β 5. γ 2. Compl. Vulg. MS.
    Am. Tol. Copt. Æth. Syr. Arm. Arr. Slav. MSS.
    *ἔμελλον) ἤμελ. A. B. C. 2. 12. 14. 33. 42. 92.

γράφειν· καὶ ἤκουσα φωνὴν ἐκ τοῦ οὐρανοῦ,
λέγουσαν ^a |· Σφράγισον ἃ ἐλάλησαν αἱ [ἑπτὰ]
βρονταὶ, καὶ μὴ ^bαὐτὰ| γράψῃς.

5 Καὶ ὁ ἄγγελος, ὃν εἶδον ἑστῶτα ἐπὶ τῆς
θαλάσσης καὶ ἐπὶ τῆς γῆς, ἦρε τὴν χεῖρα αὐτοῦ
6 ^cτὴν δεξιὰν| εἰς τὸν οὐρανὸν, καὶ ὤμοσεν ἐν τῷ
ζῶντι εἰς τοὺς αἰῶνας τῶν αἰώνων, ὃς ἔκτισε τὸν
οὐρανὸν καὶ τὰ ἐν αὐτῷ, καὶ τὴν γῆν καὶ τὰ ἐν
αὐτῇ, [καὶ τὴν θάλασσαν καὶ τὰ ἐν αὐτῇ·] "Ότι
7 χρόνος ^dοὐκέτι ἔσται·| ^eἀλλ'| ἐν ταῖς ἡμέραις
τῆς φωνῆς τοῦ ἑβδόμου ἀγγέλου, ὅταν μέλλῃ
σαλπίζειν, καὶ ^fἐτελέσθη| τὸ μυστήριον τοῦ
Θεοῦ, ὡς εὐηγγέλισε ^gτοὺς ἑαυτοῦ δούλους τοὺς
προφήτας.|

8 Καὶ ἡ φωνὴ ἣν ἤκουσα ἐκ τοῦ οὐρανοῦ,
πάλιν ^hλαλοῦσαν| μετ' ἐμοῦ, καὶ ⁱλέγουσαν|
"Υπαγε λάβε τὸ ^kβιβλίον| τὸ ἠνεῳγμένον ἐν τῇ

---

^a + [μοι.] ^b [ταῦτα.] ^c Rec.— ^d [οὐκ ἔσται ἔτι.] ^e [ἀλλὰ.] ^f [τελεσθῇ.]

4. *μοι) — A. B. C. a 23. β 6. γ 2. Compl.   Vulg. MS. Am. Harl.
  Tol. Æth. Syr. Arm. Ar. P. Slav. MSS.
  ἑπτὰ (last) — A. C.
  *ταῦτα) αὐτὰ A. C. a 20. β 5.
  γράψῃς) γράφεις 10. 17. 36. 37. 49. 91. Compl.   γράφῃς Er.
5. *αὐτοῦ) + τὴν δεξιὰν B. C. a 27. β 6. γ 3. Compl. Copt. Æth.
  Syr. Arm. Arr. Slav. MSS.
6. ἐν 1st) — B. a 19. β 4.
  καὶ τὴν γῆν καὶ τὰ ἐν αὐτῇ) — A. 12. Er.   Copt. Slav. MSS.
  καὶ τὴν θάλασσαν καὶ τὰ ἐν αὐτῇ) — A. 30. 32. 38. 40. 49.   Vulg.
  MS. Arm. Slav.
  *οὐκ ἔσται ἔτι) οὐκετι ἔσται A. C. a 24. β 7. γ 3. Compl.
7. *ἀλλὰ) ἀλλ' A. C. 13. 30. 91. Compl.
  μέλλῃ) μέλλει 35. 36. Er.

and I heard a voice from heaven saying, Seal up
those things which the [seven] thunders uttered,
and write them not.

And the angel whom I saw stand upon the sea 5
and upon the earth lifted up his right hand to
heaven, and sware by Him that liveth for ever 6
and ever, who created heaven, and the things
that are therein, and the earth, and the things that
are therein, [and the sea and the things that are
therein,] that there should be no more delay: but 7
in the days of the voice of the seventh angel, when
he should sound, the mystery of God should be
finished, as he hath given glad tidings to his
servants the prophets.

And the voice which I heard from heaven 8
I heard again speaking unto me, and saying,
Go, take the book which is open in the hand of

---

g [τοῖς ἑαυτοῦ δουλοῖς τοῖς προφήταις.]　　*h* [λαλοῦσα.]　　*i* [λέγουσα.]　　*k* [βιβλαρίδιον.]

7. καὶ) — 10.17*. 37. 49.91. Compl.　　Vulg. (not *Am.*) Syr. ed. Arm.
Ar. P.
*τελεσθῇ) ἐτελέσθη A. C. a 22. β 5.
τοῦ θεοῦ) — τοῦ C.
ὡς) δ 10. 20. 37. 49. 91. Compl.
εὐηγγέλισε) -σατο 10. 12. 17. 19. 26. 37. 49. 91. Compl.
*τοῖς ἑαυτοῦ δουλοῖς τοῖς προφήταις) τοὺς ἑ. δουλοὺς τοὺς προφητὰς
A.B.C.14.17.36.38.92. τοὺς δ. αὐτοῦ τοὺς προφ. a23. β5. Compl.
8. *λαλοῦσα . . ˙. . λέγουσα) λαλοῦσαν . . . . λέγουσαν A. C. 7. 14.
36. 92.　　Vulg. (*Am.* Et vox quam audivi dicentem de cœlo
iterum loquentem.)
*βιβλαρίδιον) βιβλίον A. C. 14. 92.　　βιβλιδάριον a 25. β 5. Compl.
ἠνεῳγμένον) ἀνεῳγμ. a 15. β 6. Compl.
ἐν τῇ χειρὶ) — C.

χειρὶ ᵃτοῦ¹ ἀγγέλου τοῦ ἑστῶτος ἐπὶ τῆς θα-
9 λάσσης καὶ ἐπὶ τῆς γῆς. καὶ ἀπῆλθον πρὸς
τὸν ἄγγελον, λέγων αὐτῷ, ᵇδοῦναί¹ μοι τὸ
ᶜβιβλαρίδιον.¹ καὶ λέγει μοι· Λάβε καὶ κατάφαγε
αὐτό· καὶ πικρανεῖ σου τὴν κοιλίαν, ἀλλ᾽ ἐν τῷ
10 στόματί σου ἔσται γλυκὺ ὡς μέλι. Καὶ ἔλαβον
τὸ βιβλαρίδιον ἐκ τῆς χειρὸς τοῦ ἀγγέλου, καὶ
κατέφαγον αὐτό· καὶ ἦν ἐν τῷ στόματί μου ὡς
μέλι, γλυκύ· καὶ ὅτε ἔφαγον αὐτὸ, ἐπικράνθη ἡ
11 κοιλία μου. καὶ ᵈλέγουσί¹ μοι· Δεῖ σε πάλιν
προφητεῦσαι ἐπὶ λαοῖς καὶ ἔθνεσι καὶ γλώσσαις
καὶ βασιλεῦσι πολλοῖς.

XI. Καὶ ἐδόθη μοι κάλαμος ὅμοιος ῥάβδῳ,
ᵉ¹ λέγων· Ἔγειραι, καὶ μέτρησον τὸν ναὸν τοῦ
Θεοῦ, καὶ τὸ θυσιαστήριον, καὶ τοὺς προσκυ-
2 νοῦντας ἐν αὐτῷ· καὶ τὴν αὐλὴν τὴν ἔξωθεν τοῦ
ναοῦ ἔκβαλε ἔξω, καὶ μὴ αὐτὴν μετρήσῃς, ὅτι
ἐδόθη τοῖς ἔθνεσι· καὶ τὴν πόλιν τὴν ἁγίαν
πατήσουσι μῆνας τεσσαράκοντα δύο.

ᵃ Rec.—   ᵇ [δός.]   ᶜ ∾ βιβλιδάριον.

---

8. *ἀγγέλου) τοῦ ἀγγ. A. C. a 18. β 3. Compl.
9. ἀπῆλθον) -θα A. 50.
  *δὸς) δοῦναι A. C. a 20. β 4.   Vulg. Syr. Slav. MSS.
  βιβλαρίδιον) βιβλιδάριον a 26. β 6. Compl.   βιβλάριον A*.
  κοιλίαν) καρδίαν A.
  τῷ) — Er.
10. βιβλαρίδιον) βιβλίον a 13. β 3.   βιβλιδάριον a 11. Compl.
  ἐν) — Er.
11. *λέγει) λέγουσι A. a 18. β 4.   Am. Harl.
  ἔθνεσι) ἐπὶ ἔθ. a 18. β 6. Compl.

the angel who standeth upon the sea and upon
the earth.   And I went unto the angel, and 9
said unto him, Give me the little book.   And
he saith unto me, Take *it*, and eat it up; and
it shall make thy belly bitter, but it shall be in
thy mouth sweet as honey.   And I took the little 10
book out of the angel's hand, and ate it up ; and
it was in my mouth sweet as honey : and when I
had eaten it, my belly was made bitter.   And it 11
was said unto me, Thou must prophesy again
against many peoples, and nations, and tongues,
and kings.

XI. And there was given me a reed like unto a
rod : saying, Rise, and measure the temple of God,
and the altar, and them that worship therein.   But 2
the court which is without the temple leave out,
and measure it not; for it is given unto the Gen-
tiles : and the holy city shall they tread under foot
forty-two months.

---

^d [λέγει.]   ^e + [καὶ ὁ ἄγγελος εἰστήκει.]

---

1. *καὶ ὁ ἄγγελος εἰστήκει) — A. a 18. β 6. γ 2. Er.   Vulg. Copt. Æth.
    Arr. Slav.   κ. εἰστ. ὁ ἄγγ. a 7. (and 14) Compl.   Syr. Arm.
    ἔγειραι) -ρε A. a 13. β 4. γ 2.

2. ἔξωθεν) ἔσωθεν 12. [34. 35. ?] 80. Er.   Slav.
    ἔξω) ἔξωθεν A. 12. 14. 26. 28. 34. 36. 37. 91. 92. Compl. Er.
    μετρήσῃς) -σεις Compl.
    ὅτι) καὶ Er.
    πατήσουσι) μετρήσουσι A.
    δύο) καὶ δύο A. a 10. β 3.

3 Καὶ δώσω τοῖς δυσὶ μάρτυσί μου, καὶ προ-
φητεύσουσιν ἡμέρας χιλίας διακοσίας ἐξήκοντα,
4 περιβεβλημένοι σάκκους. οὗτοί εἰσιν αἱ δύο
ἐλαῖαι, καὶ ^aαἱ[|] δύο λυχνίαι αἱ ἐνώπιον τοῦ
5 ^bΚυρίου[|] τῆς γῆς ^cἐστῶτες.[|] καὶ εἴ τις αὐτοὺς
^dθέλει[|] ἀδικῆσαι, πῦρ ἐκπορεύεται ἐκ τοῦ στό-
ματος αὐτῶν καὶ κατεσθίει τοὺς ἐχθροὺς αὐτῶν·
καὶ εἴ τις ^eθέλει αὐτοὺς[|] ἀδικῆσαι, οὕτω δεῖ
6 αὐτὸν ἀποκτανθῆναι. οὗτοι ἔχουσι ^fτὴν[|] ἐξου-
σίαν κλεῖσαι τὸν οὐρανὸν ἵνα μὴ ^gὑετὸς βρέχῃ[|]
^hτὰς ἡμέρας[|] ⁱτῆς προφητείας αὐτῶν·[|] καὶ ἐξου-
σίαν ἔχουσιν ἐπὶ τῶν ὑδάτων, στρέφειν αὐτὰ εἰς
αἷμα, καὶ πατάξαι τὴν γῆν ^kἐν[|] πάσῃ πληγῇ
ὁσάκις ἐὰν θελήσωσιν.

7 Καὶ ὅταν τελέσωσι τὴν μαρτυρίαν αὐτῶν, τὸ
θηρίον τὸ ἀναβαῖνον ἐκ τῆς ἀβύσσου ποιήσει
^lμετ᾽ αὐτῶν πόλεμον,[|] καὶ νικήσει αὐτοὺς, καὶ
8 ἀποκτενεῖ αὐτούς. καὶ ^mτὸ πτῶμα[|] αὐτῶν ἐπὶ
τῆς πλατείας ⁿτῆς[|] πόλεως τῆς μεγάλης, ἥτις

---

^a Rec.—   ^b [Θεοῦ.]   ^c [ἐστῶσαι.]   ^d [θέλῃ.]
ⁱ [αὐτ. τ. προφ.]   ^k Rec.—   ^l [πόλεμον

3. περιβεβλημένοι) -νους A. B. 4. 7. 32. 48.
4. ἐλαῖαι) ἀλαῖαι C.   αὐλαῖαι A.
   *δύο 2nd) αἱ δύο A. C. a 19. β 6. Compl.
   *Θεοῦ) κυρίου A. C. a 27. β 5. γ 2. Compl.   Vulg. Copt. Syr. Arr.
   — τοῦ A.
   *ἐστῶσαι) -τες A. C. a 19. β 4.
5. *θέλῃ 1st) θέλει A. C. a 21. β 3. Compl.
   *αὐτοὺς 2nd) — Er. After θέλ. A. C. a 8. β 5.
   *θέλῃ 2nd) θέλει C. a 13. β 8. γ 2. Compl.   θελήσῃ A. θελήσει 38.
   οὕτω) — A.
6. *ἐξουσίαν) τὴν ἐξου. A. C.
   ἐξου. κλεῖσαι τὸν οὐρανὸν) τ. οὐρ. ἐξου. κλει. a 15. β 4.

And I will give unto my two witnesses, and 3 they shall prophesy a thousand two hundred *and* sixty days, clothed in sackcloth. These are the 4 two olive trees, and the two candlesticks that stand before the Lord of the earth. And if any 5 man wisheth to hurt them, fire proceedeth out of their mouth and devoureth their enemies : and if any man wisheth to hurt them, he must in this manner be killed. These have authority to shut 6 heaven, that it rain not in the days of their pro- phecy : and they have authority over the waters to turn them to blood, and to smite the earth with every plague, as often as they will.

And when they shall have finished their testi- 7 mony, the beast that ascendeth out of the bottom- less pit shall make war with them, and shall overcome them, and kill them. And their dead 8 body *shall lie* in the broad way of the great city,

---

e [αὐτοὺς θέλῃ.]   *f* Rec.—   *g* [βρέχῃ ὑετὸς.]   *h* [ἐν ἡμέραις.]
μετ᾽ αὐτῶν.]   *m* [τὰ πτώματα.]   *n* Rec.—

---

6. *βρέχῃ ὑετὸς) ὑετὸς βρέχῃ A. B. C. a 20. β 6. Compl.
   *ἐν ἡμέραις) τὰς ἡμέρας A. B. C. a 25. β 5. γ 2. Compl.   ἐν ταῖς
   ἡμ. Er.
   *αὐτῶν τῆς προφητείας) τ. πρ. αὐτ. A. B. C. a 15. β 5. Compl.
   αὐτὰ) — Er.
   *πάσῃ πληγῇ ὁσάκις ἐὰν θελήσωσι) ὁσ. ἐὰν θελ. (ἐν) πασῇ. πλ. a 14.
   β 4.   ἐν πασῇ A. C. a 21. β 6. γ 2. Compl. Er.
7. θηρίον) + τὸ τέταρτον A.
   τὸ ἀναβαῖνον) — τὸ Er.   ἀναβαινῶν A.
   *πόλεμον μετ᾽ αὐτῶν) μετ᾽ αὐτ. πόλ. A. C. a 19. β 6. Compl.
8. *τὰ πτώματα) τὸ πτῶμα A. B. C. a 19. β 5.   Copt. Slav.
   *πόλεως) τῆς π. A. C. a 19. β 6. Compl.

καλεῖται πνευματικῶς Σόδομα καὶ Αἴγυπτος,
ὅπου καὶ ὁ Κύριος ^aαὐτῶν[|] ἐσταυρώθη.

9 Καὶ ^bβλέπουσιν[|] ἐκ τῶν λαῶν καὶ φυλῶν καὶ
γλωσσῶν καὶ ἐθνῶν ^cτὸ πτῶμα[|] αὐτῶν ἡμέρας
τρεῖς καὶ ἥμισυ, καὶ τὰ πτώματα αὐτῶν οὐκ
10 ^dἀφίουσι[|] τεθῆναι εἰς ^eμνῆμα.[|] Καὶ οἱ κατοι-
κοῦντες ἐπὶ τῆς γῆς ^fχαίρουσιν[|] ἐπ᾽ αὐτοῖς, καὶ
^gεὐφραίνονται.[|] καὶ δῶρα ^hπέμψουσιν[|] ἀλλήλοις
ὅτι οὗτοι οἱ δύο προφῆται ἐβασάνισαν τοὺς
κατοικοῦντας ἐπὶ τῆς γῆς.

11 Καὶ μετὰ τὰς τρεῖς ἡμέρας καὶ ἥμισυ πνεῦμα
ζωῆς ἐκ τοῦ Θεοῦ εἰσῆλθεν ⁱαὐτοῖς,[|] καὶ ἔστησαν
ἐπὶ τοὺς πόδας αὐτῶν, καὶ φόβος μέγας ^kἐπέπε-
12 σεν[|] ἐπὶ τοὺς θεωροῦντας αὐτούς. καὶ ἤκουσαν
φωνὴν μεγάλην ἐκ τοῦ οὐρανοῦ λέγουσαν αὐ-
τοῖς· ^lἈνάβατε[|] ὧδε. Καὶ ἀνέβησαν εἰς τὸν
οὐρανὸν ἐν τῇ νεφέλῃ, καὶ ἐθεώρησαν αὐτοὺς οἱ
13 ἐχθροὶ αὐτῶν. καὶ ἐν ἐκείνῃ τῇ ^mὥρα[|] ἐγένετο

a [ἡμῶν.]   b [βλέψουσιν.]   c [τὰ πτώματα.]   d [ἀφήσουσι.]
i [ἐπ᾽ αὐτούς.]   k [ἔπεσεν.]   l [ἀνάβητε.]

8. ὅπου καὶ) — καὶ 7. 12. 14. 34. 35. 36. 92. Er. Copt. Slav. MSS.
*ἡμῶν) αὐτῶν A. B. C. a 24. β 6. Compl. Vulg. Copt. Æth. Syr.
Arm. Ar. P. Slav. MSS.
9. *βλέψουσιν) -πουσιν A. C. a 26. β 6. Compl.
καὶ ἐθνῶν) — 14 Er. After αὐτῶν + καὶ οἱ ἐκ. τ. ἐθν. 14 Er.
*τὰ πτώματα) τὸ πτῶμα A. B. C. a 21. β 5. Copt.
καὶ ἥμ.) — καὶ a 21. β 4 Compl.
*ἀφήσουσι) ἀφίουσι A. C. 12. 28. 36. Er.
*μνήματα) μνῆμα A. B. a 26. β 5. Compl. Copt. Æth. Syr. Arr. Slav.
μνημεῖον C. 36.
10. *χαροῦσιν) χαίρουσιν A. B. C. a 25. β 7. Compl.
*εὐφρανθήσονται) εὐφραίνονται A. C. 12. 28. 36. εὐφρανοῦνται 14 Er.
πέμψουσιν) δώσουσιν B. a 18. β 5
ἀλλήλοις) -λους C 27.

which spiritually is called Sodom and Egypt, where their Lord also was crucified.

And *some* of the peoples and kindreds and 9 tongues and nations see their dead body three days and an half, and do not suffer their dead bodies to be put into a sepulchre.   And they that dwell upon 10 the earth rejoice over them, and make merry, and shall *ⁿ* send gifts one to another; because these two prophets tormented those that dwell on the earth.

And after the three days and an half the Spirit 11 of life from God entered into them, and they stood upon their feet; and great fear fell upon those who saw them.   And they heard a great voice 12 from heaven saying unto them, Come up hither. And they ascended up to heaven in the cloud; and their enemies beheld them.   And the same 13 *ᵒ* hour was there a great earthquake, and the tenth

---

ᵉ [μνήματα.]   *ᶠ* [χαροῦσιν.]   *ᵍ* [εὐφρανθήσονται.]   *ʰ* ∾ δώσουσιν.
ᵐ ∾ ἡμέρᾳ.   *ⁿ* ∾ give.   *ᵒ* ∾ day.

11. τὰς) — 28. 36. 37. 38. 40. 49. Compl. Er.
    ἥμισυ) τὸ ἥμ. C.
    *ἐπ' αὐτούς) ἐν αὐτοῖς A. 18. 36.   αὐτοῖς C. 7. 12. 17. 38. Er.
    (εἰσῆλ. ἐκ τ. θεοῦ αὐτοῖς C.)   εἰς αὐτοὺς B. a 17. β 4.
    *ἔπεσεν) ἐπέπεσεν A. C. a 12. (& 13.) Compl.
    τοὺς θεωροῦντας) τῶν θεωρούντων C. 17*.

12. ἤκουσαν) ἤκουσα a 18. β 6. Compl.   Copt. Syr. ed. Arm. Arr.
    φωνὴν μεγάλην) -ῆς -ῆς C. 10. 12. 17. 28 36. 37. 91.
    λέγουσαν) -σης C. 10. 12. 17. 28. 36. 91.
    αὐτοῖς) — A. 28.
    *ἀνάβητε) -βατε A. C. 26. 36. 42.

13. καὶ 1st) — a 16. β 4.
    ὥρᾳ) ἡμέρᾳ B. a 26. β 5. γ 2. Compl.   Ar. P. Slav.

σεισμὸς μέγας, καὶ τὸ δέκατον τῆς πόλεως ἔπεσε,
καὶ ἀπεκτάνθησαν ἐν τῷ σεισμῷ ὀνόματα ἀνθρώπων χιλιάδες ἑπτά· καὶ οἱ λοιποὶ ἔμφοβοι
ἐγένοντο, καὶ ἔδωκαν δόξαν τῷ Θεῷ τοῦ οὐρανοῦ.

14 Ἡ οὐαὶ ἡ δευτέρα ἀπῆλθεν· ἰδοὺ ἡ οὐαὶ ἡ
τρίτη ἔρχεται ταχύ.

15 Καὶ ὁ ἕβδομος ἄγγελος ἐσάλπισε, καὶ ἐγέ-
νοντο φωναὶ μεγάλαι ἐν τῷ οὐρανῷ ᵃλέγοντες·|
ᵇἘγένετο ἡ βασιλεία| τοῦ κόσμου, τοῦ Κυρίου
ἡμῶν, καὶ τοῦ Χριστοῦ αὐτοῦ, καὶ βασιλεύσει
εἰς τοὺς αἰῶνας τῶν αἰώνων.

16 Καὶ οἱ εἴκοσι ᶜ| τέσσαρες πρεσβύτεροι ᵈοἱ|
ἐνώπιον τοῦ Θεοῦ ᵉκάθηνται| ἐπὶ τοὺς θρόνους
αὐτῶν, ἔπεσαν ἐπὶ τὰ πρόσωπα αὐτῶν, καὶ
17 προσεκύνησαν τῷ Θεῷ, λέγοντες· Εὐχαριστοῦ-
μέν σοι, Κύριε ὁ Θεὸς ὁ παντοκράτωρ, ὁ ὢν καὶ
ὁ ἦν ᶠ|, ὅτι εἴληφας τὴν δύναμίν σου τὴν με-
18 γάλην, καὶ ἐβασίλευσας. καὶ τὰ ἔθνη ὠργί-
σθησαν, καὶ ἦλθεν ἡ ὀργή σου, καὶ ὁ καιρὸς τῶν
νεκρῶν, κριθῆναι, καὶ δοῦναι τὸν μισθὸν τοῖς
δούλοις σου τοῖς προφήταις, καὶ τοῖς ἁγίοις καὶ

ᵃ [λέγουσαι.]   ᵇ [ἐγένοντο αἱ βασιλεῖαι.]   ᶜ + [καὶ.]

13. καὶ τὸ) ὥστε τὸ C.
14. ἰδοὺ ἡ οὐαὶ ἡ τρίτη) ἡ οὐ. ἡ τρ. ἰδοὺ α20. β4. Compl.
15. ὁ) — A.
  *λέγουσαι) -οντες A. B. α12. β2.
  *ἐγένοντο αἱ βασιλεῖαι) ἐγένετο ἡ βασιλεία A. B. C. α27. β6.
    Compl. Verss.
16. οἱ εἴκ.) — οἱ A.
  *καὶ) — A. C. α10. β5. Compl. Er.
  οἱ ἐνώ.) — οἱ A. 12. 14. 46. 92. Er.

part of the city fell, and in the earthquake were slain seven thousand names of men; and the remnant were affrighted, and gave glory to the God of heaven.

The second woe is past; behold, the third woe 14 cometh quickly.

And the seventh angel sounded; and there were 15 great voices in heaven saying, The sovereignty of the world hath become our Lord's, and his Christ's; and he shall reign for ever and ever.

And the twenty-four elders, who sit before 16 God on their thrones, fell upon their faces, and worshipped God, saying, We give thee thanks, 17 O Lord God the Almighty, who art, and who wast; because thou hast taken thy great power, and hast reigned. And the nations were angry, 18 and thy wrath is come, and the time of the dead, that they should be judged, and that thou shouldest give reward unto thy servants the prophets, and to

---

^d [οἱ.]   ^e [καθήμενοι.]   ^f + [καὶ ὁ ἐρχόμενος.]

16. ἐνώπιον) + τοῦ θρόνου B. a 23. β 6.   Syr. Arr.
    *καθήμενοι) οἱ κάθηνται the same MSS. (exc. 4.)   κάθηνται
       C. 2. Arm.
    ἔπεσαν) -σον a 9. β 3. Compl.
17. *καὶ ὁ ἐρχόμενος) — A. a 23. β 5. Compl.   Vulg. MSS. Am. Harl.
       Tol. Æth. Syr. Arm. ed. Ven. Ar. P.   ὁ ἐρχ. — C.
    τὴν δυ.) — τὴν Er.
18. καιρός) κλῆρος C.
    τοῖς ἁγίοις καὶ τοῖς φοβουμένοις) τοὺς ἁγίους καὶ τοὺς φοβουμένους A.

τοῖς φοβουμένοις τὸ ὄνομά σου, τοῖς μικροῖς
καὶ τοῖς μεγάλοις, καὶ διαφθεῖραι τοὺς διαφθείροντας τὴν γῆν.

19 Καὶ ἠνοίγη ὁ ναὸς τοῦ Θεοῦ [ἐν τῷ οὐρανῷ,]
καὶ ὤφθη ἡ κιβωτὸς τῆς διαθήκης ^aαὐτοῦ| ἐν τῷ
ναῷ αὐτοῦ· καὶ ἐγένοντο ἀστραπαὶ καὶ φωναὶ
καὶ βρονταὶ καὶ σεισμὸς καὶ χάλαζα μεγάλη.

XII. Καὶ σημεῖον μέγα ὤφθη ἐν τῷ οὐρανῷ,
γυνὴ περιβεβλημένη τὸν ἥλιον, καὶ ἡ σελήνη
ὑποκάτω τῶν ποδῶν αὐτῆς, καὶ ἐπὶ τῆς κεφαλῆς
2 αὐτῆς στέφανος ἀστέρων δώδεκα· καὶ ἐν γαστρὶ
ἔχουσα κράζει ὠδίνουσα, καὶ βασανιζομένη
τεκεῖν.

3 Καὶ ὤφθη ἄλλο σημεῖον ἐν τῷ οὐρανῷ, καὶ
ἰδοὺ δράκων ^bπυῤῥὸς μέγας,| ἔχων κεφαλὰς
ἑπτὰ καὶ κέρατα δέκα· καὶ ἐπὶ τὰς κεφαλὰς
4 αὐτοῦ ^cἑπτὰ διαδήματα·| καὶ ἡ οὐρὰ αὐτοῦ
σύρει τὸ τρίτον τῶν ἀστέρων τοῦ οὐρανοῦ, καὶ
ἔβαλεν αὐτοὺς εἰς τὴν γῆν. καὶ ὁ δράκων
ἕστηκεν ἐνώπιον τῆς γυναικὸς τῆς μελλούσης

---

^a ∾ τοῦ Κυρίου. ^b [μέγας πυῤῥὸς.]

---

18. τοῖς μικροῖς καὶ τοῖς μεγάλοις) τοὺς μικροὺς κ. τοὺς μεγαλοὺς A. C.
καὶ last) — A.
διαφθείροντας) φθείροντας Er. διαφθείραντας C.
19. ἠνοίγη) ἠνοίχθη a 14. β 4. Compl.
ἐν τῷ οὐρανῷ) — A. 14. 38. 92.
ὤφθη) ἐδόθη C.
αὐτοῦ) (τοῦ) κυρίου a 26. β 5. Compl. Æth. perhaps.
καὶ σεισμὸς) — B. a 20. β 4. Compl. Arr.

the saints, and them that fear thy name, small and great ; and that thou shouldest destroy them which destroy the earth.

And the temple of God was opened ⸢in heaven,⸣ 19 and there was seen the ark of ᵈ his covenant in his temple ; and there were lightnings, and voices, and thunderings, and an earthquake, and great hail.

XII. And there was seen a great wonder in heaven ; a woman clothed with the sun, and the moon under her feet, and upon her head a crown of twelve stars : and she being with child crieth out, 2 travailing, and pained to be delivered.

And there was seen another wonder in heaven ; 3 and behold a great red dragon, having seven heads and ten horns, and seven diadems upon his heads. And his tail draweth the third part of the stars of 4 heaven, and did cast them to the earth : and the dragon stood before the woman who was ready

---

ᶜ [διαδήματα ἑπτά.]   ᵈ ∾ the Lord's.

---

1. περιβεβλημένη) -βλεπομένη A.
   ἡ σελ.) — ἡ Er.
2. κράζει) ἔκραξεν B. a 7. β 2. ἔκραζεν C. a 20. β 3. Compl. Vulg. ed.
   Syr. Æth.   + καὶ A. C.
3. *μέγας πυῤῥὸς) πυρὸς μέγας B. C. a 12. β 4. γ 2.   Copt.   πυῤῥος
   μέγας a 7. (& 33.)   Arr.
   αὐτοῦ) αὐτῶν A.
   *διαδήματα ἑπτά) ἑπτὰ διαδ. A. C. a 21. β 6. Compl.   — ἑπτὰ Er.
4. τοῦ οὐρανοῦ) — Er.

τεκεῖν, ἵνα ὅταν τέκῃ, τὸ τέκνον αὐτῆς καταφάγῃ.
5 καὶ ἔτεκεν υἱὸν ἄρρενα, ὃς μέλλει ποιμαίνειν
πάντα τὰ ἔθνη ἐν ῥάβδῳ σιδηρᾷ· καὶ ἡρπάσθη
τὸ τέκνον αὐτῆς πρὸς τὸν Θεὸν καὶ ᵃπρὸς¹ τὸν
6 θρόνον αὐτοῦ. καὶ ἡ γυνὴ ἔφυγεν εἰς τὴν
ἔρημον, ὅπου ἔχει [ᵇἐκεῖ¹] τόπον ἡτοιμασμένον
ἀπὸ τοῦ Θεοῦ, ἵνα ἐκεῖ τρέφωσιν αὐτὴν ἡμέρας
χιλίας διακοσίας ἑξήκοντα.
7 Καὶ ἐγένετο πόλεμος ἐν τῷ οὐρανῷ· ὁ Μιχαὴλ
καὶ οἱ ἄγγελοι αὐτοῦ ᶜτοῦ πολεμῆσαι¹ ᵈμετὰ¹
τοῦ δράκοντος, καὶ ὁ δράκων ἐπολέμησε, καὶ οἱ
8 ἄγγελοι αὐτοῦ, καὶ οὐκ ᵉἴσχυσεν,¹ ᶠοὐδὲ¹ τόπος
9 εὑρέθη ᵍαὐτῶν¹ ἔτι ἐν τῷ οὐρανῷ. καὶ ἐβλήθη
ὁ δράκων ὁ μέγας, ὁ ὄφις ὁ ἀρχαῖος, ὁ καλούμενος διάβολος, καὶ ὁ Σατανᾶς, ὁ πλανῶν τὴν
οἰκουμένην ὅλην, ἐβλήθη εἰς τὴν γῆν, καὶ οἱ
10 ἄγγελοι αὐτοῦ μετ᾽ αὐτοῦ ἐβλήθησαν. καὶ
ἤκουσα φωνὴν μεγάλην ʰἐν τῷ οὐρανῷ, λέ-
γουσαν·¹ Ἄρτι ἐγένετο ἡ σωτηρία καὶ ἡ δύναμις
καὶ ἡ βασιλεία τοῦ Θεοῦ ἡμῶν, καὶ ἡ ἐξουσία

ᵃ Rec.— ᵇ Rec.— ᶜ [ἐπολέμησαν.] ᵈ [κατὰ.] ᵉ [ἴσχυσαν.]

4. τεκεῖν) τίκτειν 37. 49. Compl.
καταφάγῃ) φάγῃ Er.
5. ἄρρενα) ἄρσεν A. C.
ἐν) —12. Er.
ἡρπάσθη) ἡρπάγη 10. 29. 37. 47. 49. 91. Compl.
*τὸν θρόν.) πρὸς τ. θρόν. A.C. α24. β3. Compl.   Vulg. Copt. Æth.
Syr. Arm. Arr. Slav. MSS.
6. *ἔχει) + ἐκεῖ A. α25. β5. Compl.   Slav. MSS.
ἀπὸ) ὑπὸ α21. β6.
τρέφωσιν) ἐκτρέφ. α22. β3. Compl.   -ουσιν C.
7. ὁ 1st) ὅ τε A.

to be delivered, that he might devour her child as soon as she should have brought *it* forth.   And 5 she brought forth a man child, who is to rule all nations with a rod of iron : and her child was caught up unto God and unto his throne.   And the 6 woman fled into the wilderness, where she hath a place prepared of God, that they should feed her there a thousand two hundred *and* sixty days.

And there was war in heaven : Michael and his 7 angels fought against the dragon ; and the dragon fought and his angels, and he prevailed not ; neither 8 was *ʲ*their place found any more in heaven.   And 9 the great dragon was cast out, the old serpent, that is called the Devil, and Satan, who deceiveth the whole world : he was cast out into the earth, and his angels were cast out with him.   And I 10 heard a loud voice in heaven, saying, Now is come the salvation, and the strength, and the kingdom of our God, and the authority of his

---

ʲ [οὔτε.]   *ᵍ* ~ αὐτῷ.   *ʰ* [λέγουσαν ἐν τῷ οὐρανῷ.]   *ⁱ* ~ his.

---

7. **ἐπολέμησαν) τοῦ πολεμῆσαι A. C. 7. 8. 10. 12. 17. 36. 37. 49. 91. Compl.   πολεμῆσαι B. *a*21. β 5.   Æth. Syr. Arr.
    **κατὰ) μετὰ A. B. C. *a*26. β 5. Compl.
8. **ἴσχυσαν) -σεν A. *a*22. β 3. Compl.   Copt. Æth. Erp.
    **οὔτε) οὐδὲ A. C. *a*18. β 5. Compl.
    αὐτῶν) αὐτῷ.   The MSS. &c. which read ἴσχυσεν (exc. A. 16. 38.) and 4 more.   Arr.
    9. ὁ ὄφις) — ὁ Er.
    ὁ σατ.) — ὁ *a*24. β 5. Compl.
    μετ᾽ αὐτοῦ) — Er.
10. **λέγουσαν ἐν τῷ οὐρανῷ) ἐν. τ. οὐρ. λέγ A. C. *a*17. β 6. Compl. Verss.

τοῦ Χριστοῦ αὐτοῦ· ὅτι ^aἐβλήθη| ὁ ^bκατήγωρ|
τῶν ἀδελφῶν ἡμῶν, ὁ κατηγορῶν ^cαὐτῶν| ἐνώ-
11 πιον τοῦ Θεοῦ ἡμῶν ἡμέρας καὶ νυκτός. καὶ
αὐτοὶ ἐνίκησαν αὐτὸν διὰ τὸ αἷμα τοῦ ἀρνίου,
καὶ διὰ τὸν λόγον τῆς μαρτυρίας αὐτῶν, καὶ
οὐκ ἠγάπησαν τὴν ψυχὴν αὐτῶν ἄχρι θανάτου.
12 διὰ τοῦτο εὐφραίνεσθε ^d| οὐρανοὶ καὶ οἱ ἐν
αὐτοῖς σκηνοῦντες. οὐαὶ ^e| τὴν γῆν καὶ τὴν θα-
λάσσαν ὅτι κατέβη ὁ διάβολος πρὸς ὑμᾶς ἔχων
θυμὸν μέγαν, εἰδὼς ὅτι ὀλίγον καιρὸν ἔχει.
13 Καὶ ὅτε εἶδεν ὁ δράκων ὅτι ἐβλήθη εἰς τὴν
γῆν, ἐδίωξε τὴν γυναῖκα ἥτις ἔτεκε τὸν ἄῤῥενα.
14 καὶ ἐδόθησαν τῇ γυναικὶ ^fαἱ| δύο πτέρυγες τοῦ
ἀετοῦ τοῦ μεγάλου, ἵνα πέτηται εἰς τὴν ἔρημον
εἰς τὸν τόπον αὐτῆς, ^gὅπου τρέφεται| ἐκεῖ
καιρὸν, καὶ καιροὺς, καὶ ἥμισυ καιροῦ, ἀπὸ
15 προσώπου τοῦ ὄφεως. καὶ ἔβαλεν ὁ ὄφις ^hἐκ
τοῦ στόματος αὐτοῦ ὀπίσω τῆς γυναικὸς| ὕδωρ
ὡς ποταμὸν, ἵνα ⁱαὐτὴν| ποταμοφόρητον ποιήσῃ.

---

^a [κατεβλήθη.]   ^b [κατήγορος.]   ^c ∾ αὐτούς.   ^d + [οἱ.]
^k [ὀπίσω τῆς γυναικὸς ἐκ τοῦ στόματος αὐτοῦ.]

10. Χριστοῦ) Κυρίου C.
*κατεβλήθη) ἐβλήθη A. B. C. a 22. β 6.
ὁ κατ. τ. ἀδελ ἡ.) — Er.
*κατήγορος) κατήγωρ A.
αὐτῶν) αὐτοὺς A. 28. 36. Er.
ἡμῶν last) — 14. 28. 90. 92. Er.
11. τὸν λόγον τῆς μαρτυρίας) τὴν μαρτυρίαν C.
12. *οἱ 1st) — C. a 15. β 4.
σκηνοῦντες) κατασκη. C.
*τοῖς κατοικοῦσι τὴν γῆν καὶ τὴν θάλασσαν) τῇ γῇ καὶ τῇ θαλάσσῃ
B. a 22. β 6. γ 3. Compl. — τοῖς κατ. A. C. Vulg. Copt.
Æth. Syr. Arm. Arr. Slav. MSS. γῆν) ἀγαπὴν A.

Christ : for the accuser of our brethren is cast out,
who accused them before our God day and night.
And they overcame him because of the blood of 11
the Lamb, and because of the word of their testimony ; and they loved not their lives unto the
death.   Therefore, rejoice, *ye* heavens, and ye 12
that dwell in them.   Woe to the earth and to
the sea ! for the devil is come down unto you,
having great wrath, because he knoweth that he
hath but a short time.

And when the dragon saw that he was cast out 13
unto the earth, he persecuted the woman which
brought forth the man *child*.   And there were 14
given to the woman two wings of the great eagle,
that she might fly into the wilderness, into her
place, ᵏwhere she is nourished for a time, and times,
and half a time, from the face of the serpent.   And 15
the serpent cast out of his mouth water as a flood
after the woman, that he might cause her to be

ᵉ + [τοῖς κατοικοῦσι]   ʲ Rec. —   ᵍ ∿ ὅπως τρέφηται.
   ⁱ [ταύτην.]   ᵏ ∿ that she might be nourished there.

12. ἔχων) ὁ ἔχων Er.
13. ἄρρενα) ἄρσενα C. 14. 92.   ἄρσεναν A.
14. *δύο) αἱ δύο A. C. 12. 27*. 28. 36.
    πέτηται) πέταται 38. Er.
    ὅπου τρέφεται) ὅπως τρέφηται α 23. β 4. Compl.   Arr.
    καὶ ἥμισυ καιροῦ) — C.
15. *ὀπίσω τῆς γυναικὸς ἐκ τοῦ στόματος αὐτοῦ) ἐκ τ. στόμ. αὐτ. ὀπ. τ.
    γυ. A. C. a 20. β 7. Compl.   Verss.
    *ταύτην) αὐτὴν A. B. C. a 25. β 5. Compl.   —Er. ποι. αὐτ. ποτα-
    μοφόρ. C.

16 καὶ ἐβοήθησεν ἡ γῆ τῇ γυναικὶ, καὶ ἤνοιξεν ἡ
γῆ τὸ στόμα αὐτῆς, καὶ κατέπιε τὸν ποταμὸν ὃν
17 ἔβαλεν ὁ δράκων ἐκ τοῦ στόματος αὐτοῦ. καὶ
ὠργίσθη ὁ δράκων ἐπὶ τῇ γυναικὶ, καὶ ἀπῆλθε
ποιῆσαι πόλεμον μετὰ τῶν λοιπῶν τοῦ σπέρμα-
τος αὐτῆς, τῶν τηρούντων τὰς ἐντολὰς τοῦ
Θεοῦ, καὶ ἐχόντων τὴν μαρτυρίαν ᵃ Ἰησοῦ.ˡ

18 Καὶ ᵇἐστάθηˡ ἐπὶ τὴν ἄμμον τῆς θαλάσσης,
XIII. καὶ εἶδον ἐκ τῆς θαλάσσης θηρίον ἀναβαῖνον, ἔχον ᶜκέρατα δέκα καὶ κεφαλὰς ἑπτά·ˡ
καὶ ἐπὶ τῶν κεράτων αὐτοῦ δέκα διαδήματα, καὶ
ἐπὶ τὰς κεφαλὰς αὐτοῦ ᵈὀνόματαˡ βλασφημίας.
2 καὶ τὸ θηρίον ὃ εἶδον ἦν ὅμοιον παρδάλει, καὶ
οἱ πόδες αὐτοῦ ὡς ᵉἄρκου,ˡ καὶ τὸ στόμα αὐτοῦ
ὡς στόμα λέοντος. καὶ ἔδωκεν αὐτῷ ὁ δράκων
τὴν δύναμιν αὐτοῦ, καὶ τὸν θρόνον αὐτοῦ, καὶ
3 ἐξουσίαν μεγάλην. καὶ ᶠˡ μίαν ᵍἐκˡ τῶν κεφαλῶν
αὐτοῦ ὡς ἐσφαγμένην εἰς θάνατον· καὶ ἡ
πληγὴ τοῦ θανάτου αὐτοῦ ἐθεραπεύθη, καὶ
4 ʰἐθαυμάσθηˡ ὅλη ἡ γῆ ὀπίσω τοῦ θηρίου. καὶ

ᵃ [τοῦ Ἰησοῦ Χριστοῦ.]   ᵇ ∿ [ἐστάθην.]   ᶜ [κεφαλὰς ἑπτὰ καὶ κέρατα δέκα.]

16. ἡ γῆ) — 34. 35. 36. 40. 41. 42.
   τὸν ποταμὸν ὄν) τὸ ὕδωρ ὅ A.
17. ἐπὶ) — C.
   *τοῦ Ἰησοῦ Χριστοῦ) Ἰησοῦ A. C. a25. β6. γ2. Compl.   Vulg.
   MS. Am. Copt. Syr. Ar. P. Slav. MS.   τοῦ Ἰη. 11. 14. 19.
18. *ἐστάθην) ἐστάθη A. C. 92.   Vulg. Æth. Syr. Arm. Ar. P.

   1. *κεφαλὰς ἑπτὰ καὶ κέρατα δέκα) κερ. δέκα κ. κεφ. ἑπτὰ A. C. a20. β7.
   Compl. Harl*. Copt. Æth. Syr. Arr. Slav. MSS.   δέκα) ἑπτὰ Er.
   *ὄνομα) ὀνόματα A. a26. β6. Compl.   Vulg. Syr. Ar. P. Slav.

carried away of the flood.   And the earth helped 16
the woman, and the earth opened her mouth, and
swallowed up the flood which the dragon cast out of
his mouth.   And the dragon was wroth with the 17
woman, and went to make war with the rest of
her seed, who keep the commandments of God, and
have the testimony of Jesus.

XIII.   And ᶦhe stood upon the sand of the sea,
and I saw a beast rising up out of the sea, having
ten horns and seven heads, and upon his horns
ten diadems, and upon his heads names of blasphemy.   And the beast which I saw was like unto 2
a leopard, and his feet were as *the feet* of a bear,
and his mouth as the mouth of a lion : and the
dragon gave him his power, and his throne, and
great authority.   And *I saw* one of his heads 3
as it were wounded to death ; and his deadly
wound was healed : and all the earth wondered
after the beast.   And they worshipped the 4

ᵈ [ὄνομα.]   ᵉ [ἄρκτου.]   ᶠ + [εἶδον.]   ᵍ Rec.—   ʰ [ἐθαυμάσεν.]   ᶦ ∾ I stood.

2. ἦν) — 12. 46. Er.
    *ἄρκτου) ἄρκου A. C. a 15. β 3. γ 2.
    μεγάλην) + ἔδωκεν αὐτῷ A**.
3. *εἶδον) — A. C. a 23. β 7. γ 2. Compl.   Vulg. MS. *Am. Tol.* Copt.
    Æth. Syr. Arm. Ar. P. Slav. MSS.
    *μίαν) + ἐκ A. C. a 26. β 5. Compl.   Vulg. Æth. Syr. Arm. Slav.
    ὡς) ὡσεὶ a 19. β 3. Compl.
    *ἐθαύμασεν ὅλη ἡ γῆ) ἐθαυμάσθη (-στώθη C.) ὅλη ἡ γῆ A. C.
    ἐθαυμάσθη ἐν ὅλη τῇ γῇ 12. 28. 36. Er.

προσεκύνησαν ^aτῷ δράκοντι,[|] ^bὅτι ἔδωκε τὴν[|]
ἐξουσίαν τῷ θηρίῳ, καὶ προσεκύνησαν ^cτῷ
θηρίῳ,[|] λέγοντες· Τίς ὅμοιος τῷ θηρίῳ; ^dκαὶ[|]
τίς δύναται πολεμῆσαι μετ᾽ αὐτοῦ;
5 Καὶ ἐδόθη αὐτῷ στόμα λαλοῦν μεγάλα καὶ
^eβλάσφημα·[|] καὶ ἐδόθη αὐτῷ ἐξουσία ^{f|} ποιῆσαι
6 μῆνας τεσσαράκοντα δύο· καὶ ἤνοιξε τὸ στόμα
αὐτοῦ εἰς ^gβλασφημίας[|] πρὸς τὸν Θεὸν, βλασ-
φημῆσαι τὸ ὄνομα αὐτοῦ, καὶ τὴν σκηνὴν αὐτοῦ,
7 ^{h|} τοὺς ἐν τῷ οὐρανῷ σκηνοῦντας. καὶ ἐδόθη
αὐτῷ ⁱποιῆσαι πόλεμον[|] μετὰ τῶν ἁγίων, καὶ
νικῆσαι αὐτούς· καὶ ἐδόθη αὐτῷ ἐξουσία ἐπὶ
πᾶσαν φυλὴν ^kκαὶ λαὸν[|] καὶ γλῶσσαν καὶ ἔθνος.
8 καὶ προσκυνήσουσιν ^lαὐτὸν[|] πάντες οἱ κατοι-
κοῦντες ἐπὶ τῆς γῆς, ^mὧν[|] οὐ γέγραπται ⁿτὸ
ὄνομα^{| o|} ἐν ^pτῷ βιβλίῳ[|] τῆς ζωῆς τοῦ ἀρνίου
9 ^qτοῦ[|] ἐσφαγμένου, ἀπὸ καταβολῆς κόσμου. εἴ

---

^a [τὸν δράκοντα.]   ^b [ὃς ἔδωκεν.]   ^c [τὸ θηρίον.]   ^d Rec.—
ⁱ [πόλεμον ποιῆσαι.]   ^k Rec.—   ^l [αὐτῷ.]   ^m ∾ οὗ.

---

4. *τὸν δράκοντα) τῷ δράκοντι A. B. C. a 26. β 6. γ 3. Compl.
    *ὃς ἔδωκεν) ὅτι ἔδωκε A. C. 12. 34. 35. 36. 46.   Vulg. MS. Am.
     Æth. Syr. Arm. Erp. Slav. MSS.   τῷ δεδωκότι B. a 25. β 3.
     Compl.
    *ἐξου.) τὴν ἐξου. A. B. C. a 24. β 6. Compl.
    *τὸ θηρίον) τῷ θηρίῳ C. a 26. β 6. Compl.
    *τίς 2nd) καὶ τίς A. C. a 11. β 3. Compl.   Vulg. Copt. Æth. Syr.
     Erp. Slav.
    δύναται) δυνατὸς a 22. β 5. γ 3. Compl.
5. *βλασφημίας) βλάσφημα A. 12. 28. 34. 47.   βλασφημίαν a 20. β 6.
     Compl.   Vulg. MS.
    *πόλεμον) — A. C. 12. 18. 28. 36. (and probably all the MSS.
     collated by Birch) Er.   Vulg. Syr. Slav. MSS.
    δύο) καὶ δύο A.

dragon because he gave the authority unto the
beast : and they worshipped the beast, saying,
Who *is* like unto the beast ? and who is able
to make war with him ?

And there was given unto him a mouth speaking 5
great and blasphemous things ; and authority was
given unto him to work forty *and* two months.
And he opened his mouth in blasphemies against 6
God, to blaspheme his name, and his tabernacle,
even those who dwell in heaven. And it was 7
given unto him to make war with the saints,
and to overcome them : and authority was given
him over every kindred, and people, and tongue,
and nation. And all that dwell upon the earth 8
shall worship him, whose names were not written
from the foundation of the world in the book of
life of the Lamb that was slain. He that hath 9

ᶠ [βλασφημίας.]　　ᶠ + [πόλεμον.]　　ᵍ [βλασφημίαν.]　　ʰ + [καὶ.]
ⁿ [τὰ ὀνόματα.]　　ᵒ + ∾ αὐτοῦ.　　ᵖ [τῇ βιβλῷ.]　　ᑫ Rec.—

---

6. *βλασφημίαν) -μίας A. C. 18. 34. 35.　Vulg. ed.
　καὶ τὴν σκηνὴν αὐτοῦ) — C.
　*καὶ last) — A. C. a 19. β 4.　Syr. ed. Slav. MS.
7. καὶ ἐδόθη . . . . νικῆσαι αὐτοὺς) — A. C. 12. 14. 92.
　*πόλεμον ποιῆσαι) ποι. πόλ. a 16. β 5. Compl.
　*φυλήν) + καὶ λαὸν A. B. a 23. β 5. γ 2.　Vulg. Æth. Syr. Ar. P.
　　Slav. MSS.　+ καὶ λαοὺς C.
8. *αὐτῷ) αὐτὸν A. C. a 18. β 5.
　ὧν οὐ) ὧν οὔτε B. a 7. β 2.　οὐ οὐ C.　οναι A.
　*τὰ ὀνόματα) τὸ ὄνομα A. B. C. a 26. β 4. γ 2. Compl.　Copt. Syr.
　　Arr.　+ αὐτοῦ A. C.
　*τῇ βιβλῷ) τῷ βιβλίῳ A. B. a 16. β 2. Compl.　βιβλίῳ C.
　*ἀρνίου) + τοῦ A. C. a 25. β 5. γ 2. Compl.
　ἐσφαγμένου) ἐσφαγισμένου Er.

12

10 τις ἔχει οὖς, ἀκουσάτω, εἴ ^ατις εἰς αἰχμαλω-
σίαν¹ εἰς αἰχμαλωσίαν ὑπάγει· εἴ τις ἐν
μαχαίρᾳ ἀποκτενεῖ, δεῖ αὐτὸν ἐν μαχαίρᾳ
ἀποκτανθῆναι· ὧδέ ἐστιν ἡ ὑπομονὴ καὶ ἡ
πίστις τῶν ἁγίων.

11 Καὶ εἶδον ἄλλο θηρίον ἀναβαῖνον ἐκ τῆς γῆς,
καὶ εἶχε κέρατα δύο ὅμοια ἀρνίῳ, καὶ ἐλάλει ὡς
12 δράκων. καὶ τὴν ἐξουσίαν τοῦ πρώτου θηρίου
πᾶσαν ποιεῖ ἐνώπιον αὐτοῦ· καὶ ποιεῖ τὴν γῆν
καὶ τοὺς ^bἐν αὐτῇ κατοικοῦντας¹ ἵνα ^cπροσκυνή-
σουσι¹ τὸ θηρίον τὸ πρῶτον, οὗ ἐθεραπεύθη ἡ
13 πληγὴ τοῦ θανάτου αὐτοῦ· καὶ ποιεῖ σημεῖα
μεγάλα, ἵνα καὶ πῦρ ποιῇ ^dἐκ τοῦ οὐρανοῦ κατα-
βαίνειν¹ εἰς τὴν γῆν ἐνώπιον τῶν ἀνθρώπων.
14 καὶ πλανᾷ τοὺς κατοικοῦντας ἐπὶ τῆς γῆς, διὰ
τὰ σημεῖα ἃ ἐδόθη αὐτῷ ποιῆσαι ἐνώπιον τοῦ
θηρίου, λέγων τοῖς κατοικοῦσιν ἐπὶ τῆς γῆς,
ποιῆσαι εἰκόνα τῷ θηρίῳ ^eὃ¹ ἔχει τὴν πληγὴν
15 τῆς μαχαίρας καὶ ἔζησε. καὶ ἐδόθη αὐτῷ δοῦναι

---

^a [τις αἰχμαλωσίαν συνάγει.]   ^b [κατοικοῦντας ἐν αὐτῇ.]

10. *εἴ τις αἰχμαλωσίαν συνάγει εἰς αἰχ. ὑπάγει) εἴ τις αἰχ. συνάγει C.
    εἴ τις εἰς αἰχ. εἰς αἰχ. ὑπάγει A. Slav. MS.   εἴ τις εἰς αἰχ.
    ὑπ. B. 28. 38.   εἴ τ. αἰχ. ὑπ. 32. 47. Copt. Slav. MS.   εἴ
    τις ἔχει αἰχ. ὑπ. a 17. β 3. Compl.   Slav. MS.   Variously read
    also in 7. 18. 34. 35. 36. and others.
    ἀποκτενεῖ, δεῖ) ἀποκτανθῆναι A. — ἀποκτενεῖ a 10. β 4.   Slav. MS.
    ἐν μαχαίρᾳ 2nd) — a 12. β 4.
11. ἀναβαῖνον) -βαίννον C.
    δύο) — a 14. β 3.
    ὅμοια) ὄνομα C.
12. ποιεῖ 2nd) ἐποίει a 18. β 4. Compl.   Syr. Arr.
    *κατοικοῦντας ἐν αὐτῇ) ἐν αὐτῇ κατοικ. A. a 18. β 6. Compl.

an ear, let him hear. He that *is* for cap- 10
tivity, into captivity he goeth; he that will kill
with the sword, with the sword must he be
killed.   Here is the patience and the faith of
the saints.

And I beheld another beast coming up out of 11
the earth; and he had two horns like a lamb, and
he spake as a dragon.   And he exerciseth all the 12
authority of the first beast before him, and causeth
the earth and those who dwell therein to worship
the first beast, whose deadly wound was healed.
And he doeth great wonders, so that he maketh 13
fire come down from heaven on the earth in the
sight of men; and he deceiveth those that dwell 14
on the earth through the wonders which were
given to him to do in the sight of the beast;
saying to those that dwell on the earth, that they
should make an image to the beast, which hath
the wound by a sword, and did live.   And it was 15

---

^c [προσκυνήσωσι.]   ^d [καταβαίνειν ἐκ τοῦ οὐρανοῦ.]   ^e ∽ ὅς.

12. *προσκυνήσωσι) -σοῦσι A. C. 7. 14. 30*. 36.
    τοῦ θανάτου) — A.
13. ἵνα καὶ πῦρ) καὶ πῦρ ἵνα a 21. β 3. γ 2. Compl.
    *ποιῇ καταβαίνειν ἐκ τοῦ οὐρανοῦ) ποιῇ ἐκ τ. οὐρ. καταβ. A. C. 28.
        34. 35. 38.   ἐκ τ. οὐρ. καταβαίνῃ a 24. β 4. Compl.   Vulg.
    εἰς) ἐπὶ a 18. β 4. Compl.
14. πλανᾷ) + τοὺς ἐμοὺς a 18. β 3. Compl.
    ὅ) ὅς A. C. 28. 34. 35. (36?) 92.
    ἔχει) εἶχε a 25. β 5. γ 2. Compl.
    της μαχαίρας καὶ ἔζησε) κ. ἔζ. ἀπὸ τ. μαχ. a 16. β 4.
15. αὐτῷ) αὐτῇ A. C.
    δοῦναι πνεῦμα) — δοῦναι C.   πν. δοῦ. a 16. β 3. Compl.

πνεῦμα τῇ εἰκόνι τοῦ θηρίου, ἵνα καὶ λαλήσῃ ἡ
εἰκὼν τοῦ θηρίου, καὶ ποιήσῃ ^aἵνα| ὅσοι ^bἐαν|
μὴ προσκυνήσωσι τὴν εἰκόνα τοῦ θηρίου, ^c|
16 ἀποκτανθῶσι. καὶ ποιεῖ πάντας, τοὺς μικροὺς
καὶ τοὺς μεγάλους, καὶ τοὺς πλουσίους καὶ
τοὺς πτωχοὺς, καὶ τοὺς ἐλευθέρους καὶ τοὺς
δούλους, ἵνα ^dδῶσιν| αὐτοῖς χάραγμα ἐπὶ τῆς
χειρὸς αὐτῶν τῆς δεξιᾶς, ἢ ἐπὶ ^eτὸ μέτωπον|
17 αὐτῶν, [καὶ] ἵνα μήτις δύνηται ἀγοράσαι ἢ
πωλῆσαι, εἰ μὴ ὁ ἔχων τὸ χάραγμα, ^f| τὸ ὄνομα
τοῦ θηρίου, ἢ τὸν ἀριθμὸν τοῦ ὀνόματος αὐτοῦ.
18 ὧδε ἡ σοφία ἐστίν. ὁ ἔχων ^g| νοῦν, ψηφισάτω τὸν
ἀριθμὸν τοῦ θηρίου· ἀριθμὸς γὰρ ἀνθρώπου ἐστὶ,
καὶ ὁ ἀριθμὸς αὐτοῦ ^hἑξακόσιαι ἑξήκοντα ἕξ.|

XIV. Καὶ εἶδον, καὶ ἰδοὺ ⁱτὸ| ἀρνίον ^kἑστὼς|
ἐπὶ τὸ ὄρος Σιὼν, καὶ μετ' αὐτοῦ ἑκατὸν τεσ-

---

^a Rec.—   ^b [ἂν.]   ^c + [ἵνα.]   ^d [δώσῃ.]   ^e [τῶν μετώπων.]

15. ἵνα καὶ . . . . τ. εἰκ. τ. θη.) — C.   ἵνα καὶ) καὶ ἵνα Compl.
ἡ εἰκὼν) — ἡ Compl.
*ποιήσῃ) ποιεῖ Compl.   + ἵνα A. 11. 26. 36.   Vulg. Syr. Ar. P.
   Slav. ed.
ὅσοι ἂν μὴ προσκυνήσωσι) τοὺς μὴ προσκυνοῦντας Compl.
*ἂν) ἐὰν A. a 11. β 3.
τὴν εἰκόνα) τῇ εἰκόνι a 24. β 6. γ 2. Compl.
*ἵνα) — A. a 12. β 7. γ 2.   Vulg. Syr. Arr. Slav. ed.
16. *δώσῃ) δῶσιν A. C. a 8. β 3. Compl.   δώσωσιν a 14. β 3.
χαράγμα) χαράγματα a 22. β 5. Compl.
*τῶν μετώπων) τὸ μέτωπον A. a 19. β 5.   Copt. Arm.   τοῦ μετώπου C.
17. καὶ) — C. 6. 28. 32.   Vulg. Copt. Syr. Arr. Slav.
δυνήται) δύναται a 7. β 4. Er.
*ἢ 2nd)) — A. C. a 25. β 6. γ 2.   Am. Tol. Syr. Ar. P. Slav. MS.

given to him to give breath unto the image of
the beast, that the image of the beast should
both speak, and cause that as many as would
not worship the image of the beast should be
killed. And he causeth all, both small and great, 16
and rich and poor, and free and bond, to receive
a mark in their right hand, or on their forehead :
[and] that no man might buy or sell, save he 17
that had the mark, the name of the beast, or
the number of his name. Here is wisdom. Let 18
him that hath understanding count the number
of the beast : for it is the number of a man ;
and his number *is* six hundred *and* sixty-six.

XIV. And I saw, and, behold, the Lamb stood
on the mount Sion, and with him an hundred forty

---

f + [ἦ.]   *g* + [τὸν.]   *h* [χξς´.]   *i* Rec.—   *k* [ἑστηκὸς.]

---

17. τὸ ὄνομα) τοῦ ὀνόματος C.   Vulg. MS. *Tol.* Syr.
18. *τὸν 1st) — A. C. *a* 20. β 5. Compl.
    καὶ) — *a* 18. β 5.   Slav. MSS.
    αὐτοῦ) + ἐστιν C. 10. 18. 37. 38. 49. 91. Compl.   Vulg. MS.
        Am.
    *χξς´) ἑξακόσιαι δέκα ἑξ C.   ἑξακόσιοι ἑξήκοντα ἕξ A. Compl.
        ἑξακόσια ἑ. ἕ. 17. 16. 47. &c.

1. *ἀρνίον) τὸ ἀρ. A. C. *a* 19. β 4.   Copt. Syr. Arr.
    *ἑστηκὸς) ἑστὸς A. C. Er.   ἑστὼς 12. 18. 28. 34. 35. 36. 38.
    τὸ ὄρος Σιὼν) ὄρος C.
    αὐτοῦ) + ἀριθμὸς *a* 14. β 3.   Syr. Ar. P.
    ἑκατὸν) — Er.

σαράκοντα τέσσαρες χιλιάδες, ἔχουσαι τὸ ὄνομα
ᵃαὐτοῦ, καὶ τὸ ὄνομα¹ τοῦ πατρὸς αὐτοῦ γε-
2 γραμμένον ἐπὶ τῶν μετώπων αὐτῶν. καὶ ἤκουσα
φωνὴν ἐκ τοῦ οὐρανοῦ ὡς φωνὴν ὑδάτων πολλῶν, καὶ ὡς φωνὴν βροντῆς μεγάλης· καὶ ᵇἡ
φωνὴ ἣν ἤκουσα ὡς¹ κιθαρῳδῶν κιθαριζόντων ἐν
3 ταῖς κιθάραις αὐτῶν. καὶ ᾄδουσιν ὡς ᾠδὴν
καινὴν ἐνώπιον τοῦ θρόνου, καὶ ἐνώπιον τῶν
τεσσάρων ζώων καὶ τῶν πρεσβυτέρων· καὶ
οὐδεὶς ᶜἐδύνατο¹ μαθεῖν τὴν ᾠδὴν, εἰ μὴ αἱ
ἑκατὸν τεσσαράκοντα τέσσαρες χιλιάδες, οἱ ἠγο-
4 ρασμένοι ἀπὸ τῆς γῆς. οὗτοί εἰσιν οἳ μετὰ
γυναικῶν οὐκ ἐμολύνθησαν· παρθένοι γάρ εἰσιν·
οὗτοί [εἰσιν] οἱ ἀκολουθοῦντες τῷ ἀρνίῳ ὅπου
ἂν ὑπάγῃ· οὗτοι ἠγοράσθησαν ἀπὸ τῶν ἀνθρώ-
5 πων, ἀπαρχὴ τῷ Θεῷ καὶ τῷ ἀρνίῳ· καὶ ἐν τῷ
στόματι αὐτῶν οὐχ εὑρέθη ᵈψεῦδος·¹ ἄμωμοι
[γάρ] εἰσιᵉ¹.

ᵃ Rec.—   ᵇ [φωνὴν ἤκουσα.]   ᶜ [ἠδύνατο.]

1. *ὄνομα) +αὐτοῦ καὶ τὸ ὄνομα A. B. C. α 26. β 7. γ 4. Compl.
    Vulg. Copt. Æth. Syr. Arm. Ar. P. Slav. MSS.
    γεγραμμένον) καιόμενον Er.
2. *φωνὴν ἤκουσα) ἡ φωνὴ ἣν ἤκουσα ὡς A. C. α 28. β 6. γ 2. Compl.
    Vulg. Copt. Syr. Arm. Arr. Slav. MSS.
    αὐτῶν) — C.
3. ὡς) — α 24. β 4. Compl.   Copt. Æth. Syr. Arm. Arr. Slav.
    MSS.
    καὶ τῶν πρεσβυτέρων) — C.
    *ἠδύνατο) ἐδύ. A. C. α 8. β 2. Compl.
    τεσσαρες) — C.
4. οὗτοί εἰσιν) — A.   Vulg. MS. Æth.

and four thousand, having his name and his Father's name written in their foreheads. And I 2 heard a voice from heaven, as the voice of many waters, and as the voice of a great thunder : and the voice which I heard *was* as *that* of harpers harping with their harps : and they sing as it 3 were a new song before the throne, and before the four living creatures, and the elders : and no one could learn the song but the hundred *and* forty *and* four thousand, who were redeemed from the earth.   These are those who were not defiled 4 with women ; for they are virgins.   These are they which follow the Lamb whithersoever he goeth. These were redeemed from among men, *being* the firstfruits unto God and to the Lamb.   And in 5 their mouth was found no falsehood : [for] they are blameless.

---

^d [δόλος.]   ^e + [ἐνώπιον τοῦ θρόνου τοῦ Θεοῦ.]

---

4. εἰσιν 3rd) — A. C. Er.   Vulg. Arm. Slav.
 ὅπου) + γὰρ Compl.
 ὑπάγῃ) -γει A. C. 16. 28.
 οὗτοι last) + ὑπὸ Ἰησοῦ a 26. β 5. Compl.   Syr. Ar. P.
 ἀπὸ τῶν ἀνθρώπων) — C.
5. ἐν τῷ στόματι αὐτῶν οὐχ εὑρέθη) οὐχ εὑ. ἐν τ. στ. αὐτ. a 16. β 3.
 *δόλος) ψεῦδος A. C. a 28. β 7. γ 4. Compl.   Vulg. Copt. Æth.
   Syr. Arm. Arr.
 γὰρ) — A. C. 12. 17.   Vulg. MS. *Harl.*
 *ἐνώπιον τοῦ θρόνου τοῦ Θεοῦ) — A. B. C. a 27. β 7. γ 2. Compl.
   Vulg. MS. *Harl. Tol.* Copt. Æth. Syr. Ar. P. Slav. MSS.

6 Καὶ εἶδον ἄλλον ἄγγελον "πετόμενον¹ ἐν μεσουρανήματι, ἔχοντα εὐαγγέλιον αἰώνιον, εὐαγγελίσαι ᵇἐπὶ¹ τοὺς ᶜκαθημένους¹ ἐπὶ τῆς γῆς,
καὶ ᵈἐπὶ¹ πᾶν ἔθνος καὶ φυλὴν καὶ γλῶσσαν καὶ
7 λαὸν, ᵉλέγων¹ ἐν φωνῇ μεγάλῃ· Φοβήθητε τὸν
Θεὸν, καὶ δότε αὐτῷ δόξαν, ὅτι ἦλθεν ἡ ὥρα τῆς
κρίσεως αὐτοῦ· καὶ προσκυνήσατε τῷ ποιήσαντι
τὸν οὐρανὸν καὶ τὴν γῆν καὶ θάλασσαν καὶ
πηγὰς ὑδάτων.

8 Καὶ ἄλλος ᶠ¹ ἄγγελος ἠκολούθησε, λέγων·
"Επεσεν ᵍ¹ Βαβυλὼν ʰ¹ ἡ μεγάλη· ⁱἥ¹ ἐκ τοῦ
οἴνου τοῦ θυμοῦ τῆς πορνείας αὐτῆς πεπότικε
πάντα ᵏτὰ¹ ἔθνη.

9 Καὶ ˡἄλλος ἄγγελος τρίτος¹ ἠκολούθησεν
αὐτοῖς, λέγων ἐν φωνῇ μεγάλῃ· Εἴ τις ᵐπροσ-
κυνεῖ τὸ θηρίον¹ καὶ τὴν εἰκόνα αὐτοῦ, καὶ λαμ-

ᵃ [πετώμενον.]   ᵇ Rec.—   ᶜ [κατοικοῦντας.]   ᵈ Rec.—
ʰ + [ἡ πόλις.]   ⁱ [ὅτι.]   ᵏ Rec.—

6. ἄλλον) — B. a 17. β 7. γ 2. Er.   Ar. P. Slav. MSS.
*πετώμενον) πετό. A. C, a 15. β 3. Compl.
μεσουρανήματι) -νίσματι Er.
εὐαγγελίσαι) -σασθαι 10. 28. 34. 35. 36. 49. 91. Compl.
*   + ἐπὶ A. C. 34.
*τοὺς κατοικοῦντας) τοὺς καθημένους C. a 26. β 4. Compl.   Vulg.
Slav. MSS.   τ. καθη. τ. κατοικ. Er.
*πᾶν) ἐπὶ πᾶν A. C. a 27. β 5. Compl.   Vulg. Syr. Slav. MSS.
7. *λέγοντα) λέγων A. C. a 25. β 6. γ 4. Compl.   Vulg. Copt. Slav. MSS.
ἐν) — A.
Θεὸν) Κύριον a 20. β 6.   Vulg. (not Am.) Ar. P.
προσκυνήσατε) -σαντι C.
τῷ ποιήσαντι) αὐτὸν τὸν ποιήσαντα a 17. β 5.
θάλ.) τὴν θ. A. a 21. β 7. Compl.
8. ἄλλος) + δεύτερος A. B. a 17. β 5.   Syr.   After ἄγγελος C. a 8.
β 2. Compl.   Copt. Arm.

And I saw another angel flying in the mid- 6
heaven, having the everlasting Gospel to preach
unto those that dwell on the earth, and unto every
nation, and kindred, and tongue, and people, saying 7
with a loud voice, Fear God, and give glory to
him ; for the hour of his judgment is come : and
worship him that made heaven, and earth, and sea,
and the fountains of waters.

And there followed another angel, saying, Fallen 8
is Babylon the great, who made all the nations
drink of the wine of the wrath of her fornication.

And another a third angel followed them, saying 9
with a loud voice, He that worshippeth the beast
and his image, and receiveth *his* mark in his fore-

---

e [λέγοντα.]　　　*f* ∾ + δεύτερος.　　　*g* + [ἔπεσε. See xviii. 2.]
　　l [τρίτος ἄγγελος.]　　*m* [τὸ θηρίον προσκυνεῖ.]

---

*ἔπεσε) — B. C. a 18. β 6. γ 2.　Copt. Æth. Ar. P. Slav. MSS.
8. *ἡ πόλις) — A. B. C　a 25.　β 7.　γ 3.　Compl.　Vulg. Copt. Syr.
　　Arm. Arr. Slav. MSS.
　*ὅτι) — a 15. β 6. γ 3. Compl.　Arm. Ar. P. Slav. MSS.　ἢ A. C.
　　26. 33. 34. 35. 38. 50**.　Vulg. Æth. Syr.
　τοῦ θυμοῦ) — Er.
　πορνείας) πορείας B.
　αὐτῆς) ταύτης B. a 9. β 5.
　*ἔθνη) τὰ ἔθ. A. C. a 16. β 3. γ 2. Compl.
9. *τρίτος ἄγγελος) ἄλλος ἄγγ. τρί. A. C. a 24. β 6. γ 3.　Compl.
　　Vulg. MS. *Tol.* Copt. Syr. Arm. Ar. P. Slav. MS.
　αὐτοῖς) αὐτῷ A.
　*τὸ θηρίον προσκυνεῖ) προσκ. τ. θ. A. C. a 19. β 8. Compl.　θηρίον)
　　θυσιαστήριον A.　τῷ θηρίῳ C.
　αὐτοῦ) αὐτῶν C.
　καὶ 2nd) — C. 14.

βάνει χάραγμα ἐπὶ τοῦ μετώπου αὐτοῦ, ἢ ἐπὶ
10 τὴν χεῖρα αὐτοῦ, καὶ αὐτὸς πίεται ἐκ τοῦ οἴνου
τοῦ θυμοῦ τοῦ Θεοῦ, τοῦ κεκερασμένου ἀκράτου
ἐν τῷ ποτηρίῳ τῆς ὀργῆς αὐτοῦ· καὶ βασανισθήσεται ἐν πυρὶ καὶ θείῳ ἐνώπιον ᵃἀγγέλων
11 ἁγίων,ᵃ καὶ ἐνώπιον τοῦ ἀρνίου· καὶ ὁ καπνὸς
τοῦ βασανισμοῦ αὐτῶν ᵇεἰς αἰῶνας αἰώνων
ἀναβαίνει·ᵇ καὶ ᴏὐκ ἔχουσιν ἀνάπαυσιν ἡμέρας
καὶ νυκτὸς οἱ προσκυνοῦντες τὸ θηρίον καὶ τὴν
εἰκόνα αὐτοῦ, καὶ εἴ τις λαμβάνει τὸ χάραγμα
τοῦ ὀνόματος αὐτοῦ.
12 ῞Ωδε ᶜἡᶜ ὑπομονὴ τῶν ἁγίων ἐστὶν, ᵈ οἱ
τηροῦντες τὰς ἐντολὰς τοῦ Θεοῦ καὶ τὴν πίστιν
13 Ἰησοῦ. καὶ ἤκουσα φωνῆς ἐκ τοῦ οὐρανοῦ,
λεγούσηςᵉ· Γράψον· Μακάριοι οἱ νεκροὶ οἱ
ἐν Κυρίῳ ἀποθνήσκοντες ἀπ' ἄρτι. Ναὶ, λέγει
τὸ Πνεῦμα· ἵνα ᶠἀναπαύσονταιᶠ ἐκ τῶν κόπων
αὐτῶν· τὰ ᵍγὰρᵍ ἔργα αὐτῶν ἀκολουθεῖ μετ'
αὐτῶν.
14 Καὶ εἶδον, καὶ ἰδοὺ νεφέλη λευκὴ, καὶ ἐπὶ

ᵃ [τῶν ἁγίων ἀγγέλων.] ⌐ τῶν ἀγγέλων.   ᵇ [ἀναβαίνει εἰς αἰῶνας αἰώνων.]

10. ἐν τῷ ποτηρίῳ) ἐκ τοῦ ποτηρίου Α. 16. 39.
   τῆς ὀργῆς) τὴν ὀργὴν Α.
   βασανισθήσεται) -θήσονται Α. 8. 14. 36. 92.
   *τῶν ἁγίων ἀγγέλων) ἀγγ. ἁγ. C. 38. — ἁγίων Α. 26. Vulg.
      MS. Copt. ἄγγ. τ. ἁγ. Er.
11. *ἀναβαίνει εἰς αἰῶνας αἰώνων) ε. αἰ. αἰ. ἀναβ. Α. C. a 16. β 6. γ 2.
      Compl. αἰῶνας) -να. Er. αἰῶνα αἰῶνος C.
12. *ὑπομόνη) ἡ ὑπομ. Α. C. a 21. β 2.
   *ὧδε 2nd) — Α. Β. C. a 20. β 6. Vulg. Copt. Æth. Syr. Erp.
      Slav. ed.

head, or on his hand, even he shall drink of the 10
wine of the wrath of God, which is poured out
without mixture into the cup of his indignation;
and he shall be tormented with fire and brimstone
in the presence of the holy angels, and in the
presence of the Lamb: and the smoke of their 11
torment ascendeth up for ever and ever: and they
have no rest day nor night, who worship the beast
and his image, and whosoever receiveth the mark
of his name.

Here is the patience of the saints; *here are* 12
those that keep the commandments of God, and
the faith of Jesus. And I heard a voice from 13
heaven saying, Write, Blessed *are* the dead who die
in the Lord from henceforth: Yea, saith the Spirit,
that they may rest from their labours; for their
works do follow them.

And I saw, and behold a white cloud, and 14

---

^c Rec. —   ^d +[ὧδε.]   ^e +[μοι.]   ^f [ἀναπαύσωνται.]   ^g [δὲ.]

---

12. τοῦ Θεοῦ) — Er.
    'Ιησοῦ) τοῦ 'Ιησοῦ Compl.
13. *μοι) — A. B. C. a 20. β 5.   Vulg. MS. *Am.* Copt. Æth. Syr. Arr.
    Κυρίῳ) Χριστῷ C.
    ἀπ᾽ ἄρτι· ναὶ λέγει) ἀπ᾽ ἄρτι λέγει ναὶ a 15. β 4. Compl.   Ar. P.
    ἀπ᾽ ἄρτι· λέγει ναὶ a 9. γ 2.
    *ἀναπαύσωνται) -σονται A. C. 16. 28. 30. 32. 36. 50. Er.   ἀνα-
    παήσονται A. C.
    *τὰ δὲ) τὰ γὰρ A. C. 18. 26. 38.   Vulg. Syr.
    αὐτῶν 2nd) — Er.

τὴν νεφέλην ᵃκαθήμενον ὅμοιον· υἱῷ ἀνθρώπου,
ἔχων ἐπὶ ᵇτὴν κεφαλὴν| αὐτοῦ στέφανον χρυ-
σοῦν, καὶ ἐν τῇ χειρὶ αὐτοῦ δρέπανον ὀξύ.
15 καὶ ἄλλος ἄγγελος ἐξῆλθεν ἐκ τοῦ ναοῦ,
κράζων ἐν ᶜφωνῇ μεγάλῃ| τῷ καθημένῳ ἐπὶ τῆς
νεφέλης· Πέμψον τὸ δρέπανόν σου, καὶ θέρι-
σον, ὅτι ἦλθενᵈ| ἡ ὥρα ᵉ| θερίσαι, ὅτι ἐξηράνθη
16 ὁ θερισμὸς τῆς γῆς. Καὶ ἔβαλεν ὁ καθήμενος
ἐπὶ ᶠτῆς νεφελῆς| τὸ δρέπανον αὐτοῦ ἐπὶ τὴν
γῆν, καὶ ἐθερίσθη ἡ γῆ.
17 Καὶ ἄλλος ἄγγελος ἐξῆλθεν ἐκ τοῦ ναοῦ τοῦ
ἐν τῷ οὐρανῷ, ἔχων καὶ αὐτὸς δρέπανον ὀξύ.
18 καὶ ἄλλος ἄγγελος ἐξῆλθεν ἐκ τοῦ θυσιαστηρίου, ἔχων ἐξουσίαν ἐπὶ τοῦ πυρός, καὶ ἐφώνησε
ᵍφωνῇ| μεγάλῃ τῷ ἔχοντι τὸ δρέπανον τὸ ὀξύ,
λέγων· Πέμψον σου τὸ δρέπανον τὸ ὀξύ, καὶ
τρύγησον τοὺς βότρυας τῆς ἀμπέλου τῆς γῆς,
19 ὅτι ἤκμασαν αἱ σταφυλαὶ αὐτῆς. Καὶ ἔβαλεν
ὁ ἄγγελος τὸ δρέπανον αὐτοῦ εἰς τὴν γῆν, καὶ
ἐτρύγησε τὴν ἄμπελον τῆς γῆς, καὶ ἔβαλεν εἰς

ᵃ [καθήμενος ὅμοιος.]   ᵇ [τῆς κεφαλῆς.]   ᶜ [μεγάλῃ φωνῇ.]

---

14. *καθήμενος ὅμοιος) -νον ὅμοιον A. C. a 19. β 7.
υἱῷ) υἱόν A. a 10, β 4.   υἱὸς Er.
ἔχων) ἔχον C.
*τῆς κεφαλῆς) τὴν κεφαλὴν A. a 6. (& 28. 29.)
15. ἐκ τοῦ ναοῦ κράζων) κρα. ἐ. τ. να. A.
*μεγάλῃ φωνῇ) φω. μεγ. A. C. a 16. β 6. Compl.   μεγ. τῇ φω. Er.
*σοι) — A. C. a 24. β 5. Compl.   Vulg. Copt. Æth. Arm. Arr. Slav.
*τοῦ) — A. C. a 9. β 5. Er.
16. *τὴν νεφέλην) τῆς νεφέλης A. 16*. 36. 47.
τὸ) τὸν Er.

upon the cloud *I saw one* sitting like unto the
Son of man, having on his head a golden
crown, and in his hand a sharp sickle.   And 15
another angel came out of the temple, crying
with a loud voice to him that sat on the cloud,
Thrust in thy sickle, and reap ; for the time
to reap is come ; for the harvest of the earth
is ripe.   And he that sat on the cloud thrust 16
in his sickle on the earth ; and the earth was
reaped.

And another angel came out of the temple 17
which is in heaven, he also having a sharp sickle.
And another angel came out from the altar, who 18
had power over fire ; and cried with a loud voice to
him that had the sharp sickle, saying, Thrust in thy
sharp sickle, and gather the clusters of the vine of
the earth ; for her grapes are fully ripe.   And the 19
angel thrust in his sickle into the earth, and
gathered the vine of the earth, and cast *it* into the

---

d + [σοι.]   *e* + [τοῦ.]   *f* [τὴν νεφέλην.]   *g* [κραυγῇ.]

---

17. ἄγγελος transposed after τῷ οὐρανῷ Er.
   τῷ) — C.
18. ἐξῆλθεν) — A.   Vulg. MS. *Am.*
   ἔχων) ὁ ἔχ. A.
   *κραυγῇ) ἐν κραυ. a 16. β 4.   φωνῇ A. B. 38.   Vulg. Æth.Arm. Ar.
   τῆς ἀμπέλου) — Er.
   ἤκμασαν αἱ σταφυλαὶ) ἤκμασεν ἡ σταφυλὴ B. a 17. β 6.   Æth. Arr.
   αὐτῆς) τῆς γῆς a 17. β 7.   Æth. Syr.
19. ἔβαλεν 1st) ἐξέβ. a 14. β 4.
   ἔβαλεν 2nd) ἔλαβεν Er.

τὴν ληνὸν τοῦ θυμοῦ τοῦ Θεοῦ ᵃτὸν μέγαν.¹
20 καὶ ἐπατήθη ἡ ληνὸς ᵇἔξωθεν¹ τῆς πόλεως, καὶ
ἐξῆλθεν αἷμα ἐκ τῆς ληνοῦ ἄχρι τῶν χαλινῶν
τῶν ἵππων, ἀπὸ σταδίων χιλίων ἑξακοσίων.

XV. Καὶ εἶδον ἄλλο σημεῖον ἐν τῷ οὐρανῷ
μέγα καὶ θαυμαστὸν, ἀγγέλους ἑπτὰ, ἔχοντας
πληγὰς ἑπτὰ τὰς ἐσχάτας, ὅτι ἐν αὐταῖς ἐτελέσθη ὁ θυμὸς τοῦ Θεοῦ.
2 Καὶ εἶδον ὡς θάλασσαν ὑαλίνην μεμιγμένην
πυρὶ, καὶ τοὺς νικῶντας ἐκ τοῦ θηρίου καὶ ἐκ
τῆς εἰκόνος αὐτοῦ καὶ ᶜ¹ ἐκ τοῦ ἀριθμοῦ τοῦ
ὀνόματος αὐτοῦ, ἑστῶτας ἐπὶ τὴν θάλασσαν τὴν
3 ὑαλίνην, ἔχοντας κιθάρας τοῦ Θεοῦ. καὶ ᾄδουσι
τὴν ᾠδὴν ᵈΜωϋσέως¹ ᵉτοῦ¹ δούλου τοῦ Θεοῦ,
καὶ τὴν ᾠδὴν τοῦ ἀρνίου, λέγοντες· Μεγάλα
καὶ θαυμαστὰ τὰ ἔργα σου, Κύριε ὁ Θεὸς ὁ
παντοκράτωρ· δίκαιαι καὶ ἀληθιναὶ αἱ ὁδοί
4 σου, ὁ βασιλεὺς τῶν ᶠἐθνῶν.¹ τίς οὐ μὴ φο-
βηθῇ ᵍ¹, Κύριε, καὶ δοξάσῃ τὸ ὄνομά σου; ὅτι

ᵃ [τὴν μεγάλην.]   ᵇ [ἔξω.]   ᶜ + [ἐκ τοῦ χαράγματος αὐτοῦ.]

19. ληνὸν) ἀλῶναν C.
*τὴν μεγάλην) τὸν μέγαν A. C. a 20. β 5. Compl.
20. *ἔξω) ἔξωθεν A. C. a 24. β 8. Compl.
ἑξακοσίων) — C**. 11.

1. αὐταῖς) αὐτοῖς Er.
2. μεμιγ. πυρὶ) π. μεμ. Compl.
ἐκ τοῦ θηρίου καὶ ἐκ τῆς εἰκόνος) ἐκ τ. εἰκ. κ. ε. τ. θη. B. a 12. β 5.
*ἐκ τοῦ χαράγματος αὐτοῦ) — A. B. C. a 24. β 4. Compl. Vulg.
Copt. Æth. Syr. Arr.
κιθάρας) τὰς κιθ. a 8. β 2.

great winepress of the wrath of God. And the 20
winepress was trodden without the city, and blood
came out of the winepress, even unto the horse
bridles, by the space of a thousand *and* six hundred
furlongs.

XV. And I saw another wonder in heaven, great
and marvellous, seven angels having the seven
last plagues; for in them is filled up the wrath
of God.

And I saw as it were a sea of glass mingled 2
with fire, and those that had gotten the victory
over the beast, and over his image, and over
the number of his name, standing on the sea of
glass, having the harps of God. And they sing 3
the song of Moses the servant of God, and the
song of the Lamb, saying, Great and marvellous
are thy works, O Lord God, the Almighty; just
and true *are* thy ways, thou King of the nations.
Who shall not fear, O Lord, and glorify thy name? 4

---

[d] [Μωσέως.]   [e] Rcc.—   [f] [ἁγίων.] ∾ αἰώνων.   [g] + [σε.]

---

3. καὶ ᾄδουσι . . . . τοῦ Θεοῦ) — C.
*Μωσέως) Μωϋσέως A. α 17. β 3. Compl.
+ τοῦ A. α 8. (& 12.) Compl.
τὰ ἔργα) — τὰ Er. κύριε) κύριος Er.
*ἁγίων) ἐθνῶν A. B. α 27. β 9. γ 3. Compl. Copt. Æth. Arm. Ar. P. Slav. MSS. αἰώνων C. 18. Vulg. Syr. Arm. ed. in m. Erp. It is probable that ΕΘΝΩΝ was in some MS. written ΑΙΘΝΩΝ and then ΑΙΟΝΩΝ, which was corrected into ΑΙΩΝΩΝ.

4. *σε) — A. B. C. 12. 14. 36. 47. 92. Er. Vulg. MS. *Am. Tol.* Æth. Arm.
δοξάσῃ) -σει A. C. α 9. β 5.

μόνος ὅσιος· ὅτι πάντα τὰ ἔθνη ἥξουσι, καὶ
προσκυνήσουσιν ἐνώπιόν σου· ὅτι τὰ δικαιώματά
σου ἐφανερώθησαν.

5 Καὶ μετὰ ταῦτα εἶδον, καὶ ᵃ| ἠνοίγη ὁ ναὸς
6 τῆς σκηνῆς τοῦ μαρτυρίου ἐν τῷ οὐρανῷ· καὶ
ἐξῆλθον οἱ ἑπτὰ ἄγγελοι ᵇοἱ| ἔχοντες τὰς ἑπτὰ
πληγὰς ⌊ἐκ τοῦ ναοῦ⌉, ἐνδεδυμένοι λίνον κα-
θαρὸν ᶜ| λαμπρὸν, καὶ περιεζωσμένοι περὶ τὰ
7 στήθη ζώνας χρυσᾶς. καὶ ἓν ἐκ τῶν τεσσάρων
ζώων ἔδωκε τοῖς ἑπτὰ ἀγγέλοις ἑπτὰ φιάλας
χρυσᾶς, γεμούσας τοῦ θυμοῦ τοῦ Θεοῦ τοῦ
8 ζῶντος εἰς τοὺς αἰῶνας τῶν αἰώνων. καὶ ἐγε-
μίσθη ὁ ναὸς καπνοῦ ἐκ τῆς δόξης τοῦ Θεοῦ,
καὶ ἐκ τῆς δυνάμεως αὐτοῦ· καὶ οὐδεὶς ᵈἐδύνατο|
εἰσελθεῖν εἰς τὸν ναὸν, ἄχρι τελεσθῶσιν αἱ ἑπτὰ
πληγαὶ τῶν ἑπτὰ ἀγγέλων.

XVI. Καὶ ἤκουσα ᵉμεγάλης φωνῆς| ⌊ἐκ τοῦ
ναοῦ,⌉ λεγούσης τοῖς ἑπτὰ ἀγγέλοις· Ὑπά-

ᵃ [ἰδού.]   ᵇ Rec.—   ᶜ+[καὶ.]

---

4. ὅσιος) ἅγιος B. a26. β7. γ2. Compl.   + εἶ. a4. (& 36.) Compl.
     Vulg. Syr.
     πάντα τὰ ἔθνη) πάντες B. a21. β7.   Ar. P.
     σου) + κύριε A.
5. *ἰδού) — A. B. C. a27. β9. Compl. Æth. Syr. Arm. Slav. MSS.
6. *ἄγγελοι) + οἱ A. C. a21. β 8. Compl.
     ἐκ τοῦ ναοῦ) — B. a19. β4.   ἐ. τ. οὐρανοῦ. Compl.   + οἱ ἦσαν
     B. a17. B. 7. γ2. Compl.
     λίνον) λίθον A. C. 38**, 48. 90.   Vulg. MS. Am. Slav. MSS.
     λινοῦν B. 14. 18. 36. 92.   + καὶ Comp.
     *καὶ λαμ.) — καὶ A. B. C. a16. β7. Er.   Vulg. MS. Am. Tol.
     Copt. Syr. Arr. Slav. MS.

for *thou* only *art* holy : for all the nations shall come and worship before thee ; for thy judgments have been made manifest.

And after that I saw, and the temple of the 5 tabernacle of the testimony in heaven was opened : and the seven angels who had the seven plagues, 6 came out ⸢of the temple⸥ clothed in pure white linen, and having their breasts girded with golden girdles.   And one of the four living creatures 7 gave unto the seven angels seven cups of gold full of the wrath of God, who liveth for ever and ever.   And the temple was filled with smoke 8 from the glory of God, and from his power ; and no one was able to enter into the temple, till the seven plagues of the seven angels were fulfilled.

XVI. And I heard a great voice ⸢out of the temple⸥ saying to the seven angels, Go your ways,

---

---

6. περὶ) — 12 Er.
7. ἐκ) — 11. 12. 16. Er.
8. ναὸς) + ἐκ τοῦ a 17. β 4.
    *ἠδύνατο) ἐδύνατο A. C. a 8. (& 6.)
    εἰς τὸν ναὸν) ἐν τῷ ναῷ Er.
    ἄχρι) ἄχρις οὗ C.
    ἑπτὰ last) — 10. 12. 17. 18. 38. 49. Compl.

1. *φωνῆς μεγάλης) μεγ. φω. A. B. C. a 6. β 3.
    ἐκ τοῦ ναοῦ) — B. a 18. β 5.   Syr. (in some copies), Ar. P.
       Slav. MSS.

γετε, καὶ "ἐκχέετε¹ τὰς ᵇἑπτὰ¹ φιάλας τοῦ θυμοῦ τοῦ Θεοῦ εἰς τὴν γῆν.

2 Καὶ ἀπῆλθεν ὁ πρῶτος, καὶ ἐξέχεε τὴν φιάλην αὐτοῦ ᶜεἰς¹ τὴν γῆν· καὶ ἐγένετο ἕλκος κακὸν καὶ πονηρὸν ᵈἐπὶ¹ τοὺς ἀνθρώπους τοὺς ἔχοντας τὸ χάραγμα τοῦ θηρίου, καὶ τοὺς ᵉπροσκυνοῦντας τῇ εἰκόνι αὐτοῦ.¹

3 Καὶ ὁ δεύτερος ᶠ¹ ἐξέχεε τὴν φιάλην αὐτοῦ εἰς τὴν θάλασσαν· καὶ ἐγένετο αἷμα ὡς νεκροῦ, καὶ πᾶσα ψυχὴ ᵍ[ζωῆς]¹ ἀπέθανεν ʰτὰ¹ ἐν τῇ θαλάσσῃ.

4 Καὶ ὁ τρίτος ⁱ¹ ἐξέχεε τὴν φιάλην αὐτοῦ εἰς τοὺς ποταμοὺς καὶ ᵏ¹ τὰς πηγὰς τῶν 5 ὑδάτων· καὶ ἐγένετο αἷμα. καὶ ἤκουσα τοῦ ἀγγέλου τῶν ὑδάτων, λέγοντος· Δίκαιος ˡ¹ εἶ, ὁ ὢν καὶ ὁ ἦν ᵐ¹ ὅσιος, ὅτι ταῦτα ἔκρινας.

6 ὅτι αἷμα ἁγίων καὶ προφητῶν ἐξέχεαν, καὶ αἷμα αὐτοῖς ⁿδέδωκας¹ πιεῖν· ἄξιοί ᵒ¹ εἰσι.

ᵃ [ἐκχέατε.]   ᵇ Rec.—   ᶜ [ἐπὶ.]   ᵈ [εἰς.]   ᵉ [τῇ εἰκόνι αὐτοῦ
· + [ἄγγελος.]   ᵏ + [εἰς.]   ᶠ + [κύριε.]

1. καὶ ἐκχ.) — καὶ α 9. β 3. Er. Compl.   Vulg. MS. Copt. Arm.
*ἐκχέατε) -ετε A. C. 12. 14. Er.
*τὰς) + ἐπτὰ A. B. C. α 20. β 7.   Vulg. Syr. Arm. Arr.
τοῦ Θεοῦ) — 12 Er.

2. ὁ) — Er.
*ἐπὶ) εἰς A. C. α 19. β 7.   Vulg. Syr. Ar. P.
κακὸν) — A.
*εἰς) ἐπὶ A. C. α 21. β 6.   Syr. Arm. Arr.
*τῇ εἰκόνι αὐτοῦ προσκυνοῦντας) προσκ. τῇ εἰκ. αὐ. A. C. α 17. β 7.
Compl.   τὴν εἰκόνα προσκ. αὐ. Er.

3. *ἄγγελος) — A. C. 18.   Vulg. MS. Am. Tol. Æth.
ψυχὴ) -χῆς A.
*ζῶσα) — α 19. β 4.   Slav. MSS.   ζωῆς A. C. Syr.

and pour out the seven cups of the wrath of God upon the earth.

And the first went, and poured out his cup 2
upon the earth; and there was a noisome and grievous sore upon the men who had the mark of the beast, and *upon* those who worshipped his image.

And the second poured out his cup into the 3
sea; and it became blood as of a dead *man;* and every [living] soul died *as to* the things in the sea.

And the third poured out his cup into the 4
rivers and fountains of waters; and they became
blood. And I heard the angel of the waters 5
say, Thou art righteous, who art, and who wast
holy, because thou hast judged thus. For they 6
have shed the blood of saints and prophets, and thou hast given them blood to drink; they are

---

προσκυνοῦντας.] [f] + [ἄγγελος.] [g] [ζῶσα.] [h] Rec.— [m] + [καὶ ὁ.] [n] [ἔδωκας.] [o] + [γὰρ.]

---

3. *ἀπέθανεν) + τὰ A. C. Syr. Slav. MS.

4. *ἄγγελος) — A. C. *α*18. *β*6. Vulg. Æth. Ar. P.
 *εἰς 2nd) — A. C. 10. 43. 49. 91. Compl. Copt.
 ἐγένετο) -οντο A. 36.

5. τῶν ὑδάτων) — Er.
 *κύριε) — A. C. *α*25. *β*6. *γ*3. Compl. Vulg. MS. *Am. Tol.* Copt. Syr. Ar. P. Slav. MSS.
 ὁ 2nd) ὃς B. *α*9. *β*2.
 *ἦν καὶ) — καὶ A. B. C. *α* 25. *β* 7. *γ* 3. Compl. Vulg. Arm. Slav. MS.
 *ὁ ὅσ.) — ὁ A. B. C. *α*19. *β*5. Syr. Arm.

6. *ἔδωκας) δέδωκας A. C.
 *γὰρ) — A. C. *α*25. *β*8. *γ*3. Compl. *Tol.* Copt. Slav. MS.

7 Καὶ ἤκουσα ^a| τοῦ θυσιαστηρίου λέγοντος·
Ναὶ, Κύριε ὁ Θεὸς ὁ παντοκράτωρ, ἀληθιναὶ
καὶ δίκαιαι αἱ κρίσεις σου.

8 Καὶ ὁ τέταρτος ^b| ἐξέχεε τὴν φιάλην αὐτοῦ
ἐπὶ τὸν ἥλιον· καὶ ἐδόθη αὐτῷ καυματίσαι τοὺς
9 ἀνθρώπους ἐν πυρί· καὶ ἐκαυματίσθησαν οἱ
ἄνθρωποι καῦμα μέγα, καὶ ἐβλασφήμησαν τὸ
ὄνομα τοῦ Θεοῦ τοῦ ἔχοντος ^c τὴν| ἐξουσίαν
ἐπὶ τὰς πληγὰς ταύτας, καὶ οὐ μετενόησαν δοῦναι αὐτῷ δόξαν.

10 Καὶ ὁ πέμπτος ^d| ἐξέχεε τὴν φιάλην αὐτοῦ
ἐπὶ τὸν θρόνον τοῦ θηρίου· καὶ ἐγένετο ἡ βασιλεία αὐτοῦ ἐσκοτωμένη· καὶ ἐμασσῶντο τὰς
11 γλώσσας αὐτῶν ἐκ τοῦ πόνου, καὶ ἐβλασφήμησαν τὸν Θεὸν τοῦ οὐρανοῦ ἐκ τῶν πόνων αὐτῶν
καὶ ἐκ τῶν ἑλκῶν αὐτῶν, καὶ οὐ μετενόησαν ἐκ
τῶν ἔργων αὐτῶν.

12 Καὶ ὁ ἕκτος ^e| ἐξέχεε τὴν φιάλην αὐτοῦ ἐπὶ
τὸν ποταμὸν τὸν μέγαν τὸν Εὐφράτην· καὶ
ἐξηράνθη τὸ ὕδωρ αὐτοῦ, ἵνα ἑτοιμασθῇ ἡ ὁδὸς
τῶν βασιλέων τῶν ἀπὸ ^f ἀνατολῆς| ἡλίου.　καὶ

---

7. *ἄλλου ἐκ) — A. B. C. a 26. β 7. γ 2. (Compl. ἐκ)　　Vulg. MS.
　　Copt. Syr. Ar. P. Slav. MSS.
8. ὁ) ὅτε) Er.
　　*ἄγγελος) — A. C. a 12. β 3.　　Vulg. MS. Tol. Æth. Syr. Ar. P.
　　τοὺς ἀνθρώπους ἐν πυρὶ) ἐν. π. τ. ἀνθ. a 12. β 3.
9. ἐβλασφήμησαν) + οἱ ἄνθρωποι B. a 22. β 6. Compl.　　Syr. Ar. P.
　　Slav. MS.
　　τὸ ὄνομα) ἐνώπιον A.
　　*ἐξουσίαν) τὴν ἐξου. A. 10. 12. 36. 37. 49. 91. Compl

worthy.   And I heard the altar say, Even so, 7
O Lord God the Almighty, true and righteous *are*
thy judgments.

And the fourth poured out his cup upon the 8
sun; and *power* was given unto him to scorch men
with fire.   And men were scorched with great 9
heat, and blasphemed the name of God, who hath
power over these plagues: and they repented not to
give him glory.

And the fifth poured out his cup upon the throne 10
of the beast; and his kingdom was darkened, and
they gnawed their tongues for pain, and they 11
blasphemed the God of heaven because of their
pains and their sores, and repented not of their
deeds.

And the sixth poured out his cup upon the 12
great river Euphrates; and the water thereof
was dried up, that the way of the kings might
be prepared from the sunrising.   And I saw 13

---

^d + [ἄγγελος.]   ^e + [ἄγγελος.]   ^f [ἀνατολῶν.]

---

9. οὐ) οὐχὶ C.
10. *ἄγγελος) — A. C. a 18. β 6.   Vulg. MS. *Am.* Æth. Syr. Ar. P.
    ἐσκοτωμένη) -τισμένη B. 29.
    ἐμασσῶντο) ἐμασῶντο A. C. a 7. β 2. Er.
12. *ἄγγελος) —A. C. a 19. β 4. Er.   Vulg. MS. *Am. Tol.* Æth. Syr.
    Ar. P.
    μέγαν τὸν) — τὸν a 15. β 6. Compl.
    ὕδωρ αὐτοὺ) — αὐτοῦ 12. 36. Er.
    *ἀνατολῶν) -λῆς C. a 22. β 6.

εἶδον ἐκ τοῦ στόματος τοῦ δράκοντος, καὶ ἐκ τοῦ
στόματος τοῦ θηρίου, καὶ ἐκ τοῦ στόματος τοῦ
ψευδοπροφήτου, πνεύματα τρία ἀκάθαρτα, ᵃ ὡς
14 βάτραχοι·¹ εἰσὶ γὰρ πνεύματα ᵇδαιμονίων¹
ποιοῦντα σημεῖα ἃ ἐκπορεύεται ἐπὶ τοὺς βασιλεῖς ᶜ¹ τῆς οἰκουμένης ὅλης, συναγαγεῖν αὐτοὺς
εἰς ᵈτὸν¹ πόλεμον τῆς ἡμέρας [ἐκείνης] τῆς
15 μεγάλης τοῦ Θεοῦ τοῦ παντοκράτορος. Ἰδοὺ
ἔρχομαι ὡς κλέπτης, μακάριος ὁ γρηγορῶν, καὶ
τηρῶν τὰ ἱμάτια αὐτοῦ, ἵνα μὴ γυμνὸς περι-
πατῇ, καὶ βλέπωσι τὴν ἀσχημοσύνην αὐτοῦ.
16 Καὶ συνήγαγεν αὐτοὺς εἰς τὸν τόπον τὸν καλού-
μενον Ἑβραϊστὶ ᵉἈρμαγεδών.¹
17 Καὶ ὁ ἕβδομος ᶠ¹ ἐξέχεε τὴν φιάλην αὐτοῦ
ᵍἐπὶ¹ τὸν ἀέρα· καὶ ἐξῆλθε φωνὴ μεγάλη ʰεκ¹
τοῦ ναοῦ [τοῦ οὐρανοῦ,] ἀπὸ τοῦ θρόνου, λέ-
18 γουσα· Γέγονε. Καὶ ἐγένοντο ⁱἀστραπαι καὶ
φωναὶ καὶ βρονταὶ¹ καὶ σεισμὸς ⸢ἐγένετο⸣ μέγας,
οἷος οὐκ ἐγένετο ἀφ᾽ οὗ ᵏἄνθρωπος ἐγένετο¹ ἐπὶ

ᵃ [ὅμοια βατράχοις.]   ᵇ [δαιμόνων.]   ⸳ +[τῆς γῆς καὶ.]
ʰ [ἀπὸ.]   ⁱ [φωναὶ καὶ βρονταὶ καὶ ἀστραπαὶ.]

13. τοῦ δράκοντος καὶ ἐκ τοῦ στόματος) — C. 9. 27. 39.
   τρία ἀκάθαρτα) ἀκάθ. τρ. Β. a 16. β 4.
   *ὅμοια βατράχοις) ὡς βάτραχοι Α. Β. a 25. β 7. γ 2. Compl.   Vulg.
   Æth. Arm. Ar. P. Slav.
14. *δαιμόνων) δαιμονίων Α. a 17. β 6.
   ἃ ἐκπορεύεται) ἃ ἐκπορεύονται Β. 16. 36. 39.   ἐκπορεύεσθαι 18. Er.
   *τῆς γῆς καὶ) — Α. Β. a 28. β 8. γ 2. Compl.   Vulg. (Copt.) Æth.
   Syr. (Arm. Erp.) Slav.
   *πόλεμον) τὸν πόλ. Α. a 18. β 6. Compl.
   ἐκείνης) — Α. 14. 38. 92.   Vulg. Copt. Æth. Arm. Erp.   τῆς
   μεγάλης ἡμέρας Α.
16. τόπον) ποταμὸν Α.   τὸν τόπον) — τὸν Compl.

three unclean spirits as it were frogs *come* out
of the mouth of the dragon, and out of the
mouth of the beast, and out of the mouth of
the false prophet.   For they are the spirits of 14
demons, working miracles, which go forth unto
the kings of the whole world, to gather them
to the battle of [that] great day of the Almighty God.   Behold, I come as a thief; blessed 15
is he that watcheth, and keepeth his garments,
lest he walk naked, and they see his shame.   And 16
he gathered them together into the place which
is called in the Hebrew tongue Armagedon.

And the seventh poured out his cup upon the 17
air ; and there came a great voice out of the temple
[of heaven,] from the throne, saying, It is done.
And there were lightnings and voices, and thunders, 18
and there was a great earthquake, such as was
not since ᶦthere was a man upon the earth, so

---

d Rec. —   *e* ['Αρμαγεδδών.]   *f* + [ἄγγελος.]   *g* [εἰς.]
      k ∿ [οἱ ἄνθρωποι ἐγένοντο.]   *l* ∿ [men were.]

---

16. **'Αρμαγεδδών.) 'Αρμαγεδών. A. a 11. β 3. Compl. Eras.   Μαγεδὼν
          B. a 14. β 3.   Vulg. MS. Slav. MSS.
      **ἄγγελος) — A. a 19. β 6.   Vulg. MS. Am. Tol. Syr.
17. **εἰς) ἐπὶ A. a 22. β 5.
      μεγάλη) — A. 12. 46. Er.
      **ἀπὸ) ἐκ A. 12. 18. 36. 38. 46. Er.
      τοῦ ναοῦ) — 12. 18. 28. 36. 47. Er.
      τοῦ οὐρανοῦ) — A. 10. 14. 92.   Vulg. Copt. Syr. Erp. Slav. MS.
18. **φωναὶ καὶ βρονταὶ καὶ ἀστραπαὶ) ἀστρ. κ. φω. κ. βρ. A. 2. 6. 7. 11.
          13. 26. 36. 40. 92.   ἀστ. κ. βρ. κ. φω. a 16. β 5. Compl.
      ἐγένετο) — a 18. β 3.   Ar. P. Slav. MS.
      **οἱ ἄνθρωποι ἐγένοντο) ἄνθρωπος ἐγένετο A. 38. Copt. Arm. + καὶ Er.

19 τῆς γῆς, τηλικοῦτος σεισμὸς οὕτω μέγας. καὶ
ἐγένετο ἡ πόλις ἡ μεγάλη εἰς τρία μέρη, καὶ αἱ
πόλεις τῶν ἐθνῶν ᵃἔπεσαν·| καὶ Βαβυλὼν ἡ
μεγάλη ἐμνήσθη ἐνώπιον τοῦ Θεοῦ, δοῦναι
αὐτῇ τὸ ποτήριον τοῦ οἴνου τοῦ θυμοῦ τῆς
20 ὀργῆς αὐτοῦ· καὶ πᾶσα νῆσος ἔφυγε, καὶ ὄρη
21 οὐχ εὑρέθησαν· καὶ χάλαζα μεγάλη ὡς ταλαν-
τιαία καταβαίνει ἐκ τοῦ οὐρανοῦ ἐπὶ τοὺς
ἀνθρώπους· καὶ ἐβλασφήμησαν οἱ ἄνθρωποι τὸν
Θεὸν, ἐκ τῆς πληγῆς τῆς χαλάζης· ὅτι μεγάλη
ἐστὶν ἡ πληγὴ αὐτῆς σφόδρα.

XVII. Καὶ ἦλθεν εἷς ἐκ τῶν ἑπτὰ ἀγγέλων
τῶν ἐχόντων τὰς ἑπτὰ φιάλας, καὶ ἐλάλησε μετ᾽
ἐμοῦ, λέγων ᵇ|· Δεῦρο, δείξω σοι τὸ κρίμα τῆς
πόρνης τῆς μεγάλης, τῆς καθημένης ἐπὶ [τῶν]
2 ὑδάτων [τῶν] πολλῶν· μεθ᾽ ἧς ἐπόρνευσαν οἱ
βασιλεῖς τῆς γῆς, καὶ ἐμεθύσθησαν ᶜοἱ κατοι-
κοῦντες τὴν γῆν ἐκ τοῦ οἴνου τῆς πορνείας αὐτῆς.|
3 Καὶ ἀπήνεγκέ με εἰς ἔρημον ἐν πνεύματι· καὶ
εἶδον γυναῖκα καθημένην ἐπὶ θηρίον κόκκινον,
γέμον ᵈτὰ ὀνόματα| βλασφημίας, ἔχον κεφαλὰς

ᵃ [ἔπεσον.]   ᵇ +[μοι.]   ᶜ [ἐκ τοῦ οἴνου τῆς πορνείας

19. *ἔπεσον) -σαν Α. 16. 27. 28. 42. 49.
21. αὐτῆς) αὕτη α6. β2. γ2.

1. ἦλθεν) ἐξῆλθεν Α.
    *μοι) — Α. α 26. β 6. Compl.   Vulg. Copt. Syr. Arm. Arr.
    Slav. MSS.
    τῶν ὑδάτων τῶν πολ.) ὑδ. πολ. Α. 12. 28. 34. 35. 36. Er.

mighty an earthquake, *and* so great.   And the great 19
city was *divided* into three parts, and the cities
of the nations fell: and great Babylon came in
remembrance before God, to give unto her the cup
of the wine of the fierceness of his wrath.   And 20
every island fled away, and the mountains were not
found.   And there fell upon men a great hail out of 21
heaven, *every stone* about the weight of a talent: and
men blasphemed God because of the plague of the
hail; for the plague thereof was exceeding great.

XVII. And there came one of the seven angels
which had the seven cups, and talked with me, saying, Come hither; I will shew unto thee the judgment of the great harlot that sitteth upon many
waters: with whom the kings of the earth have 2
committed fornication, and the inhabitants of the
earth have been made drunk with the wine of her
fornication.   So he carried me away in the spirit 3
into the wilderness: and I saw a woman sitting
upon a scarlet coloured beast, full of names of
blasphemy, having seven heads and ten horns.

αὐτῆς οἱ κατοικοῦντες τὴν γῆν.]   *d* [ὀνομάτων.]

2. *ἐκ τοῦ οἴνου τῆς πορνείας αὐτῆς οἱ κατ. τὴν γῆν) οἱ κ. τ. γ. ἐκ τ. οἴ.
    τ. πορ. αὐ. A. a 17. β 7. Compl.

3. εἶδον) ἶδα A.
    *ὀνομάτων) τὰ ὀνόματα. A. 7. 8. 9. 13.   ὀνόματα a 15. β 5.
    ἔχον) ἔχων A.
    κεφ. ἑπτὰ καὶ) — Er.

4 ἑπτὰ καὶ κέρατα δέκα. καὶ ἡ γυνὴ ᵃ ἦν¹ περιβεβλημένη ᵇπορφυροῦν καὶ κόκκινον,¹ καὶ
κεχρυσωμένη ᶜχρυσίῳ¹ καὶ λίθῳ τιμίῳ καὶ
μαργαρίταις, ἔχουσα ᵈποτήριον χρυσοῦν¹ ἐν τῇ
χειρὶ αὐτῆς, γέμον βδελυγμάτων, καὶ ᵉτὰ ἀκά-
5 θαρτα τῆς¹ πορνείας αὐτῆς, καὶ ἐπὶ τὸ μέτωπον
αὐτῆς ὄνομα γεγραμμένον, μυστήριον· Βαβυλὼν ἡ μεγάλη, ἡ μήτηρ τῶν πορνῶν καὶ τῶν
6 βδελυγμάτων τῆς γῆς. Καὶ εἶδον τὴν γυναῖκα
μεθύουσαν ἐκ τοῦ αἵματος τῶν ἁγίων καὶ ἐκ τοῦ
αἵματος τῶν μαρτύρων Ἰησοῦ· καὶ ἐθαύμασα,
ἰδὼν αὐτὴν, θαῦμα μέγα.

7 Καὶ εἶπέ μοι ὁ ἄγγελος· Διατί ἐθαύμασας;
ἐγὼ ᶠἐρῶ σοι¹ τὸ μυστήριον τῆς γυναικὸς, καὶ
τοῦ θηρίου τοῦ βαστάζοντος αὐτὴν, τοῦ ἔχοντος
τὰς ἑπτὰ κεφαλὰς καὶ τὰ δέκα κέρατα.

8 ᵍΤὸ¹ θηρίον ὃ εἶδες, ἦν, καὶ οὐκ ἔστι, καὶ
μέλλει ἀναβαίνειν ἐκ τῆς ἀβύσσου, καὶ εἰς
ἀπώλειαν ὑπάγειν· καὶ θαυμάσονται οἱ κατοικοῦντες ἐπὶ τῆς γῆς, ὧν οὐ γέγραπται ʰτὸ ὄνομα¹

ᵃ [ἡ.]   ᵇ [πορφύρᾳ καὶ κοκκίνῳ.]   ᶜ [χρυσῷ.]   ᵈ [χρυσοῦν ποτήριον.]

4. *ἡ 2nd) ἦν A. B. a20. β3. Compl.   Vulg. Æth. Syr. Arm. Arr. Slav.
   *πορφύρᾳ καὶ κοκκίνῳ) πορφυροῦν καὶ κόκκινον A. B. a20. β6.
   πορφύραν καὶ κόκκινον a7. β3. γ2. Compl.
   καὶ κεχρ.) — καὶ a13. β4. Compl.
   *χρυσῷ) -σίῳ A. a16. β5.
   *χρυσοῦν ποτήριον) ποτ. χρυ. A. a17. β5.
   *ἀκαθάρτητος) τὰ ἀκάθαρτα τῆς A. B. a26. β8. γ3.   Compl.
   πορνείας) πορείας B.
   αὐτῆς) τῆς γῆς B. a16. β5.   Copt. Syr. Ar. P. Slav. MS.
6. εἶδον) ἴδα A.
   ἐκ) — a11. β4.

And the woman was clothed in purple and 4
scarlet, and decked with gold and precious
stones and pearls, having a golden cup in her
hand full of abominations and the filthiness of
her fornication, and upon her forehead a name 5
written, a Mystery, Babylon the Great, the
Mother of the Harlots and the Abominations
of the Earth.   And I saw the woman drunken 6
with the blood of the saints, and with the blood
of the martyrs of Jesus; and when I saw her,
I wondered with great wonder.

And the angel said unto me, Wherefore didst 7
thou wonder?   I will tell thee the mystery of the
woman, and of the beast that carrieth her, which
hath the seven heads and ten horns.

The beast that thou sawest, was, and is not, and 8
is to ascend out of the bottomless pit, and to go
into perdition : and they that dwell on the earth
shall wonder, whose names were not written in the

---

^e [ἀκαθάρτητος.]   ^f [σοι ἐρῶ.]   ^g Rec.—   ^h [τὰ ὀνόματα.]

6. καὶ ἐκ) — καὶ a 15. β 3.
   μαρτύρων) μαρτυρίων A.
7. *σοι ἐρῶ) ἐρῶ σοι A. a 15. β 4.
   αὐτὴν) + καὶ Er.
8. *θηρίον) τὸ θη. A. a 24. β 7. Compl.
   ἦν) ἦ A.
   ὑπάγειν) -γει A. 12. Er.
   θαυμάσονται) -σθήσονται A.
   ἐπὶ τῆς γῆς) τὴν γὴν a 15. β 6.
   οὐ γέγραπται) οὐκ ἐγέγραπται A.
   *τὰ ὀνόματα) τὸ ὄνομα A. a 15. β 5.   Copt. Syr. Erp. Slav. MS.

ἐπὶ τὸ βιβλίον τῆς ζωῆς ἀπὸ καταβολῆς κόσμου,
*βλεπόντων¹ τὸ θηρίον, ὅτι ἦν, καὶ οὐκ ἔστι,
ᵇκαὶ πάρεσται¹.

9 ˮΩδε ὁ νοῦς ὁ ἔχων σοφίαν. αἱ ἑπτὰ κεφαλαὶ
ᶜἑπτὰ ὄρη εἰσιν¹, ὅπου ἡ γυνὴ κάθηται ἐπ'
10 αὐτῶν· καὶ βασιλεῖς ἑπτά εἰσιν· οἱ πέντε
ἔπεσαν, ᵈ¹ ὁ εἷς ἐστιν, ὁ ἄλλος οὔπω ἦλθε, καὶ
11 ὅταν ἔλθῃ, ὀλίγον αὐτὸν δεῖ μεῖναι. καὶ τὸ
θηρίον ὃ ἦν, καὶ οὐκ ἔστι, καὶ αὐτὸς ὄγδοός
ἐστι, καὶ ἐκ τῶν ἑπτά ἐστι, καὶ εἰς ἀπώλειαν
ὑπάγει.

12 Καὶ τὰ δέκα κέρατα ἃ εἶδες, δέκα βασιλεῖς
εἰσιν, οἵτινες βασιλείαν ᵉοὔπω¹ ἔλαβον, ἀλλ'
ἐξουσίαν ὡς βασιλεῖς μίαν ὥραν λαμβάνουσι
μετὰ τοῦ θηρίου.

13 Οὗτοι μίαν ᶠγνώμην ἔχουσι¹, καὶ τὴν δύναμιν
καὶ [τὴν] ἐξουσίαν ᵍαὐτῶν¹ τῷ θηρίῳ ʰδιδόασιν¹.

14 οὗτοι μετὰ τοῦ ἀρνίου πολεμήσουσι, καὶ τὸ
ἀρνίον νικήσει αὐτούς, ὅτι Κύριος κυρίων ἐστὶ
καὶ Βασιλεὺς βασιλέων· καὶ οἱ μετ' αὐτοῦ,
κλητοὶ καὶ ἐκλεκτοὶ καὶ πιστοί.

ᵃ [βλέποντες.]   ᵇ [καίπερ ἐστίν.]   ᶜ [ὄρη εἰσὶν ἑπτά.]   ᵈ +[καὶ.]

8. τὸ βιβλίον) τοῦ βιβλίον a 16. β 6.
   *βλέποντες) βλεπόντων A. B. a 21. β 7. γ 3.
   τὸ θηρίον ὅτι ἦν) ὅτι ἦν τὸ θηρίον B. a 18. β 6.
   *καίπερ ἐστίν) καὶ πάρεσται A. B. a 24. β 6. γ 2. Compl.
   κ. πάρεστιν 11. 12. 16. 36. 43. 47.
9. *ὄρη εἰσὶν ἑπτά) ἑπτὰ ὄρη εἰσὶν A. a 16. β 5. Compl.
10. ἑπτὰ εἰσιν) εἰσιν ἑπτὰ a 10. β 4.
    ἔπεσαν) -σον a 9. β 2. Compl.

book of life from the foundation of the world, when they behold the beast, because it was, and is not, and shall be present.

Here *is* the mind which hath wisdom. The 9 seven heads are seven mountains, on which the woman sitteth; and there are seven kings: five 10 are fallen, one is, *and* the other is not yet come; and when he shall have come he must continue a short space. And the beast that was, and is not, 11 even he is the eighth, and is of the seven, and goeth into perdition.

And the ten horns which thou sawest are ten 12 kings, which have *ⁱ* not yet received a kingdom; but they receive power as kings one hour with the beast.

These have one mind, and give their power and 13 authority unto the beast. These shall make war 14 with the Lamb, and the Lamb shall overcome them: for he is Lord of lords, and King of kings: and they that are with him *are* called, and chosen, and faithful.

ᵉ ∾ οὐκ.　　ᶠ ∾ ἔχουσι γνώμην.　　ᵍ [ἑαυτῶν.]　　ʰ [διαδιδώσουσιν.]　　ⁱ ∾ not.

---

10. *καὶ ὁ εἷς) — καὶ A. a 26. β 6. Compl.　Vulg. ed. Syr.
　　αὐτὸν δεῖ) δεῖ αὐτ. a 10. β 3.
11. αὐτὸς) οὗτος a 13. β 4.
12. οὔπω) οὐκ A. Er.　Vulg. MS. Erp. Slav.
　　ἀλλ') ἀλλὰ A.
13. γνώμην ἔχουσι) ἔχ. γνώ. a 16. β 6.
　　τὴν ἐξου.) — τὴν A. a 14. β 5.
　　*ἑαυτῶν) αὐτῶν A. a 18. β 5. Compl.
　　*διαδιδώσουσιν) διδόασιν A. a 24. β 6. γ 2. Compl.

15 Καὶ λέγει μοι· Τὰ ὕδατα ἃ εἶδες, οὗ ἡ πόρνη
κάθηται, λαοὶ καὶ ὄχλοι εἰσὶ, καὶ ἔθνη καὶ γλῶσ-
16 σαι· καὶ τὰ δέκα κέρατα ἃ εἶδες, ᵃκαὶ¹ τὸ
θηρίον, οὗτοι μισήσουσι τὴν πόρνην, καὶ ἠρημω-
μένην ποιήσουσιν αὐτὴν καὶ γυμνὴν, καὶ τὰς
σάρκας αὐτῆς φάγονται, καὶ αὐτὴν κατακαύ-
17 σουσιν ἐν πυρί. ὁ γὰρ Θεὸς ἔδωκεν εἰς τὰς
καρδίας αὐτῶν ποιῆσαι τὴν γνώμην αὐτοῦ, καὶ
ποιῆσαι ᵇγνώμην μίαν,¹ καὶ δοῦναι τὴν βασιλείαν αὐτῶν τῷ θηρίῳ, ἄχρι ᶜτελεσθήσονται¹
ᵈοἱ λόγοι¹ τοῦ Θεοῦ.
18 Καὶ ἡ γυνὴ ἣν εἶδες, ἔστιν ἡ πόλις ἡ μεγάλη,
ἡ ἔχουσα βασιλείαν ἐπὶ τῶν βασιλέων τῆς
γῆς.

XVIII. [Καὶ] μετὰ ταῦτα εἶδον ᵉἄλλον¹
ἄγγελον καταβαίνοντα ἐκ τοῦ οὐρανοῦ, ἔχοντα
ἐξουσίαν μεγάλην· καὶ ἡ γῆ ἐφωτίσθη ἐκ τῆς
2 δόξης αὐτοῦ. καὶ ἔκραξεν ᶠἐν ἰσχυρᾷ φωνῇ,¹
λέγων· Ἔπεσεν ⸢ἔπεσε⸣ Βαβυλὼν ἡ μεγάλη,

ᵃ [ἐπὶ.]   ᵇ [μίαν γνώμην.]   ᶜ [τελεσθῇ.]

---

16. *ἐπὶ) καὶ A. B. a 27. β 6. Compl.   Vulg. MS. Am. Copt. Æth.
Syr. Ar. P. Slav. MSS.
γυμνὴν) + ποιήσουσιν αὐτὴν B. a 16. β 4. Compl.
κατακαύσουσιν) καύσουσιν 12. 38. Er.
17. καὶ ποι. μίαν γνώ.) — A.   Vulg.
*μίαν γνώμην) γνώ. μίαν a 15. β 4. Compl.
αὐτῶν) αὐτῷ A.
*τελεσθῇ) -θήσονται A. a 8. γ 2. Compl.   -θῶσιν B. a 18.
β 7. γ 2.
*τὰ ῥήματα) οἱ λόγοι A. B. a 26. β 7. Compl.

And he saith unto me, The waters which thou 15
sawest, where the harlot sitteth, are peoples, and
multitudes, and nations, and tongues. And the ten 16
horns which thou sawest and the beast, these shall
hate the harlot, and shall make her desolate and
naked, and shall eat her flesh, and burn her with
fire. For God hath put into their hearts to fulfil his 17
mind, and to make one mind, and to give their
kingdom unto the beast, until the words of God
shall be fulfilled.

And the woman whom thou sawest is that great 18
city, which holdeth the rule over the kings of the
earth.

XVIII. [And] after these things I saw another angel coming down from heaven, having
great authority ; and the earth was lightened
with his glory. And he cried with a strong 2
voice, saying, Fallen, ⌈fallen,⌉ is Babylon the great,

---

^d [τὰ ῥήματα.] ^e Rec.— ^f [ἐν ἰσχύϊ φωνῇ μεγάλῃ.]

---

18. τῆς γῆς) ἐπὶ τ. γ. a 11. β 4.

1. καὶ 1st) — A. a 17. β 6. Copt. Syr. Slav. MS.
*εἶδον) + ἄλλον A. B. a 17. β 5. γ 2. Compl. Er. Vulg. Copt.
Æth. Syr. Arm. Ar. P. Slav. After ἄγγελον a 8.
2. ἔκραξεν) ἐκέκραξεν A.
*ἐν ἰσχύϊ φωνῇ μεγάλῃ) ἐν ἰσχυρᾷ φωνῇ A. a 13. (& 13.) γ 2.
Compl. Vulg. MS. Am. Copt. Æth. Syr. Arm. Arr. ἰσχ.
φω. B. a 9. β 3.
ἔπεσε) — B. a 18. β 6. Copt. Æth. Arr. Slav. MSS.

καὶ ἐγένετο κατοικητήριον δαιμόνων, καὶ φυ-
λακὴ παντὸς πνεύματος ἀκαθάρτου, καὶ φυ-
λακὴ παντὸς ὀρνέου ἀκαθάρτου καὶ μεμισημένου·
3 ὅτι ἐκ [τοῦ οἴνου] τοῦ θυμοῦ τῆς πορνείας αὐ-
τῆς ᵃπεπώκασι| πάντα τὰ ἔθνη, καὶ οἱ βασιλεῖς
τῆς γῆς μετ᾽ αὐτῆς ἐπόρνευσαν, καὶ οἱ ἔμποροι
τῆς γῆς ἐκ τῆς δυνάμεως τοῦ στρήνους αὐτῆς
ἐπλούτησαν.

4 Καὶ ἤκουσα ἄλλην φωνὴν ἐκ τοῦ οὐρανοῦ,
λέγουσαν· ᵇἘξελθὲ| ἐξ αὐτῆς ὁ λαός μου, ἵνα
μὴ συγκοινωνήσητε ταῖς ἁμαρτίαις αὐτῆς, καὶ
5 ᶜἐκ τῶν πληγῶν αὐτῆς ἵνα μὴ λάβητε·| ὅτι
ᵈἐκολλήθησαν| αὐτῆς αἱ ἁμαρτίαι ἄχρι τοῦ
οὐρανοῦ, καὶ ἐμνημόνευσεν ὁ Θεὸς τὰ ἀδικήματα
6 αὐτῆς. ἀπόδοτε αὐτῇ ὡς καὶ αὐτὴ ἀπέδωκε ᵉ|,
καὶ διπλώσατε ᶠ| ᵍ[τὰ]| διπλᾶ κατὰ τὰ ἔργα
αὐτῆς· ἐν τῷ ποτηρίῳ ᾧ ἐκέρασε, κεράσατε αὐτῇ
7 διπλοῦν. ὅσα ἐδόξασεν ʰαὐτὴν| καὶ ἐστρηνίασε,

ᵃ [πέπωκε.]   ᵇ [ἐξέλθετε.]   ᶜ [ἵνα μὴ λάβητε ἐκ τῶν πληγῶν αὐτῆς.]

---

2. δαιμόνων) -μονίων Α.
ἀκαθάρτου 1st) + καὶ μεμισημένου Α. 16.
ὀρνέου) θηρίου Α.
3. τοῦ οἴνου) — Α. C.   Vulg. MS. *Am. Tol.* Æth.   After θυμοῦ
   36. 37. 47. 49. Compl.   Arm. Slav. MS.
τοῦ θυ. τῆς πορ.) τ. πορ. τ. θυ. C.
*πέπωκε) πεπώκασι α 15. β 2.   πεπτώκασι α 6. β 4.   πέπτωκαν
   Α. C. Copt. Æth.   πεπότικε 18. 36. 37. Compl.
τῆς γης last) αὐτῆς Er.
στρήνους) -νου C. 47. Compl. Er.
ἄλλην φωνήν) ἄλλης φωνῆς C.
4. *ἐξέλθετε) ἔξελθε C. α 16. β 4.   ἐξέλθατε Α.
ἐξ αὐτῆς) —12. Er.   After ὁ λαός μου C. 38.
καὶ ἐκ) — καὶ 12. Er.

and is become the habitation of demons, and the hold of every unclean spirit, and a cage of every unclean and hateful bird. For all the nations 3 have drunk of [the wine of] the wrath of her fornication, and the kings of the earth have committed fornication with her, and the merchants of the earth have waxed rich through the power of her delicacies.

And I heard another voice from heaven, saying, 4 Come out of her, my people, that ye may have no fellowship with her sins, and that ye receive not of her plagues. For her sins have reached unto 5 heaven, and God hath remembered her iniquities. Reward her even as she rewarded, and double 6 twofold according to her works : in the cup which she hath filled fill to her double. How 7 much she hath glorified herself, and lived deli-

---

^d [ἠκολούθησαν.]   ^e + [ὑμῖν.]   ^f + [αὐτῇ.]   ^g Rec.—   ^h [ἑαυτὴν.]

4. *ἵνα μὴ λάβητε ἐκ τῶν πληγῶν αὐτῆς) ἐκ. τ. πλ. a. ἵνα μὴ λάβ. A. C. a 20. β 6. Compl.

5. *ἠκολούθησαν) ἐκολλήθησαν A. C. a 27. β 5. Compl. (Vulg.) Copt. Æth. Syr. (Arm.) Arr. Slav.
   ὁ θεὸς τὰ ἀδική. αὐτῆς. ἀπόδοτε) αὐτ. ὁ θ. Τὰ ἀδικ. αὐτ. ἀπόδ. a 10. β 3. Compl.

6. *ὑμῖν) — A. C. a 20. β 5.   Vulg. MS. Am. Tol. Copt. Æth. Syr. Arr. Slav. MSS.
   *αὐτῇ 2nd) — A. C. 2. 8. 9. 14. 19. 92.   Vulg. Slav. MSS.
   * + τὰ C. a 10. β 3.
   διπλᾶ) + ὡς καὶ αὐτὴ καὶ a 13. β 4.   Slav. MSS.
   ποτηρίῳ) + αὐτῆς a 17. β 3.   Slav. MS.

7. *ἑαυτὴν) αὐτὴν A. C. a 10. β 2.

τοσοῦτον δότε αὐτῇ βασανισμὸν καὶ πένθος· ὅτι ἐν τῇ καρδίᾳ αὐτῆς λέγει· ^aὍτι[|] κάθημαι βασίλισσα καὶ χήρα οὐκ εἰμὶ, καὶ πένθος οὐ μὴ 8 ἴδω. Διὰ τοῦτο ἐν μιᾷ ἡμέρᾳ ἥξουσιν αἱ πληγαὶ αὐτῆς, θάνατος καὶ πένθος καὶ λιμός· καὶ ἐν πυρὶ κατακαυθήσεται· ὅτι ἰσχυρὸς [Κύριος] ὁ Θεὸς ὁ ^bκρίνας[|] αὐτήν.

9 Καὶ ^cκλαύσουσι[|] ^{d|} καὶ κόψονται ^eἐπ᾽ αὐτὴν[|] οἱ βασιλεῖς τῆς γῆς, οἱ μετ᾽ αὐτῆς πορνεύσαντες καὶ στρηνιάσαντες, ὅταν βλέπωσι τὸν καπνὸν 10 τῆς πυρώσεως αὐτῆς, ἀπὸ μακρόθεν ἑστηκότες διὰ τὸν φόβον τοῦ βασανισμοῦ αὐτῆς, λέγοντες· Οὐαὶ, οὐαὶ ἡ πόλις ἡ μεγάλη Βαβυλὼν, ἡ πόλις ἡ ἰσχυρὰ, ὅτι ^{f|} μιᾷ ὥρᾳ ἦλθεν ἡ κρίσις σου. 11 Καὶ οἱ ἔμποροι τῆς γῆς κλαίουσι καὶ πενθοῦσιν ^gἐπ᾽ αὐτὴν,[|] ὅτι τὸν γόμον αὐτῶν οὐδεὶς 12 ἀγοράζει οὐκέτι· γόμον χρυσοῦ, καὶ ἀργύρου, καὶ λίθου τιμίου, καὶ μαργαρίτου, καὶ ^hβυσσίνου,[|] καὶ ⁱπορφύρας,[|] καὶ σηρικοῦ, καὶ κοκ-

---

^a Rec.—   ^b [κρίνων.]   ^c [κλαύσονται.]   ^d + [αὐτήν.]

7. τοσοῦτον δότε) κεράστε Er.
    καὶ πένθος) — 10. 12. 37. 49. 91. Compl.
    *λέγει) + ὅτι A. C. a 24. β 5. Compl.
    κάθημαι) καθὼς a 10.
    βασιλίσσα) -λεύουσα C.
8. καὶ πεν.) — καὶ B. a 16. β 3.
    κύριος) — A.   Vulg. Æth.
    *κρίνων) κρίνας A. C. a 19. β 5. Compl.   Vulg. MS. Copt. Syr. Arm. Arr. Slav. MSS.
9. *κλαύσονται) -σοῦσι B. C. a 25. β 4. Compl.
    *αὐτὴν)—A.B.C. a 21. β 5. Compl.   Vulg. Copt. Syr. Arm. Arr. Slav.
    *ἐπ᾽ αὐτῇ) ἐπ᾽ αὐτὴν C. a 24. β 3. Compl.
10. τὸν) — Er.

cately, so much torment and sorrow give her : because she saith in her heart, I sit a queen, and am not a widow, and shall see no mourning. Therefore 8 shall her plagues come in one day, death, and mourning, and famine ; and she shall be utterly burned with fire : for strong *is* ⸢the Lord⸣ God who hath judged her.

And the kings of the earth, who with her have 9 committed fornication and lived delicately, shall mourn, and lament over her, when they shall see the smoke of her burning, standing afar off because 10 of the fear of her torment, saying, Alas, alas that great city Babylon, that mighty city! for in one hour is thy judgment come.

And the merchants of the earth weep and 11 mourn over her ; for no man buyeth their merchan- dise any more : the merchandise of gold, and of 12 silver, and of precious stones, and of pearls, and of fine linen, and of purple, and of silk, and of scarlet,

---

ᵉ [ἐπ' αὐτῇ.]   ᶠ + [ἐν.]   ᵍ [ἐπ' αὐτῇ.]   ʰ [βύσσου.]   ⁱ ⌐ πορφύρου.

*ἐν) — A. B. C. a 26. β 6. Compl.   Vulg. Slav. MSS.
μιᾷ ὥρᾳ ἦλθεν) μίαν ὥραν A.
11. κλαίουσι καὶ πενθοῦσιν) κλαύσουσι καὶ πενθήσουσιν a 21. β 5.
     Vulg. Arr.
   *ἐπ' αὐτῇ) ἐν αὐτῇ A.   ἐπ' αὐτὴν C. 16**. 18. 32. 39.   ἐπ'
     αὐτοὺς B.   ἐν ἑαυτοῖς Er.
12. γόμον) γόμος Er.   γόμον χρυσοῦν καὶ ἀργυροῦν καὶ λίθους τιμίους
     καὶ μαργαρίτας C.
   καὶ μαρ.) οὔτε μαρ. Er.
   μαργαρίτου) -ταις A.
   *βύσσου) βυσσίνου A. C. a 22. β 5.
   πορφύρας) -ροῦ a 21. β 4. Compl. Er.   —A.
   καὶ σηρικοῦ) — Er.

κίνου· καὶ πᾶν ξύλον θύϊνον, καὶ πᾶν σκεῦος
ἐλεφάντινον, καὶ πᾶν σκεῦος ἐκ ξύλου τιμιω-
τάτου, καὶ χαλκοῦ, καὶ σιδήρου, καὶ μαρμάρου,
13 καὶ κινάμωμον, "καὶ ἄμωμον,¹ καὶ θυμιάματα, καὶ
μύρον, καὶ λίβανον, καὶ οἶνον, καὶ ἔλαιον, καὶ σε-
μίδαλιν, καὶ σῖτον, καὶ κτήνη, καὶ πρόβατα, καὶ
ἵππων, καὶ ῥεδῶν, καὶ σωμάτων, καὶ ψυχὰς ἀν-
14 θρώπων. καὶ ἡ ὀπώρα ᵇ σου τῆς ἐπιθυμίας τῆς
ψυχῆς¹ ἀπῆλθεν ἀπὸ σοῦ, καὶ πάντα τὰ λιπαρὰ
καὶ τὰ λαμπρὰ ᶜἀπώλετο¹ ἀπὸ σοῦ, καὶ οὐκέτι οὐ
15 μὴ ᵈαὐτὰ εὑρήσουσιν.¹ Οἱ ἔμποροι τούτων οἱ
πλουτήσαντες ἀπ᾽ αὐτῆς ἀπὸ μακρόθεν στήσον-
ται διὰ τὸν φόβον τοῦ βασανισμοῦ αὐτῆς, κλαί-
16 οντες καὶ πενθοῦντες, ᵉ¹ λέγοντες· Οὐαὶ, οὐαὶ ἡ
πόλις ἡ μεγάλη, ἡ περιβεβλημένη βύσσινον καὶ
πορφυροῦν καὶ κόκκινον, καὶ ⌐κεχρυσωμένη [ἐν]
ᶠχρυσίῳ¹ καὶ λίθῳ τιμίῳ καὶ μαργαρίταις· ὅτι
μιᾷ ὥρᾳ ἠρημώθη ὁ τοσοῦτος πλοῦτος.

ᵃ Rec.—   ᵇ [τῆς ἐπιθυμίας τῆς ψυχῆς σου.]   ᶜ [ἀπῆλθεν.]

ξύλον) σκεῦος A.
ἐκ) — C. 18.
ξύλου) λίθου A.
καὶ μαρμάρου) — Er.
13. *κινάμωμον) -μώμου a 15. β 2.   + κ. ἄμωμον A. C. 6. 11. 12. 17. 19.
34. 35. 36.   Vulg. MS. Am. Tol. Syr. Æth. Slav. MSS.
καὶ μύρον) — C.
παὶ οἶνον) — a 12. β 4.
κτήνη καὶ πρόβ.) πρ. κ. κτ. a 12. β 3.
ῥεδῶν) ῥαίδων, or ῥαιδῶν a 21. β 4.   Compl.
ἡ ὀπ. — ἡ C.
14. *τῆς ἐπιθ. τ. ψυ. σου) σου τ. ἐπιθ. τ. ψυ. A. C. 35.
τά λαμ.) — τὰ C.

and all thyine wood, and all vessels of ivory, and all
vessels of most precious wood, and of brass, and of 13
iron, and of marble, and cinnamon, and spice, and
odours, and ointments, and frankincense, and wine,
and oil, and fine flour, and wheat, and cattle, and
sheep, and of horses, and of chariots, and of bodies,
and souls of men. And the fruits that thy soul 14
lusted after are departed from thee, and all things
which were dainty and goodly have perished from
thee, and they shall find them no more at 15
all. The merchants of these things, which
were made rich by her, shall stand afar off for
the fear of her torment, weeping and wailing,
saying, Alas, alas that great city, that was 16
clothed in fine linen, and purple, and scarlet,
and decked with gold, and precious stones, and
pearls! for in one hour so great riches is come 17
to nought.

---

d [εὑρήσῃς αὐτά.]   e +[καὶ.]   f [χρυσῷ.]

14. *ἀπῆλθεν) ἀπώλετο A. C. a 19. β 6.   Copt. Arr. Slav. MS.   ἀπώ-
λοντο a 8. Compl.   Vulg. Syr. Slav. MS.
*οὐ μὴ εὑρ. αὐτ.) αὐτ. οὐ μὴ εὑρ. C. a 7. β 3.   οὐ μὴ αὐτ. εὑρ. A. 38.
*εὑρήσῃς) εὕρῃς a 15. β 7.   εὑρήσεις 37. 49. Compl. Er.   εὑρή-
σουσιν A. C. 34. 35. 36. 90.   Vulg. Syr.
15. αὐτῆς) +καὶ a 10. β 5.
16. *καὶ λέγ.) — καὶ A. C. a 11. β 5.   Copt. Syr. Arr. Slav. MS.
οὐαὶ) — a 15. β 4.
ἡ 3rd) — A.
βύσσινον) βύσσον a 12. β 4.   κοκ. κ. πορ. κ. βύσ. A.
*ἐν χρυσῷ) χρυσίῳ A. a 19. β 4.   ἐν χρυσίῳ C. 6. 8. 16.
μαργαρίταις) -τῃ A. C.

17 Καὶ πᾶς κυβερνήτης, καὶ πᾶς ^aὁ ἐπὶ τόπον
πλέων,[|] καὶ ναῦται, καὶ ὅσοι τὴν θάλασσαν
18 ἐργάζονται, ἀπὸ μακρόθεν ἔστησαν, καὶ ^bἔκραξαν[|]
^cβλέποντες[|] τὸν καπνὸν τῆς πυρώσεως αὐτῆς,
19 λέγοντες· Τίς ὁμοία τῇ πόλει τῇ μεγάλῃ; καὶ
ἔβαλον χοῦν ἐπὶ τὰς κεφαλὰς αὐτῶν, καὶ ^dἔκ-
ραξαν[|] κλαίοντες καὶ πενθοῦντες, λέγοντες·
Οὐαὶ, οὐαὶ ἡ πόλις ἡ μεγάλη, ἐν ᾗ ἐπλούτησαν
πάντες οἱ ἔχοντες ^eτὰ[|] πλοῖα ἐν τῇ θαλάσσῃ ἐκ
τῆς τιμιότητος αὐτῆς, ὅτι μιᾷ ὥρᾳ ἠρημώθη.
20 Εὐφραίνου ^fἐπ᾽ αὐτῇ[|], οὐρανὲ, καὶ οἱ ἅγιοι
^gκαὶ οἱ[|] ἀπόστολοι καὶ οἱ προφῆται, ὅτι ἔκρινεν
ὁ Θεὸς τὸ κρίμα ὑμῶν ἐξ αὐτῆς.
21 Καὶ ἦρεν εἷς ἄγγελος ἰσχυρὸς λίθον ὡς
^hμύλινον[|] μέγαν, καὶ ἔβαλεν εἰς τὴν θάλασσαν,
λέγων· Οὕτως ὁρμήματι βληθήσεται Βαβυλὼν
22 ἡ μεγάλη πόλις, καὶ οὐ μὴ εὑρεθῇ ἔτι. καὶ
φωνὴ κιθαρῳδῶν καὶ μουσικῶν καὶ αὐλητῶν καὶ
σαλπιστῶν οὐ μὴ ἀκουσθῇ ἐν σοὶ ἔτι, καὶ πᾶς
τεχνίτης πάσης τέχνης οὐ μὴ εὑρεθῇ ἐν σοὶ ἔτι,
καὶ φωνὴ μύλου οὐ μὴ ἀκουσθῇ ἐν σοὶ ἔτι,

---

^a [ἐπὶ τῶν πλοίων ὁ ὅμιλος.]   ^b [ἔκραζον.]   ^c [ὁρῶντες.]   ^d [ἔκραζον.]

17. *ἐπὶ τῶν πλοίων ὁ ὅμιλος) ὁ ἐπὶ τόπον πλέων A. (τὸν τ. B.) C. a 18.
β 5.   Vulg. MS. Am. Anglosax. Syr. Arm. Slav. MSS.
ἐπὶ τῶν πλοίων πλέων a 8. β 2. γ 2. Compl.   Slav. ed.
καὶ ὅσοι) — Er.   ἐργάζονται) -ζοντες Er.
18. *ἔκραζον) ἔκραξαν A. C. 35.
*ὁρῶντες) βλέποντες A. C. a 26. β 7. γ 2.   Compl.
καπνὸν) τόπον A. 10.   Vulg.
τίς) — C.
πόλει) + ταύτῃ C.   Vulg. Arm.
19. ἔβαλον) ἐπέβαλον A. Syr.   ἔβαλαν C.

And every shipmaster, and every passenger
and sailors, and as many as trade by sea,
stood afar off, and cried when they saw the 18
smoke of her burning, saying, What *city is* like 19
unto this great city! And they cast dust on their
heads, and cried, weeping and mourning, saying,
Alas, alas that great city, wherein were made rich
all that had ships in the sea by reason of her costli
ness! for in one hour is she made desolate.

Rejoice over her, *thou* heaven, and *ye* saints and 20
apostles and prophets; for God hath avenged you
of her.

And a mighty angel took up a stone like a great 21
millstone, and cast *it* into the sea, saying, Thus with
violence shall that great city Babylon be cast down,
and shall be found no more at all. And the voice 22
of the harpers, and musicians, and of pipers, and
trumpeters, shall be heard no more at all in thee;
and no craftsman, of whatsoever craft *he be*, shall be
found any more in thee; and the sound of a
millstone shall be heard no more at all in thee;

ᵉ Rec. —   ᶠ [ἐπ' αὐτήν.]   ᵍ Rec. —   ʰ [μύλον.]

---

19. *ἔκραζον) ἔκραξαν A. C. 35.
    κλαίοντες καὶ πενθοῦντες) — A.   + καὶ a 17. β 5. Compl.   Vulg.
        MS. *Am.* Æth. Syr. Slav. MS.
    *πλοῖα) τὰ πλ. A. C. a 17. β 5. Compl.
20. *ἐπ' αὐτὴν) ἐπ' αὐτῇ C. a 26. β 5. Compl.   ἐν αὐτῇ A.
    *ἅγιοι) + καὶ οἱ A. a 26. β 5. Compl.   Vulg. MS. *Am.* Copt. Syr.
21 ἰσχυρὸς) — A. Syr.
    *μύλον) μύλινον A.   Vulg. Copt. Syr. ed.   μύλικον C.
22. πασῆς τέχνης) — A.   Copt. Arr. Slav. MS
    ἀκουσθῇ) εὑρεθῇ B.

23 καὶ φῶς λύχνου οὐ μὴ φανῇ ἐν σοὶ ἔτι, καὶ φωνὴ
νυμφίου καὶ νύμφης οὐ μὴ ἀκουσθῇ ἐν σοὶ ἔτι·
ὅτι οἱ ἔμποροί σου ἦσαν οἱ μεγιστᾶνες τῆς γῆς,
ὅτι ἐν τῇ φαρμακείᾳ σου ἐπλανήθησαν πάντα
24 τὰ ἔθνη. καὶ ἐν αὐτῇ ᵃαἷμαˡ προφητῶν καὶ
ἁγίων εὑρέθη, καὶ πάντων τῶν ἐσφαγμένων ἐπὶ
τῆς γῆς.

XIX. ᵇˡ Μετὰ ταῦτα ἤκουσα ὡς φωνὴν ᶜμεγά-
λην ὄχλου πολλοῦˡ ἐν τῷ οὐρανῷ, ᵈλεγόντων·ˡ
Ἀλληλούϊα· ἡ σωτηρία καὶ ἡ δόξα ᵉˡ καὶ ἡ δύ-
2 ναμιςᶠτοῦ Θεοῦˡ ἡμῶν· ὅτι ἀληθιναὶ καὶ δίκαιαι
αἱ κρίσεις αὐτοῦ· ὅτι ἔκρινε τὴν πόρνην τὴν
μεγάλην, ἥτις ᵍᵎἔφθειρεˡ τὴν γῆν ἐν τῇ πορνείᾳ
αὐτῆς, καὶ ἐξεδίκησε τὸ αἷμα τῶν δούλων αὐτοῦ
3 ἐκ ʰˡ χειρὸς αὐτῆς. καὶ δεύτερον εἴρηκαν· Ἀλ-
ληλούϊα· καὶ ὁ καπνὸς αὐτῆς ἀναβαίνει εἰς
4 τοὺς αἰῶνας τῶν αἰώνων. καὶ ἔπεσον οἱ πρεσβύτεροι οἱ εἴκοσι ⁱˡ τέσσαρες, καὶ τὰ τέσσαρα
ζῶα, καὶ προσεκύνησαν τῷ Θεῷ τῷ καθημένῳ ἐπὶ

ᵃ ∽ αἵματα.   ᵇ +[καὶ.]   ᶜ [ὄχλου πολλοῦ μεγάλην.]   ᵈ [λέγοντος.]

23. καὶ φῶς . . . . ἐν σοὶ ἔτι) — A. 26. Er.   ἐν — C.
νύμφης) φωνὴ νύμφ. C.
οἱ ἐμπ.) — οἱ A.
24. αἷμα) αἵματα a 26. β 6. Compl.   Arr. Slav. MS.

1. *καὶ 1st) — A. C. a 21. β 5. γ 2.   Vulg. Copt. Syr. Slav. MS.
ὡς) — 12. 16. 18. a 47. 91. Er.   Syr. Arm. Slav. ed.
*ὄχλου πολλοῦ μεγάλην) μεγ. ὄχ. πολ. A. C. a 17. β 4.   —μεγ. 40.
Er.   Vulg. ed. (not Am.)
*λέγοντος) λεγόντων A. C. a 26. β 5. Compl.   Syr.   + τὸ Er.
*δόξα καὶ ἡ τιμὴ καὶ ἡ δύναμις) δύναμις καὶ ἡ δόξα a 20. β 5. γ 2.

and the light of a candle shall shine no more at all in 23
thee; and the voice of the bridegroom and of the bride
shall be heard no more at all in thee ; for thy merchants were the great men of the earth ; for by thy
sorceries were all the nations deceived.   And in her
was found the blood of prophets, and of saints, and 24
of all that were slain upon the earth.

XIX. After these things I heard as it were a
great voice of much people in heaven, saying, Alleluia ; the salvation, and glory, and power, of our
God : for true and righteous *are* his judgments ; for 2
he hath judged the great harlot, who did corrupt
the earth with her fornication, and hath avenged
the blood of his servants at her hand.   And the 3
second time they said, Alleluia !   And her smoke
goeth up for ever and ever.   And the twenty-four 4
elders and the four living creatures fell down and
worshipped God that sitteth on the throne, saying,

ᵉ +[καὶ ἡ·τιμὴ.]   ᶠ [κυρίῳ τῷ Θεῷ.]   ᵍ ∼ διέφθειρε.   ʰ +[τῆς.]   ⁱ +[καὶ.]

Compl.   Vulg. MS. Syr. Slav. MS.   Also—κ. ἡ τι. A. C.
    4. 8. 9. 17. 18. 25. 38.   Vulg. Slav. MSS.
1. *κυρίῳ τῷ Θεῷ) τοῦ‸Θεοῦ A. C. a 24. β 4. γ 2. Compl. Copt.
    Slav. MS.   τῷ Θεῷ 36. 47. Vulg. Æth. Syr. Arm. Arr.
    Slav. MS.
2. ἔφθειρε) διέφθ. a 26. β 5. Compl.   ἔκρινε A.
    *τῆς χειρ.) — τῆς A. C. a 14. β 4. Compl.
3. εἴρηκαν) εἴρηκεν a 17. β 4. Compl.   εἶπαν C. 38.
    αὐτῆς) — 47. Er.   Æth. Slav. MS.
4. οἱ 2nd) — A.
    *καὶ 2nd) — A. C. a 13. β 5. Compl.   οἱ εἴκ. τέσσ. πρεσ. A.

5 ᵃτῷ θρόνῳ| λέγοντες· Ἀμήν· ἀλληλούϊα. Καὶ
φωνὴ ᵇἀπὸ| τοῦ θρόνου ἐξῆλθε, λέγουσα· Αἰ-
νεῖτε ᶜτῷ Θεῷ| ἡμῶν πάντες οἱ δοῦλοι αὐτοῦ, καὶ
οἱ φοβούμενοι αὐτὸν ᵈ| οἱ μικροὶ καὶ οἱ μεγάλοι.

6 Καὶ ἤκουσα ὡς φωνὴν ὄχλου πολλοῦ, καὶ
ὡς φωνὴν ὑδάτων πολλῶν, καὶ ὡς φωνὴν βρον-
τῶν ἰσχυρῶν, λεγόντων· Ἀλληλούϊα, ὅτι ἐβασί-
λευσε Κύριος ὁ Θεὸς ᵉ[ἡμῶν]| ὁ παντοκράτωρ.

7 χαίρωμεν καὶ ᶠἀγαλλιώμεθα,| καὶ δῶμεν τὴν
δόξαν αὐτῷ· ὅτι ἦλθεν ὁ γάμος τοῦ ἀρνίου, καὶ
8 ἡ γυνὴ αὐτοῦ ἡτοίμασεν ἑαυτήν. καὶ ἐδόθη
αὐτῇ ἵνα περιβάληται βύσσινον ᵍλαμπρὸν [καὶ]
καθαρόν·| τὸ γὰρ βύσσινον τὰ δικαιώματὰ ʰτῶν
9 ἁγίων ἐστί.| καὶ λέγει μοι· Γράψον· Μακάριοι
οἱ εἰς τὸ δεῖπνον τοῦ γάμου τοῦ ἀρνίου κεκλη-
μένοι. Καὶ λέγει μοι· Οὗτοι οἱ λόγοι ἀληθινοὶ
10 ⁱτοῦ Θεοῦ εἰσί.| Καὶ ᵏἔπεσα| ἔμπροσθεν τῶν
ποδῶν αὐτοῦ προσκυνῆσαι αὐτῷ· καὶ λέγει
μοι· Ὅρα μή· σύνδουλός σου εἰμὶ καὶ τῶν

ᵃ [τοῦ θρόνου.]   ᵇ [ἐκ.]   ᶜ [τὸν Θεὸν.]   ᵈ +[καὶ.]   ᵉ Rec.—   ᶠ ∽ ἀγαλλιῶμεν.

4. *τοῦ θρόνου) τῷ θρόνῳ A. C. a 17. β 4.
5. *ἐκ) ἀπὸ A. C. a 16. β 4.
   λέγουσα) — 12. 47. Er.
   *τὸν Θεὸν) τῷ Θεῷ A. C. 9. 12. 14. 27. 36. 41. 42. 92.
   αὐτοῦ καὶ) — καὶ C.
   *αὐτὸν καὶ) — καὶ A. C. a 21. β 5. Compl.   Vulg. Copt. Æth. Syr.
      Arm. Slav. MSS.
6. ὡς 1st) — 6. 8. 12. 35. Er.
   ὡς 2nd) — A. 12.
   λεγόντων) λέγοντες B. a 14. β 3.   -τας a 7. Er.
   Κύριος) — 8. 12. 36. Er.

Amen ; Alleluia.   And a voice came out from the 5
throne, saying, Praise our God, all ye his servants,
and ye that fear him, small and great.

And I heard as it were the voice of a great 6
multitude, and as the voice of many waters, and
as the voice of mighty thunderings, saying, Alleluia : for the Lord [our] God the Almighty hath
reigned.   Let us be glad and rejoice, and give 7
honour to him : for the marriage of the Lamb is
come, and his wife hath made herself ready.   And 8
to her was granted that she should be arrayed
in fine linen, bright and clean : for the fine linen
is the righteousness of saints.   And he saith 9
unto me, Write, Blessed *are* those who have
been called unto the marriage supper of the Lamb.
And he saith unto me, These are the true sayings of God.   And I fell before his feet to 10
worship him.   And he said unto me, See *thou
do it* not : I am the fellowservant of thee, and

---

^g [καθαρὸν καὶ λαμπρόν.]   ^h [ἐστι τῶν ἁγίων.]   ⁱ [εἰσι τοῦ Θεοῦ.]   ^k [ἔπεσον.]

---

6. *Θεὸς) + ἡμῶν a 25. β 6. Compl.   Vulg. Syr. Arm. Ar. P. Slav. MS.
7. ἀγαλλιώμεθα) -ῶμεν A. 12. 18. 35. 36.
      δῶμεν) δώσομεν A. 36.
      αὐτοῦ) — 7. 12. 16. 39. Er.
8. *καθαρὸν καὶ λαμπρόν) λαμ. καθ. A. 7. 91. 92.   Vulg. MS. *Am. Æth.
         Syr. Erp. Slav. MSS.   λαμ. καὶ καθ. a 21. β 4. Compl. Vulg. ed.
      *ἐστι τῶν ἁγίων) τ. ἁγ. ἐστί. A. a 17. β 5. Compl.
9. γράψον) — Er.   Vulg. MS.
      τοῦ γάμου) — 16. 36. 39. Er.
      *εἰσι τοῦ Θεοῦ) τ. θε. εἰσι A. a 16. β 5.
10. *ἔπεσον) -σα A. a 8. β 2.   Er.

ἀδελφῶν σου τῶν ἐχόντων τὴν μαρτυρίαν ^a|
Ἰησοῦ· τῷ Θεῷ προσκύνησον· ἡ γὰρ μαρτυρία
^b| Ἰησοῦ ἐστι τὸ πνεῦμα τῆς προφητείας.

11 Καὶ εἶδον τὸν οὐρανὸν ^cἠνεῳγμένον,| καὶ
ἰδοὺ ἵππος λευκὸς, καὶ ὁ καθήμενος ἐπ' αὐτὸν,
καλούμενος πιστὸς καὶ ἀληθινὸς, καὶ ἐν δικαιο-
12 σύνῃ κρίνει καὶ πολεμεῖ. οἱ δὲ ὀφθαλμοὶ αὐτοῦ
ὡς φλὸξ πυρὸς, καὶ ἐπὶ τὴν κεφαλὴν αὐτοῦ
διαδήματα πολλά· ἔχων ὄνομα γεγραμμένον ὃ
13 οὐδεὶς οἶδεν εἰ μὴ αὐτός· καὶ περιβεβλημένος
ἱμάτιον βεβαμμένον αἵματι· καὶ ^dκέκληται| τὸ
14 ὄνομα αὐτοῦ· Ὁ Λόγος τοῦ Θεοῦ. Καὶ τὰ
στρατεύματα τὰ ἐν τῷ οὐρανῷ ἠκολούθει αὐτῷ ἐφ'
ἵπποις λευκοῖς, ἐνδεδυμένοι βύσσινον λευκὸν ^e|
15 καθαρόν. καὶ ἐκ τοῦ στόματος αὐτοῦ ἐκπορεύεται
ῥομφαία ὀξεῖα, ἵνα ἐν αὐτῇ ^fπατάξῃ| τὰ ἔθνη· καὶ
αὐτὸς ποιμανεῖ αὐτοὺς ἐν ῥάβδῳ σιδηρᾷ· καὶ
αὐτὸς πατεῖ τὴν ληνὸν τοῦ οἴνου τοῦ θυμοῦ
^g| τῆς ὀργῆς τοῦ Θεοῦ τοῦ παντοκράτορος.

---

^a + [τοῦ.]   ^b + [τοῦ.]   ^c [ἀνεῳγμένον.]

10. σου 2nd) + καὶ 12. Er.
  *τοῦ Ἰησοῦ 1st) — τοῦ A. a 18. β 5. Compl.
  *τοῦ Ἰησοῦ 2nd) — τοῦ A. 12. 14. 16. 36. 91. 92. Er.
11. *ἀνεῳγμένον) ἤνεῳγ. A. 42**.
  καλούμενος) — A. 4. 6. 12. 17*. 32. 48. Er. Vulg. MS. (Arm.)
  Slav. ed.
12. ὡς) — a 21. β 5. γ 2. Compl. Arm.
  ἔχων) + ὀνόματα γεγραμμένα καὶ B. a 17. β 2 Compl. Syr.
13. *καλεῖται) κέκληται A. B. a 16. β 3. Vulg. MS. Æth. Syr.
  Ar. P.
14. τὰ 2nd) — a 5. β 2. γ 2. Er.

thy brethren that have the testimony of Jesus :
worship God : for the testimony of Jesus is the
spirit of prophecy.

And I saw heaven opened, and behold a white 11
horse ; and he that sat upon him *was* called
Faithful and True, and in righteousness he doth
judge, and make war. His eyes *were* as a flame 12
of fire, and on his head *were* many diadems ; and
he had a name written, that no man knew, but
he himself. And he *was* clothed with a vesture 13
dipped in blood : and his name hath been called
The Word of God. And the armies which were 14
in heaven followed him upon white horses, clothed
in fine linen, white *and* clean. And out of his 15
mouth goeth a sharp sword, that with it he
should smite the nations : and he shall rule
them with a rod of iron : and he treadeth the
winepress of the fierceness of the wrath of God the

[καλεῖται.]   *e* + [καί.]   *f* [πατάσσῃ.]   *g* + [καί.]

14. ἠκολούθει) -θουν 38. (90.) Er.
   ἐφ' ἵπποις) ἐπὶ ἵπ. a 12. (& 13.) Compl.
   βύσσινον λευκὸν) λευ. βύσσ. A.
   *καὶ last) — A. a 22. β 5. γ 2. Compl. Vulg. MS. *Am.* Copt.
      Æth. Syr. Arr.
15. ῥομφαία) + δίστομος B. a 26. β 6. γ 3. Compl. Vulg. ed. (not
      Am.) Æth. Syr. Ar. P. Slav. MS.
   *πατάσσῃ) πατάξῃ A. a 25. β 6. Compl.
   *καὶ last) — A. a 25. β 5. Compl. Vulg. Copt. Æth. Syr. Arm.
      Erp. Slav. MSS.
   τοῦ last) 29. Er.

16 καὶ ἔχει ἐπὶ τὸ ἱμάτιον καὶ ἐπὶ τὸν μηρὸν αὐτοῦ
ᵃ| ὄνομα γεγραμμένον· Βασιλεὺς βασιλέων καὶ
Κύριος κυρίων.

17 Καὶ εἶδον ἕνα ἄγγελον ἑστῶτα ἐν τῷ ἡλίῳ·
καὶ ἔκραξε φωνῇ μεγάλῃ, λέγων πᾶσι τοῖς
ὀρνέοις τοῖς ᵇπετομένοις| ἐν μεσουρανήματι·
Δεῦτε ᶜσυνάχθητε| εἰς τὸ δεῖπνον ᵈτὸ μέγα τοῦ|
18 Θεοῦ· ἵνα φάγητε σάρκας βασιλέων, καὶ σάρκας
χιλιάρχων, καὶ σάρκας ἰσχυρῶν, καὶ σάρκας
ἵππων καὶ τῶν καθημένων ἐπ᾽ αὐτῶν, καὶ σάρ-
κας πάντων, ἐλευθέρων ᵉτε| καὶ δούλων, καὶ
μικρῶν καὶ μεγάλων.

19 Καὶ εἶδον τὸ θηρίον, καὶ τοὺς βασιλεῖς τῆς
γῆς, καὶ τὰ στρατεύματα αὐτῶν συνηγμένα
ποιῆσαι ᶠτὸν| πόλεμον μετὰ τοῦ καθημένου ἐπὶ
τοῦ ἵππου, καὶ μετὰ τοῦ στρατεύματος αὐτοῦ.

20 καὶ ἐπιάσθη τὸ θηρίον, καὶ μετ᾽ ᵍαὐτοῦ| ὁ ψευ-
δοπροφήτης ὁ ποιήσας τὰ σημεῖα ἐνώπιον
αὐτοῦ, ἐν οἷς ἐπλάνησε τοὺς λαβόντας τὸ χά-

ᵃ + [τὸ.]   ᵇ [πετωμένοις.]   ᶜ [καὶ συνάγεσθε.]

---

16. ἐπὶ τὸ ἱμάτιον καὶ) — Α. Æth.
*τὸ ὄν.) — τὸ Α. a 24. β 6. γ 2. Compl.
17. ἕνα) — Β. a 16. β 5. γ 2. Syr.
τῷ) — Er.
φωνῇ) ἐν φωνῇ a 10. β 3.
*πετωμένοις) πετομένοις Α. a 14. β 4. Compl.
μεσουρανήματι) -νίσματι Er.
*καὶ συνάγεσθε) συνάχθητε Α. a 28. β 7. γ 2. Compl.   Vulg. MS.
    Am. Copt. Æth. Syr. Erp. Slav. MS.
*τοῦ μεγάλου) τὸ μέγα τοῦ Α. a 25. β 5. Compl.   Vulg. Copt. Syr.
    Erp. Slav. MSS.

Almighty.   And he hath on *his* vesture and on 16
his thigh a name written, King of kings, and
Lord of lords.

And I saw an angel standing in the sun; and he 17
cried with a loud voice, saying to all the fowls that
fly in the midst of heaven, Come *and* be gathered
together unto the great supper of God; that ye 18
may eat the flesh of kings, and the flesh of captains, and the flesh of mighty men, and the flesh of
horses, and of those that sit on them, and the flesh
of all *men*, both free and bond, both small and
great.

And I saw the beast, and the kings of the 19
earth, and their armies, gathered together to
make war against him that sat on the horse,
and against his army.   And the beast was taken, 20
and with him the false prophet that wrought
miracles before him, with which he deceived
those that had received the mark of the beast,

---

^d [τοῦ μεγάλου.]   ^e Rec.—   ^f Rec.—   ^g [τούτου.]

---

18. σάρκας 2nd) — Er.
   αὐτῶν) αὐτοὺς A. 14. 92.
   *ἐλευθέρων) + τε A. a 18. β 7. Compl.
   καὶ μικρῶν) — καὶ 9. 14. 30. 36. 47. 92. Compl.   Slav. MSS.
      + τε a 21. β 6. Compl.   Slav. MSS.
19. αὐτῶν) αὐτοῦ A. 6. 11.
   *ποιῆσαι) + τὸν A. a 12. β 4.
20. *μετὰ τούτου ὁ) οἱ μετ᾽ αὐτοῦ ὁ A. 41.   μετ᾽ αὐτοῦ ὁ. 14. 37. 38.
      49**. Compl.   Vulg. Slav.   ὁ μετ᾽ αὐτοῦ a 18. β 5.

ραγμα τοῦ θηρίου, καὶ τοὺς προσκυνοῦντας τῇ
εἰκόνι αὐτοῦ· ζῶντες ἐβλήθησαν οἱ δύο εἰς τὴν
λίμνην τοῦ πυρὸς τὴν καιομένην ἐν ^a| θείῳ.
21 καὶ οἱ λοιποὶ ἀπεκτάνθησαν ἐν τῇ ῥομφαίᾳ τοῦ
καθημένου ἐπὶ τοῦ ἵππου, τῇ ^bἐξελθούσῃ| ἐκ
τοῦ στόματος αὐτοῦ· καὶ πάντα τὰ ὄρνεα ἐχορ-
τάσθησαν ἐκ τῶν σαρκῶν αὐτῶν.

XX. Καὶ εἶδον ἄγγελον καταβαίνοντα ἐκ τοῦ
οὐρανοῦ, ἔχοντα τὴν ^cκλεῖν| τῆς ἀβύσσου, καὶ
2 ἄλυσιν μεγάλην ἐπὶ τὴν χεῖρα αὐτοῦ. καὶ
ἐκράτησε τὸν δράκοντα, τὸν ὄφιν τὸν ἀρχαῖον,
ὅς ἐστι διάβολος καὶ ^dὁ| Σατανᾶς, καὶ ἔδησεν
3 αὐτὸν χίλια ἔτη, καὶ ἔβαλεν αὐτὸν εἰς τὴν
ἄβυσσον, καὶ ἔκλεισε ^e| καὶ ἐσφράγισεν ἐπάνω
αὐτοῦ, ἵνα μὴ ^fπλανᾷ| ^gἔτι τὰ ἔθνη,| ἄχρι τε-
λεσθῇ τὰ χίλια ἔτη· ^h| μετὰ ταῦτα δεῖ ⁱλυθῆναι
αὐτὸν| μικρὸν χρόνον.

4 Καὶ εἶδον θρόνους, καὶ ἐκάθισαν ἐπ᾽ αὐτούς,

---

^a + [τῷ.]   ^b [ἐκπορευομένῃ.]   ^c [κλεῖδα.]   ^d Rec. —

20. ἐβλήθησαν) βληθήσονται 36. 38. Er.
    τὴν καιομένην) τῆς καιομένης A.
    *τῷ θείῳ) — τῷ A. a 18. β 5.   Compl.

21. τοῦ 1st) — Er.
    *ἐκπορευομένῃ) ἐξελθούσῃ A. B. a 28. β 6. γ 2.   Compl.
    τὰ ὄρνεα) — τὰ 12. Er.

1. *κλεῖδα) κλεῖν A. a 25. β 2.   Compl.

2. τὸν ὄφιν τὸν ἀρχαῖον) ὁ ὄφις ὁ ἀρχαῖος A

and those that worship his image. These both were cast alive into the lake of fire burning with brimstone. And the remnant were 21 slain with the sword of him that sat upon the horse, which *sword* proceeded out of his mouth : and all the fowls were filled with their flesh.

XX. And I saw an angel coming down from heaven, having the key of the bottomless pit and a great chain in his hand. And he laid hold on 2 the dragon, that old serpent, which is the Devil, and Satan, and bound him a thousand years, and 3 cast him into the bottomless pit, and shut *him* up, and set a seal upon him, that he should deceive the nations no more, till the thousand years should be fulfilled : after that he must be loosed a little season.

And I saw thrones, and they sat upon them, 4

---

^e +[αὐτὸν.]   ^f [πλανήσῃ.]   ^g [τὰ ἔθνη ἔτι.]   ^h + [καὶ.]   ⁱ [αὐτὸν λυθῆναι.]

---

2. *σατανᾶς) ὁ σατ. A. a 14. Compl.   + ὁ πλανῶν τὴν οἰκουμένην ὅλην
    B. a 26. Compl.   Syr. Ar. P. Slav. MSS.
3. ἔκλεισε) ἔδησεν 3. 12. Er.
    *αὐτὸν) — A. a 27. β 5. γ 2. Compl.   Vulg. Æth. Syr. Arm. Ar. P.
        Slav. MSS.
    ἐπάνω αὐτοῦ) ἐμμενῶς αὐτόν A.
    *πλανήσῃ) πλανᾷ a 28. β 5.   Compl.
    *τὰ ἔθνη ἔτι) ἔτι τὰ ἔθνη A. a 24. β 5. Compl.
    τὰ χιλ.) — τὰ 12. Er.
    *καὶ last) — A. a 11. β 3.   Vulg. MS. Am. Tol. Syr.
    *αὐτὸν λυθῆναι) λυθ. αὐτ. A. a 10. β 2.

καὶ κρίμα ἐδόθη αὐτοῖς· καὶ τὰς ψυχὰς τῶν
πεπελεκισμένων διὰ τὴν μαρτυρίαν Ἰησοῦ, καὶ
διὰ τὸν λόγον τοῦ Θεοῦ, καὶ οἵτινες οὐ προσ-
εκύνησαν ᵃτὸ θηρίον,| ᵇ οὐδὲ| ᶜτὴν εἰκόνα| αὐτοῦ,
καὶ οὐκ ἔλαβον τὸ χάραγμα ἐπὶ τὸ μέτωπον ᵈ|
καὶ ἐπὶ τὴν χεῖρα αὐτῶν· καὶ ἔζησαν, καὶ ἐβασί-
5 λευσαν μετὰ τοῦ Χριστοῦ ᵉ| χίλια ἔτη· ᶠ⌈καὶ⌉
οἱ| λοιποὶ τῶν νεκρῶν οὐκ ᵍἔζησαν| ʰἄχρι|
τελεσθῇ τὰ χίλια ἔτη. αὕτη ἡ ἀνάστασις ἡ
6 πρώτη. μακάριος καὶ ἅγιος ὁ ἔχων μέρος ἐν τῇ
ἀναστάσει τῇ πρώτῃ· ἐπὶ τούτων ὁ ⁱδεύτερος
θάνατος| οὐκ ἔχει ἐξουσίαν, ἀλλ᾽ ἔσονται ἱερεῖς
τοῦ Θεοῦ καὶ τοῦ Χριστοῦ, καὶ βασιλεύσουσι
μετ᾽ αὐτοῦ χίλια ἔτη.
7 Καὶ ὅταν τελεσθῇ τὰ χίλια ἔτη, λυθήσεται ὁ
8 Σατανᾶς ἐκ τῆς φυλακῆς αὐτοῦ, καὶ ἐξελεύσεται
πλανῆσαι τὰ ἔθνη τὰ ἐν ταῖς τέσσαρσι γωνίαις
τῆς γῆς, τὸν Γὼγ καὶ τὸν Μαγὼγ, συναγαγεῖν
αὐτοὺς εἰς ᵏτὸν| πόλεμον, ὧν ὁ ἀριθμὸς ˡαὐ-

ᵃ [τῷ θηρίῳ.]   ᵇ [οὔτε.]   ᶜ [τῇ εἰκόνι.]   ᵈ + [αὐτῶν.]   ᵉ + [τὰ.]   ᶠ [οἱ δὲ.]

4. πεπελεκισμένων) πεπολεμημένων A.
 *τῷ θηρίῳ) τὸ θηρίον A. a 18. β 3.
 *οὔτε) οὐδε A. a 16. β 3.
 *τῇ εἰκόνι) τὴν εἰκόνα A. a 18. β 2. Er.
 *αὐτῶν 1st) — A. a 23. β 4.   Vulg. ed. Syr. Slav. MS.
 τοῦ Χριστ.) — τοῦ 32. Er.
 *τὰ χιλ.) ⌐τὰ A. 12. 32. 34. 49. 91. Compl. Er.
5. οἱ δὲ . . . . ἔτη) — a 14. β 4. Syr.
 *οἱ δὲ) οἱ A.   καὶ οἱ B. a 11. (& 10. 13.) Compl.
 νεκρῶν) ἀνθρώπων B 32. 34.
 *ἀνέζησαν) ἔζησαν A.B. a 13. (& 12. 13.) Compl. Vulg.Copt.Slav.MS.

and judgment was given unto them : and *I saw* the souls of those that were beheaded because of the testimony of Jesus, and because of the word of God, and such as had not worshipped the beast, neither his image, neither had received the mark upon *their* foreheads, and on their hands ; and they lived and reigned with Christ a thousand years. ⌈And⌉ 5 the rest of the dead lived not until the thousand years were finished. This *is* the first resurrection. Blessed and holy *is* he that hath part in 6 the first resurrection : on such the second death hath no power, but they shall be priests of God and of Christ, and shall reign with him a thousand years.

And when the thousand years are expired, 7 Satan shall be loosed out of his prison, and shall 8 go out to deceive the nations which are in the four quarters of the earth, Gog and Magog, to gather them together to battle : the number of

---

^g [ἀνέζησαν.]   ^h [ἕως.]   ⁱ [θάνατος ὁ δεύτερος.]   ^k Rec.—   ^l Rec.—

5. *ἕως) ἄχρι A. B. *a* 10. (& 12. 13.) Compl.
    ἔτη) + ἄχρι Er.
6. *ὁ θάνατος ὁ δεύτερος) ὁ δεύτερος θάν. A. *a* 22. β 5.   Compl.
    βασιλεύσουσι) -εύουσι A.
    μετ᾽ αὐτοῦ) μετὰ ταῦτα *a* 14.
7. ὅταν τελεσθῇ) μετὰ B. *a* 16. β 5.   Arm. Slav. MS.   ὅτε ἐτελέσ-
    θησαν Er.
8. ταῖς) — 12. 37. Er.
    τὸν Μα.) — τὸν A. Er.
    *πόλεμον) τὸν πολ. A. *a* 20. β 3.   Compl.
    *ἀριθμὸς) + αὐτῶν A. B. *a* 19. β 4.

9 τῶν | ὡς ἡ ἄμμος τῆς θαλάσσης. καὶ ἀνέβησαν
ἐπὶ τὸ πλάτος τῆς γῆς, καὶ ᵃἐκύκλευσαν | τὴν
παρεμβολὴν τῶν ἀγίων, καὶ τὴν πόλιν τὴν
ἠγαπημένην· καὶ κατέβη πῦρ ᵇἐκ τοῦ οὐρανοῦ
10 ἀπὸ τοῦ Θεοῦ, | καὶ κατέφαγεν αὐτούς· καὶ ὁ
διάβολος ὁ πλανῶν αὐτοὺς ἐβλήθη εἰς τὴν
λίμνην τοῦ πυρὸς καὶ θείου, ὅπου ᶜκαὶ| τὸ
θηρίον καὶ ὁ ψευδοπροφήτης· καὶ βασανισθή-
σονται ἡμέρας καὶ νυκτὸς εἰς τοὺς αἰῶνας τῶν
αἰώνων.

11 Καὶ εἶδον θρόνον ᵈμέγαν λευκὸν, | καὶ τὸν
καθήμενον ἐπ᾽ αὐτοῦ, οὗ ἀπὸ προσώπου ἔφυγεν
ἡ γῆ καὶ ὁ οὐρανὸς, καὶ τόπος οὐχ εὑρέθη αὐ-
12 τοῖς. καὶ εἶδον τοὺς νεκροὺς, ᵉτοὺς μεγάλους
καὶ τοὺς μικροὺς | ἐστῶτας ἐνώπιον τοῦ ᶠθρόνου, |
καὶ βιβλία ᵍἠνοίχθησαν· | καὶ ʰἄλλο βιβλίον |
ⁱἠνοίχθη | ὅ ἐστι τῆς ζωῆς· καὶ ἐκρίθησαν οἱ νεκροὶ
ἐκ τῶν γεγραμμένων ἐν τοῖς βιβλίοις, κατὰ
13 τὰ ἔργα αὐτῶν. καὶ ἔδωκεν ἡ θάλασσα τοὺς

ᵃ [ἐκύκλωσαν.]   ᵇ [ἀπὸ τοῦ Θεοῦ ἐκ τοῦ οὐρανοῦ.]   ᶜ Rec.—   ᵈ [λευκὸν μέγαν.]

9. *ἐκύκλωσαν) ἐκύκλευσαν Α. a 14. β 2.   Compl.
   *ἀπὸ τοῦ Θεοῦ ἐκ τοῦ οὐρανοῦ) ἐκ τ. οὐρ. ἀπὸ τ. Θεοῦ a 18. β 4.
      Compl.   Vulg. MS. Copt. Arm. Erp.
   ἀπὸ τ. Θε.) — Α. 12. 18.   Vulg. MS. Ar. P. Slav. MS.
10. ὁ διαβ.) — ὁ Er.
   *ὅπου) + καὶ Α. a 26 β 3. Compl.   Vulg. ed. Syr.
11. *λευκὸν μέγαν) μέγ. λευκ. Α. a 17. β 3. Compl.   Vulg. Copt. Æth.
      Syr. Arr. Slav.
   αὐτοῦ) αὐτὸν a 26. β 3.   Compl.
   ἀπὸ) + τοῦ Α.

whom *is* as the sand of the sea. And they went 9
up on the breadth of the earth, and compassed the
encampment of the saints about, and the beloved
city : and fire came down out of heaven, ¦from
God¦ and devoured them. And the devil that 10
deceived them was cast into the lake of fire and
brimstone, were both the beast and the false
prophet *are*, and they shall be tormented day
and night for ever and ever.

And I saw a great white throne, and him that 11
sat on it, from whose face the earth and the heaven
fled away ; and there was found no place for them.
And I saw the dead, great and small, standing 12
before the throne ; and the books were opened :
and another book was opened, which is *the book* of
life : and the dead were judged out of those things
which were written in the books, according to their
works.   And the sea gave up the dead which were 13

ᵉ [μικροὺς καὶ μεγάλους.]   ᶠ [Θεοῦ.]   ᵍ [ἠνεῴχθησαν.]   ʰ [βιβλίον ἄλλο.]   ⁱ [ἠνεῴχθη.]

11· ἡ γη καὶ ὁ οὐρ.) ὁ οὐρ. κ. ἡ. γ. 10. 37. 49. 91. Compl.   *Tol.* Æth.
        Ar. P. Slav. MS.
12. *μικροὺς καὶ μεγάλους) — a 7. (& 29.) τοὺς μεγ. κ. τ. μικ. A.
        a 10. β 2. γ 2. Compl.   Vulg. Æth. Syr. Arm. Ar. P. Slav.
        MSS.
    *Θεοῦ) θρόνου A. B. a 28. β 4. Compl.   Vulg. Copt. Æth. Syr.
        Arm. Arr. Slav. MSS.
    *ἠνεῴχθησαν) ἠνοίχθησαν A. a 5. (& 11. 14.) Er.   ἀνεωχ. Compl.
        ἤνοιξαν a 8.
    *βιβλίον ἄλλο) ἄλλο βιβλίον A. a 19. β 3.   Compl.
    *ἠνεῴχθη) ἠνοίχθη A. 3. 7. 11. 29. 35. 40. Er   ἀνεώχ. Compl.

^aνεκροὺς τοὺς ἐν αὐτῇ,¹ καὶ ὁ θάνατος καὶ ὁ ᾄδης
ἔδωκαν τοὺς ^bνεκροὺς τοὺς ἐν αὐτοῖς·¹ καὶ ἐκρίθη-
14 σαν ἕκαστος κατὰ τὰ ἔργα αὐτῶν. καὶ ὁ θάνατος
καὶ ὁ ᾄδης ἐβλήθησαν εἰς τὴν λίμνην τοῦ πυρός·
οὗτος ^cὁ θάνατος ὁ δεύτερός ἐστιν¹ ^dἡ λίμνη
15 τοῦ πυρός.¹ καὶ εἴ τις οὐχ εὑρέθη ἐν τῇ βίβλῳ
τῆς ζωῆς γεγραμμένος, ἐβλήθη εἰς τὴν λίμνην
τοῦ πυρός.

XXI. Καὶ εἶδον οὐρανὸν καινὸν καὶ γῆν και-
νήν· ὁ γὰρ πρῶτος οὐρανὸς καὶ ἡ πρώτη γῆ
2 ^eἀπῆλθον,¹ καὶ ἡ θάλασσα οὐκ ἔστιν ἔτι. καὶ ^f¹
τὴν πόλιν τὴν ἁγίαν Ἰερουσαλὴμ καινὴν ^gεἶδον¹
καταβαίνουσαν ^hἐκ τοῦ οὐρανοῦ, ἀπὸ τοῦ Θεοῦ¹,
ἡτοιμασμένην ὡς νύμφην κεκοσμημένην τῷ ἀνδρὶ
3 αὐτῆς. καὶ ἤκουσα φωνῆς μεγάλης ἐκ τοῦ
ⁱοὐρανοῦ,¹ λεγούσης· Ἰδοὺ ἡ σκηνὴ τοῦ Θεοῦ
μετὰ τῶν ἀνθρώπων, καὶ σκηνώσει μετ᾿. αὐτῶν·
καὶ αὐτοὶ ^kλαὸς¹ αὐτοῦ ἔσονται, καὶ αὐτὸς ὁ

^a [ἐν αὐτῇ νεκρούς.] ^b [ἐν αὐτοῖς νεκρούς.] ^c [ἔστιν ὁ δεύτερος θάνατος.]
^h [ἀπὸ τοῦ Θεοῦ ἐκ τοῦ οὐρανοῦ.] ⁱ ∾ θρόνου.

13. *ἐν αὐτῇ νεκρούς) νεκ. τοὺς ἐν αὐτῇ Α. a 20. β 4. τοὺς ἐν αὐτοῖς
νεκ. Er. (38.)
ἔδωκαν) ἔδωκεν Α. 2. 48.
*ἐν αὐτοῖς νεκρούς) νεκ. τοὺς ἐν αὐτοῖς. Α. a 17. β 3. ἑαυτῶν νεκ-
ρούς Compl.
αὐτῶν) αὐτοῦ a 10. β 2.
14. *ἔστιν ὁ δεύτερος θάνατος) ὁ θάν. ὁ δεύτ. ἐστ. Α. a 16. β 3. γ2.
ἐστιν ὁ θάν. ὁ δεύτ. 9. 10. 37. 49. Compl.
* + ἡ λίμνη τοῦ πυρός Α. a 24. β 3. γ 2. Compl. Vulg. MS. (Am.)
Tol. Æth. Syr. Ar. P. Slav. MSS.
15. τῇ βίβλῳ) τῷ βιβλίῳ a 17. β 3.

in it; and death and hades gave up the dead
which were in them: and they were judged every
man according to their works. And death and hades 14
were cast into the lake of fire. This is the second
death, the lake of fire. And whosoever was not 15
found written in the book of life was cast into the
lake of fire.

XXI. And I saw a new heaven and a new
earth : for the first heaven and the first earth
were passed away ; and there was no more sea. 2
And I saw the holy city, New Jerusalem, coming down out of heaven from God, prepared as 3
a bride adorned for her husband. And I heard
a great voice out of *heaven saying, Behold,
the tabernacle of God *is* with men, and he will
dwell with them, and they shall be his people,

---

e Rec.—   *d* [παρῆλθε.]   *f* + [ἐγὼ Ἰωάννης εἶδον.]   *g* Rec.—
        k [λαοί.]   *l* ∖ the throne.

---

1. *παρῆλθε) ἀπῆλθαν A.   -θον a 18. β 2.   -θε 2. 4. 11. 35. 47.
    Vulg. Copt. Æth. Syr.
2. *ἐγὼ Ἰωάννης) — A. B. a 26. β 3. γ 3. Compl.   Vulg. MS. *Am.*
    Tol. Copt. Æth. Syr. Arm. Arr. Slav. MS.
    *εἶδον τὴν πόλιν τὴν ἁγίαν Ἰερουσαλὴμ καινὴν) τ. π. τ. ἁ. Ἰ. κ. εἶδ.
    A. B. a 27. β 3. γ 4. Compl.
    *ἀπὸ τοῦ Θεοῦ ἐκ τοῦ οὐρ.) ἐκ τ. οὐρ. ἀ. τ. Θε. A. B. a 17. β 3.
    Vulg. Copt. Æth. Syr. Arr. Slav. MSS.
3. οὐρανοῦ) θρόνου A. 18.   Vulg. Arm. ed. in m.
    *λαοί) λαὸς a 24. β 3. γ 2. Compl.   Vulg. Copt. Æth. Syr. Arr.

4 Θεὸς ^aμετ' αὐτῶν ἔσται,[|] ^b[αὐτῶν Θεὸς][|], καὶ
ἐξαλείψει [ὁ Θεὸς] πᾶν δάκρυον ἀπὸ τῶν ὀφ-
θαλμῶν αὐτῶν, καὶ ὁ θάνατος οὐκ ἔσται ἔτι·
οὔτε πένθος, οὔτε κραυγὴ, οὔτε πόνος οὐκ ἔσται
ἔτι· ὅτι τὰ πρῶτα ἀπῆλθον.
5 Καὶ εἶπεν ὁ καθήμενος ἐπὶ ^cτῷ θρόνῳ·[|]
Ἰδοὺ, καινὰ ^dποιῶ πάντα.[|] Καὶ λέγει ^e|·
Γράψον· ὅτι οὗτοι οἱ λόγοι ^fπιστοὶ καὶ
6 ἀληθινοί[|] εἰσι. Καὶ εἶπέ μοι· ^gΓέγοναν.[|]
Ἐγώ εἰμι τὸ ^hἌλφα[|] καὶ τὸ Ὦ, ἡ ἀρχὴ καὶ
τὸ τέλος. ἐγὼ τῷ διψῶντι δώσω ⁱ[αὐτῷ[|]] ἐκ
7 τῆς πηγῆς τοῦ ὕδατος τῆς ζωῆς δωρεάν. ὁ
νικῶν κληρονομήσει ^kταῦτα,[|] καὶ ἔσομαι αὐτῷ
8 Θεὸς, καὶ αὐτὸς ἔσται μοι [ὁ] υἱός. ^lτοῖς δὲ
δειλοῖς[|] καὶ ἀπίστοις ^m| καὶ ἐβδελυγμένοις καὶ

---

^a [ἔσται μετ' αὐτῶν.]   ^b [Θεὸς αὐτῶν.]   ^c [τοῦ θρόνου.]   ^d [πάντα ποιῶ.]
    ⁱ Rec.—   ^k [πάντα.]   ^l [δειλοῖς δὲ.]

3. *ἔσται μετ' αὐτῶν) μ. α. ἔστ. A. B. a 13. β 3.
    *Θεὸς αὐτῶν) — a 22. β 2. Compl. Copt. Erp. Slav. MS.   αὐτῶν
        Θεὸς A.
4. ὁ Θεὸς) — B. a 24. β 3. γ 2. Compl. Copt. Æth. Syr. Arm. Arr.
        Slav. MSS.   + ἀπ' αὐτῶν B. a 11. β 2.
    ἀπὸ) ἐκ A.
    ἔτι 1st) — Er.
    ὅτι) — A.   Slav. MSS.
    ἀπῆλθον) -θεν a 11. β 3.   -θαν A.
5. *τοῦ θρόνου) τῷ θρόνῳ A. a 18. β 2. γ 3.   + καὶ A.
    *καινὰ πάντα ποιῶ) πάντα καίνα ποιῶ a 15. β 2.   και. π. πάν. A. 35.
        37. 38. 49. 91.   Compl.
    *μοι) — A. B. a 9. β 3.   Vulg. MS. Am. Tol. Syr. Ar. P.
    *ἀληθινοὶ καὶ πιστοὶ) π. κ. ἀλ. A. B. a 16. β 3.   Vulg. Æth. Syr.
        Ar. P. Slav. MSS.   + τοῦ Θεοῦ B. a 17. β 3.   Syr. Ar. P.
6. *γέγονε. ἐγώ εἰμι τὸ) γέγοναν· (γεγόνασι· 38.) ἐγώ εἰμι τὸ A. 38.

and God himself shall be with them, ⸢*and be* their⸣ 4
God.⸣   And ⸢God⸣ shall wipe away all tears from
their eyes; and there shall be no more death, neither
sorrow, nor crying, neither shall there be any more
pain : for the former things are passed away.

And he that sitteth upon the throne said, 5
Behold, I make all things new.   And he said,
Write : for these words are faithful and true.
And he said unto me, They are done.   I am 6
Alpha and Omega, the beginning and the end.
I will give unto him that is athirst of the foun-
tain of the water of life freely.   He that over- 7
cometh shall inherit these things; and I will
be his God, and he shall be my son.   But the 8
cowardly, and unbelieving, ″and the abominable,

---

^e + [μοι.]   ^f [ἀληθινοὶ καὶ πιστοί.]   ^g [Γέγονε.]   ^h [A.]
      ^m ∾ + καὶ ἁμαρτωλοῖς.   ⁿ ∾ + and sinners.

γέγονα ἐγὼ τὸ *a* 7. (& 13.) γ 2.   Syr.   γέγονα τὸ *a* 17. Compl.
[Versions read very variously.]
6. *A) ἄλφα A. 8. 13. 34. 35.
ἡ, τὸ) — 32. 37. 46. 48. 49.   Compl.
*δώσω) + αὐτῷ B. *a* 14.
τῆς πηγῆς) — A.   Slav. MS.
τοῦ ὑδ.) — τοῦ Er.
7. κληρονομήσει) δώσω αὐτῷ B. *a* 19. β 3. γ 2.   Slav. MSS.
*πάντα) ταῦτα A. B. *a* 27. β 2. γ 3. Compl.   Vulg. Copt. Æth.
Syr. Arr. Slav. MSS.
αὐτῷ) αὐτῶν A.
αὐτὸς) — A.
ὁ υἱ.) — ὁ A. *a* 13. β 3. Compl.
8. *δειλοῖς δὲ) τοῖς δὲ δειλοῖς A. B. *a* 25. β 3. γ 3.   Compl.
ἀπίστοις) καὶ ἁμαρτωλοῖς B. *a* 28. β 3. γ 2. Compl.   Syr. Ar. P.
Slav. MS.

φονεῦσι καὶ πόρνοις καὶ ªφαρμακοῖς¹ καὶ εἰδω-
λολάτραις, καὶ πᾶσι τοῖς ψευδέσι, τὸ μέρος
αὐτῶν ἐν τῇ λίμνῃ τῇ καιομένῃ πυρὶ καὶ θείῳ,
ὅ ἐστιν ᵇὁ θάνατος ὁ δεύτερος.¹

9 Καὶ ἦλθεν ᶜ¹ εἷς ᵈἐκ¹ τῶν ἑπτὰ ἀγγέλων τῶν
ἐχόντων τὰς ἑπτὰ φιάλας τὰς γεμούσας τῶν ἑπτὰ
πληγῶν τῶν ἐσχάτων, καὶ ἐλάλησε μετ᾽ ἐμοῦ, λέ-
γων· Δεῦρο, δείξω σοι τὴν νύμφην ᵉτὴν γυναῖκα
10 τοῦ ἀρνίου.¹ Καὶ ἀπήνεγκέ με ἐν πνεύματι ᶠἐπὶ¹
ὄρος μέγα καὶ ὑψηλὸν, καὶ ἔδειξέ μοι τὴν πόλιν
ᵍ¹ τὴν ἁγίαν Ἱερουσαλὴμ, καταβαίνουσαν ἐκ
11 τοῦ οὐρανοῦ ἀπὸ τοῦ Θεοῦ, ἔχουσαν τὴν δόξαν
τοῦ Θεοῦ· ʰ¹ ὁ φωστὴρ αὐτῆς ὅμοιος λίθῳ
τιμιωτάτῳ, ὡς λίθῳ ἰάσπιδι κρυσταλλίζοντι·
12 ⁱἔχουσα¹ τεῖχος μέγα καὶ ὑψηλὸν, ᵏἔχουσα¹
πυλῶνας δώδεκα, καὶ ἐπὶ τοῖς πυλῶσιν ἀγγέλους δώδεκα, καὶ ὀνόματα ἐπιγεγραμμένα, ἃ
ἐστι ˡτὰ ὀνόματα¹ τῶν δώδεκα φυλῶν ᵐ¹ υἱῶν

ª [φαρμακεῦσι.]   ᵇ [δεύτερος θάνατος.]   ᶜ +[πρός με.]
ᵍ +[τὴν μεγάλην.]   ʰ +[καὶ.]   ⁱ [ἔχουσάν τε.]

8. *φαρμακεῦσι) -κοῖς A. a 28. β 3. γ 2. Compl. Er.
ψευδέσι) ψεύσταις A.
*δεύτερος θάνατος) ὁ θάν. ὁ δεύτ. A. a 16. β 3. γ 2. Compl.
9. *πρός με) — A. B. a 24. β 2. γ 4. Compl.   Vulg. Copt. Æth. Syr.
Slav. MS.
*εἷς) + ἐκ A. a 19. β 3. γ 3. Compl.   Vulg. Æth. Syr. Erp. Slav.
τὰς 2nd) — a 11. β 2. Compl.   τὰς γεμούσας) τῶν γεμόντων A. 12.
τῶν ἐπ.) — τῶν a 12. β 3.
*τὴν νύμφην τοῦ ἀρνίου τὴν γυναῖκα) τ. νύμ. τ. γυ. τ. ἀρν. A. 34. 35.
38.   Vulg. Copt. Æth. Syr. Erp.   τ. γυ. τ. νυμ. τ. ἀρν. a 21.
β 3. Compl.   Ar. P.
10. *ἐπ᾽) ἐπὶ A
*τὴν μεγάλην) — A. B. a 20. β 2. Vulg. Copt. Æth. Syr. Arr. Slav. MS.

and murderers, and whoremongers, and sorcerers, and idolaters, and all liars, shall have their part in the lake which burneth with fire and brimstone : which is the second death.

And there came one of the seven angels who 9 had the seven cups full of the seven last plagues, and talked with me, saying, Come hither, I will show thee the bride, the Lamb's wife. And he 10 carried me away in the spirit to a great and high mountain, and showed me the holy city, Jerusalem, descending out of heaven from God, having the glory of God : her light *was* like 11 unto a stone most precious, even like a jasper stone, clear as crystal ; and it had a wall great 12 and high, *and* had twelve gates, and at the gates twelve angels, and names written thereon, which are the names of the twelve tribes of the

---

d Rec.—   *e* [τοῦ ἀρνίου τὴν γυναῖκα.]   *f* [ἐπ'.]
  k [ἔχουσαν.]   *l* Rec.—   *m* + [τῶν.]

---

10. τὴν ἀγ.) — τὴν Compl.
    ἀπὸ) ἐκ *a* 16. β 2.
11. ἔχου. . . . . Θεοῦ) — A.
    *καὶ) — A. *a* 23. β 3. Compl.   Vulg. MS. *Am. Tol.* Copt.
    Slav. MSS.
    ὡς λίθῳ) — 7. 12. 17*. 18. 38. 49. Er.
12. *ἔχουσάν τε) ἔχουσα A. *a* 21. β 2.   -σά τε Er.   — τε. Compl.
    ἔχουσαν) ἔχουσα A. *a* 23. β 3. Er.
    καὶ ἐπὶ . . . . δώδεκα) — A. Syr.
    *ἅ ἐστι) + τὰ ὀνόματα A. *a* 7. (& 11. 13.)   ὀνόματα, *a* 13. (& 29.)
        Vulg. Copt. Syr. Ar. P. Slav. MS.
    *τῶν υἱ.) — τῶν A. *a* 14. β 2.

13 Ἰσραήλ. ᵃἀπὸ¹ ᵇἀνατολῆς¹ πυλῶνες τρεῖς·
ᶜκαὶ¹ ἀπὸ βοῤῥᾶ, πυλῶνες τρεῖς· ᵈκαὶ¹ ἀπὸ
νότου, πυλῶνες τρεῖς· ᵉκαὶ¹ ἀπὸ δυσμῶν, πυ-
14 λῶνες τρεῖς. καὶ τὸ τεῖχος τῆς πόλεως ἔχον
θεμελίους δώδεκα, καὶ ᶠἐπ᾽ αὐτῶν¹ ᵍδώδεκα¹
ὀνόματα τῶν δώδεκα ἀποστόλων τοῦ ἀρνίου.

15 Καὶ ὁ λαλῶν μετ᾽ ἐμοῦ, εἶχε ʰμέτρον¹ κάλα-
μον χρυσοῦν, ἵνα μετρήσῃ τὴν πόλιν, καὶ τοὺς
16 πυλῶνας αὐτῆς, καὶ τὸ τεῖχος αὐτῆς. καὶ ἡ
πόλις τετράγωνος κεῖται, καὶ τὸ μῆκος αὐτῆς ⁱ¹
ὅσον καὶ τὸ πλάτος. καὶ ἐμέτρησε τὴν πόλιν τῷ
καλάμῳ ἐπὶ σταδίους δώδεκα χιλιάδων· τὸ
μῆκος καὶ τὸ πλάτος καὶ τὸ ὕψος αὐτῆς ἴσα ἐστί.
17 καὶ ἐμέτρησε τὸ τεῖχος αὐτῆς ἑκατὸν τεσσαράκοντα τεσσάρων πηχῶν, μέτρον ἀνθρώπου, ὅ
ἐστιν ἀγγέλου.

18 Καὶ ἦν ἡ ἐνδόμησις τοῦ τείχους αὐτῆς, ἴασπις·
καὶ ἡ πόλις χρυσίον καθαρὸν ᵏὅμοιον¹ ὑάλῳ κα-

ᵃ [ἀπ᾽.]   ᵇ ∾ ἀνατολῶν.   ᶜ Rec.—   ᵈ Rec.—   ᵉ Rec.—

13. *ἀπ᾽ ἀνατολῆς) ἀπὸ ἀνατολῶν a 22. β 2. γ 2. Compl.   ἀπ᾽) ἀπὸ A.
*τρεῖς) + καὶ (three times) A. a 25. β 3. Compl.   Vulg. ed. Copt.
Syr. Arm. Arr. Slav. MS.
νότου) μεσημβρίας Er.   (δυσμῶν π. τ. κ. ἀπὸ νότου A.   Am.)
14. τὸ τεῖχ.) — τὸ Er.
*ἐν αὐτοῖς) ἐπ᾽ αὐτῶν A. a 27. β 3. Compl.   Vulg. MS. Copt.
Syr. Arr.
* + δώδεκα A. a 22. β 3. (& 25.)   δεκαδύο 18. 19. ιβ΄ 92.   Vulg.
Syr. Arm. Ar. P. Slav. MS.
15. *εἶχε) + μέτρον A. a 23. β 3. γ 2. Compl.   Vulg. Æth. Syr. Ar. P.
Slav. MSS.
καὶ τὸ τεῖχος αὐτῆς) — B. a 17. β 3. Compl.

children of Israel : on the east three gates ; and 13
on the north three gates ; and on the south
three gates; and on the west three gates.   And 14
the wall of the city had twelve foundations, and
on them the twelve names of the twelve apostles
of the Lamb.

And he that talked with me had a golden 15
measuring reed to measure the city, and the
gates thereof, and the wall thereof.   And the 16
city lieth foursquare, and the length is as large
as the breadth : and he measured the city with
the reed, twelve thousand furlongs.   The length
and the breadth and the height of it are equal.
And he measured the wall thereof, an hundred 17
and forty *and* four cubits, *according to* the measure of a man, that is, of the angel.

And the building of the wall of it was *of* 18
jasper : and the city *was* pure gold, like unto

ƒ [ἐν αὐτοῖς.]   g Rec.—   h Rec.—   i +[τοσοῦτόν ἐστιν.]   k [ὁμοία.]

16. *τοσοῦτόν ἐστιν) — A. B. a 28. β 3. γ 3. Compl. Æth. Syr. Ar. P.
        Slav. MSS.
      ὅσον) ὁσοῦτον Er.
      καὶ τὸ πλ.) — καὶ B. a 24. β 3. Compl.
      πόλιν) + ἐν 11. 12. 32. Er.
      σταδίους) σταδίων Er.
      δώδεκα) δεκαδύο a 17. β 3.
      τὸ μῆκος) δώδεκα τὸ μῆ. B. a 19. β 2. Compl.   Syr.
17. ἐμέτρησε) — a 19. β 2.
      ἐκ. τεσσ. τεσσ.) δ′ καὶ ἐκ. καὶ τεσσ. A.
18. ἦν) — A. Æth. Syr.
      *ὁμοία) ὅμοιον A. a 20. β 5. Compl.   Vulg. (Syr.) Slav. MSS.

142 ΑΠΟΚΑΛΥΨΙΣ. Κεφ. κα'.

19 θαρῷ. ^a| οἱ θεμέλιοι τοῦ τείχους τῆς πόλεως
παντὶ λίθῳ τιμίῳ κεκοσμημένοι. ὁ θεμέλιος ὁ
πρῶτος, ἴασπις· ὁ δεύτερος, σάπφειρος· ὁ τρίτος,
20 χαλκηδών· ὁ τέταρτος, σμάραγδος· ὁ πέμπτος,
σαρδόνυξ· ὁ ἕκτος, σάρδιος· ὁ ἕβδομος, χρυ-
σόλιθος· ὁ ὄγδοος, βήρυλλος· ὁ ἔννατος, τοπά-
ζιον· ὁ δέκατος, χρυσόπρασος· ὁ ἑνδέκατος,
21 ὑάκινθος· ὁ δωδέκατος, ἀμέθυστος. καὶ οἱ
δώδεκα πυλῶνες, δώδεκα μαργαρῖται· ἀνὰ εἷς
ἕκαστος τῶν πυλώνων ἦν ἐξ ἑνὸς μαργαρίτου·
καὶ ἡ πλατεῖα τῆς πόλεως, χρυσίον καθαρὸν, ὡς
ὕαλος ^bδιαυγής.|
22 Καὶ ναὸν οὐκ εἶδον ἐν αὐτῇ· ὁ γὰρ Κύριος ὁ
Θεὸς ὁ παντοκράτωρ, ναὸς αὐτῆς ἐστι, καὶ τὸ
23 ἀρνίον. καὶ ἡ πόλις οὐ χρείαν ἔχει τοῦ ἡλίου,
οὐδὲ τῆς σελήνης, ἵνα φαίνωσιν ^c| αὐτῇ· ἡ γὰρ
δόξα τοῦ Θεοῦ ἐφώτισεν αὐτὴν, καὶ ὁ λύχνος
24 αὐτῆς τὸ ἀρνίον. καὶ ^dπεριπατήσουσι τὰ ἔθνη
διὰ τοῦ φωτὸς αὐτῆς·| καὶ οἱ βασιλεῖς τῆς γῆς
25 φέρουσι τὴν δόξαν ^e| αὐτῶν εἰς αὐτήν. καὶ οἱ
πυλῶνες αὐτῆς οὐ μὴ κλεισθῶσιν ἡμέρας· νὺξ

---

^a +[καὶ.]   ^b [διαφανὴς.]   ^c +[ἐν.]   ^d [τὰ ἔθνη

19. *καὶ) — A. a 16. β 3.   Vulg. MS. Am. Slav. MS.
20. σάρδιος) σάρδιον A. a 16. β 3.
    χρυσόπρασος) -σον. A.   χρυσόπασος 2. 29. 30. 50.
    ὑάκινθος) -θινος Compl.
    ἀμέθυστος) -σος a 14. β 2. Er.
21. ἀνὰ) ἵνα A.
    *διαφανὴς) διαυγὴς A. a 27. β 3. Compl.
22. ναὸς) ὁ ναὸς A.
23. *ἐν) — A. B. a 15. (& 39.) γ 2. Er.

clear glass.   The foundations of the wall of the 19
city *were* adorned with all manner of precious
stones.   The first foundation *was* a jasper ;   the
second, a sapphire ;   the third, a chalcedony ;
the fourth, an emerald ;   the fifth, a sardonyx ; 20
the sixth, a sardius ;   the seventh, a chrysolyte ;   the
eighth, a beryl ;   the ninth, a topaz ;   the tenth,
a chrysoprasus ;   the eleventh, a jacinth ;   the
twelfth, an amethyst.   And the twelve gates 21
were twelve pearls ;   every several gate was of
one pearl :   and the broadway of the city *was*
pure gold, as it were transparent glass.

And I saw no temple therein : for the Lord 22
God the. Almighty and the Lamb are the temple
of it.   And the city had no need of the sun, 23
neither of the moon, to shine in it : for the glory
of God did lighten it, and the Lamb *is* the light
thereof.   And the nations shall walk by means 24
of the light thereof : and the kings of the earth
do bring their glory unto it.   And the gates of 25
it shall not be shut at all by day : for there

τῶν σωζομένων ἐν τῷ φωτὶ αὐτῆς περιπατήσουσι.]   ᶜ + [καὶ τὴν τιμὴν.]

---

23. αὐτῇ· ἡ γὰρ) αὐτὴ γὰρ ἡ B. a 19. β 3. γ 3.
     αὐτὴν) αὐτῇ Er.
24. *τὰ ἔθνη τῶν σωζομένων ἐν τῷ φωτὶ αὐτῆς περιπατήσουσι) περιπατ.
     τ. ἔθ. διὰ τοῦ φωτὸς αὐτῆς A. a 27. β 2. γ 4. Compl.   Vulg.
     Copt. Æth. Syr. (some copies) Arm. Ar. P. Slav. MSS.
     φέρουσι) — τὴν & + αὐτῷ a 15. β 3. γ 2.
     *καὶ τὴν τιμὴν) — A. 10. 11. 17. 18. 38. 47. Er.   Copt. Æth. Erp.
     αὐτῶν) τῶν ἐθνῶν a 19. β 3. γ 2.   Syr. Slav. MS.
25. οἱ πυ.) — οἱ Er.

26 γὰρ οὐκ ἔσται ἐκεῖ. καὶ οἴσουσι τὴν δόξαν καὶ
27 τὴν τιμὴν τῶν ἐθνῶν εἰς αὐτήν. καὶ οὐ μὴ
εἰσέλθῃ εἰς αὐτὴν πᾶν ªκοινὸν,ᴵ καὶ ᵇποιῶνᴵ βδέ-
λυγμα, καὶ ψεῦδος· εἰ μὴ οἱ γεγραμμένοι ἐν τῷ
βιβλίῳ τῆς ζωῆς τοῦ ἀρνίου.

XXII Καὶ ἔδειξέ μοι ᶜᴵ ποταμὸν ὕδατος
ζωῆς, λαμπρὸν ὡς κρύσταλλον, ἐκπορευόμενον
2 ἐκ τοῦ θρόνου τοῦ Θεοῦ καὶ τοῦ ἀρνίου. ἐν
μέσῳ τῆς πλατείας αὐτῆς, καὶ τοῦ ποταμοῦ,
ἐντεῦθεν καὶ ᵈἐκεῖθενᴵ, ξύλον ζωῆς, ποιοῦν καρ-
ποὺς δώδεκα, κατὰ μῆνα ᵉᴵ ἕκαστον ἀποδιδοῦν
τὸν καρπὸν αὐτοῦ· καὶ τὰ φύλλα τοῦ ξύλου εἰς
3 θεραπείαν τῶν ἐθνῶν. καὶ πᾶν ᶠκατάθεμαᴵ οὐκ
ἔσται ἔτι· καὶ ὁ θρόνος τοῦ Θεοῦ καὶ τοῦ ἀρνίου
ἐν αὐτῇ ἔσται· καὶ οἱ δοῦλοι αὐτοῦ λατρεύσου-
4 σιν αὐτῷ· καὶ ὄψονται τὸ πρόσωπον αὐτοῦ, καὶ
5 τὸ ὄνομα αὐτοῦ ἐπὶ τῶν μετώπων αὐτῶν. καὶ
νὺξ οὐκ ἔσται ᵍ[ἔτι·]ᴵ καὶ ʰοὐχ ἕξουσι χρείανᴵ

ª [κοινοῦν.]   ᵇ [ποιοῦν.]   ᶜ +[καθαρὸν.]   ᵈ [ἐντεῦθεν.]

---

26. —— ver. Er.
  εἰς αὐτὴν) +ἵνα εἰσέλθωσι a 17. β 3.   Slav. MS.
27. *κοινοῦν) κοινὸν A. a 25. β 3. γ 2. Compl.   Vulg. Slav.
  *ποιοῦν) ποιῶν A. 18. 41. 68. 92.   (Vulg. Syr.) Arr.   ὁ ποιῶν
  a 12. β 3.

1. *καθαρὸν) — A. B. a 17. β 3. γ 4.   Vulg. Copt. Æth. Syr. Erp.
  Slav. MS.   After ποταμὸν 26. 32. 34. 38. 46. 48. 49. 91.
  Compl.   Slav. MSS.
2. ἐν μέσῳ) ἐμμέσῳ A.

shall be no night there. And they shall bring the 26
glory and honour of the nations unto it. And there 27
shall in no wise enter into it any thing common,
neither *whosoever* worketh abomination, or a lie:
but those who are written in the Lamb's book of life.

XXII. And he showed me the river of the
water of life, bright as crystal, proceeding out
of the throne of God and of the Lamb. In the 2
midst of the broadway of it, and of the river,
on this⁷ side and on that side, *was there* the tree
of life, which bare twelve *manner of* fruits, *and*
yielded its fruit every month : and the leaves
of the tree *were* for the healing of the nations.
And there shall be no more curse : but the 3
throne of God and of the Lamb shall be in it ;
and his servants shall serve him : and they shall 4
see his face ; and his name *shall be* on their
foreheads. And there shall be no ⸢more⸣ night; 5

ᵉ + [ἕνα.] ᶠ [καταυάθεμα.] ᵍ [ἐκεῖ.] ʰ [χρείαν οὐκ ἔχουσι.] ∾ οὐ χρέια.

---

2. *καὶ ἐντεῦθεν) καὶ ἐκεῖθεν A. B. a 17. β 3. γ 4.   Syr. Arm. Slav. MSS.
   ποιοῦν) ποιῶν A. 18
   *ἕνα) — A. a 23. β 3. γ 3. Compl.   Slav.
   ἕκαστον ἀποδιδοῦν) ἀποδιδ. ἔκαστ. B. a 5.   ἕκαστον) -τῳ B. 39.
   40.   Slav. MS.   ἀποδιδοῦν) -δοῦς B. a 17. Compl.   ἀπο-
   διδόντα 29. Er.   Vulg. MS. Slav. MS.
   τὸν) — 29. 30. 40. Er.
3. *καταυάθεμα) κατάθεμα A. a 27. β 2. γ 2. Compl.
   ἔτι) ἐκεῖ a 12. γ 2. Compl.   Ar. P.
5. *ἐκεῖ) ἔτι A. 2. 19. 68.   Vulg. Syr.   — a 13. (& 13.)
   *χρείαν οὐκ ἔχουσι) οὐχ ἔξουσι χρείαν A.   Vulg. Copt. Syr. Arr.

^a[φωτὸς] λύχνου καὶ ^bφωτὸς[|] ἡλίου, ὅτι Κύριος ὁ Θεὸς ^cφωτίσει [ἐπ'][|] αὐτούς· καὶ βασιλεύσουσιν εἰς τοὺς αἰῶνας τῶν αἰώνων.

6 Καὶ εἶπέ μοι· Οὗτοι οἱ λόγοι πιστοὶ καὶ ἀληθινοί· καὶ Κύριος ὁ Θεὸς τῶν ^dπνευμάτων τῶν[|] προφητῶν ἀπέστειλε τὸν ἄγγελον αὐτοῦ δεῖξαι τοῖς δούλοις αὐτοῦ ἃ δεῖ γενέσθαι ἐν τά- 7 χει. ^eκαὶ[|] ἰδοὺ ἔρχομαι ταχύ. μακάριος ὁ τηρῶν τοὺς λόγους τῆς προφητείας τοῦ βιβλίου τούτου.

8 ^fΚἀγὼ[|] Ἰωάννης ὁ ^gἀκούων καὶ βλέπων ταῦτα·[|] καὶ ὅτε ἤκουσα καὶ ^hἔβλεπον[|], ἔπεσον προσκυνῆσαι ἔμπροσθεν τῶν ποδῶν τοῦ ἀγγέλου 9 τοῦ δεικνύοντός μοι ταῦτα. καὶ λέγει μοι· Ὅρα μή· σύνδουλός σου ⁱεἰμὶ, καὶ τῶν ἀδελφῶν σου τῶν προφητῶν, καὶ τῶν τηρούντων τοὺς λόγους τοῦ βιβλίου τούτου· τῷ Θεῷ προσκύνησον.

10 Καὶ λέγει μοι· Μὴ σφραγίσῃς τοὺς λόγους τῆς προφητείας τοῦ βιβλίου τούτου· ^kὁ καιρὸς 11 γὰρ[|] ἐγγύς ἐστιν. ὁ ἀδικῶν, ἀδικησάτω ἔτι·

---

a Rec.—   b ∾φὼς.   c ∾φωτιεῖ [φωτίζει.]   d [ἁγίων.]   e Rec.—   f Καὶ ἐγὼ.

οὐ χρεία a 15. β 2.   + φωτὸς A. 18. (38.) 47.   Vulg. Copt. Æth. Syr. Erp. Slav. MSS.

5. φωτὸς) φὼς A. 11. 12. 32. 35. 48.
ἡλίου) — a 13. β 2.   Ar. P. Slav. MSS.
*φωτίζει) φωτιεῖ a 22. β 2. Compl.   Vulg. ed. Slav. MSS.
φωτίσει A. 12. 42.
+ ἐπ' A.

6. εἶπε) λέγει a 22. β 2. Compl.
Κύριος) ὁ Κυ. A. 92.
*ἁγίων) πνευμάτων τῶν A. B. a 26. β 2. γ 2. Compl.   Vulg. (Copt.) Æth. Syr. Arr. Slav. MSS.
δεῖξαι τοῖς δούλοις αὐτοῦ) — a 9.

7. *ἰδοὺ) καὶ ἰδοὺ A. a 18. β 2.   Vulg. ed. Æth. Syr. Ar. P. Slav. MSS.

and they shall not need [the light of] candle, nor
light of the sun ; for the Lord God will give them
light : and they shall reign for ever and ever.

And he said unto me, These sayings *are* faithful 6
and true : and the Lord God of the spirits of the
prophets hath sent his angel to show unto his servants the things which must come to pass shortly.
And behold, I come quickly : blessed *is* he that 7
keepeth the words of the prophecy of this book.

And I John heard and saw these things. 8
And when I had heard and seen, I fell down
to worship before the feet of the angel who
showed me these things.   And he saith unto 9
me, See *thou do it* not : I am the fellow-servant
of thee and thy brethren the prophets, and of those
who keep the words of this book : worship God.

And he saith unto me, Seal not the words 10
of the prophecy of this book : for the time is
at hand.   He that is unjust, let him be unjust 11

---

^g [βλέπων ταῦτα καὶ ἀκούων.]   ^h [ἔβλεψα.] ∾εἶδον.   ⁱ +[γὰρ.]   ^k [ὅτι ὁ καιρὸς.]

8. *καὶ ἐγὼ) κἀγὼ A. *a* 8. (& 13.) Compl.
   *βλέπων ταῦτα καὶ ἀκούων) ἀκ. κ. βλ. ταῦ. A. *a* 17. β 2. γ 3. Compl.
       Vulg. Syr.
   *καὶ ἔβλεψα) κ. ἔβλεπον A.   κ. ὅτε εἶδον B. *a* 14. β 2.
   ἔπεσον) ἔπεσα 16. 30. 35. 38. 68. Er.
   ἔμπροσθεν τῶν) πρὸ A.
9. *γὰρ) — A. *a* 25. β 2. γ 2. Compl.   Vulg. MS. *Am.* Copt. Syr.
       Arr. Slav. MSS.
   τῶν πρ.) — τῶν Er.
   καὶ last) *a* 9. γ 2. Compl.   Slav. MSS.
10. *ὅτι ὁ καιρὸς) ὁ καιρὸς γὰρ A. *a* 16. β 2.   Vulg. Copt. Syr. Slav.
       MSS.   ὁ καιρὸς 4. 16. 27. 39. 48. 68.   ὁ καὶ) — ὁ Er.

[καὶ ὁ ᵃ ῥυπαρὸς ῥυπαρευθήτω | ἔτι·] καὶ ὁ δί-
καιος, ᵇ δικαιοσύνην ποιησάτω | ἔτι· καὶ ὁ ἅγιος,
12 ἁγιασθήτω ἔτι. ᶜ | Ἰδοὺ ἔρχομαι ταχὺ, καὶ ὁ
μισθός μου μετ᾽ ἐμοῦ, ἀποδοῦναι ἑκάστῳ ὡς τὸ
13 ἔργον ᵈ ἐστὶν αὐτοῦ |. ἐγὼ ᵉ | τὸ ᶠ Ἄλφα | καὶ τὸ
Ὦ, ᵍ ὁ πρῶτος καὶ ὁ ἔσχατος, ἀρχὴ καὶ τέλος. |
14 Μακάριοι οἱ ʰ πλύνοντες τὰς στολὰς αὐτῶν |, ἵνα
ἔσται ἡ ἐξουσία αὐτῶν ἐπὶ τὸ ξύλον τῆς ζωῆς,
καὶ τοῖς πυλῶσιν εἰσέλθωσιν εἰς τὴν πόλιν·
15 ἔξω ⁱ | οἱ κύνες καὶ οἱ φαρμακοὶ καὶ οἱ πόρνοι
καὶ οἱ φονεῖς καὶ οἱ εἰδωλολάτραι, καὶ πᾶς ᵏ |
φιλῶν καὶ ποιῶν ψεῦδος.
16 Ἐγὼ Ἰησοῦς ἔπεμψα τὸν ἄγγελόν μου μαρ-
τυρῆσαι ὑμῖν ταῦτα ˡ ἐν | ταῖς ἐκκλησίαις· ἐγώ
εἰμι ἡ ῥίζα καὶ τὸ γένος ᵐ | ⁿ Δαυὶδ, | ὁ ἀστὴρ ὁ
17 λαμπρὸς [καὶ] ᵒ ὁ πρωϊνός. | Καὶ τὸ Πνεῦμα καὶ
ἡ νύμφη λέγουσιν· ᵖ Ἔρχου· | καὶ ὁ ἀκούων

ᵃ [ῥυπῶν ῥυπωσάτω.]   ᵇ [δικαιωθήτω.]   ᶜ +[καὶ.]   ᵈ [αὐτοῦ ἔσται.]
ʰ [ποιοῦντες τὰς ἐντολὰς αὐτοῦ.]   ⁱ +[δὲ.]   ᵏ +[ὁ.]   ˡ [ἐπὶ.]

11. *καὶ ὁ ῥυπῶν ῥυπωσάτω ἔτι) — A. [20?] 21. 34. 35. 68.   κ. ὁ ῥυπαρὸς
    ῥυπαρευθήτω a 23. β 2. Compl.
    *δικαιωθήτω) δικαιοσύνην ποιησάτω A. a 26. β 2. γ 3. Compl.
    Vulg. MS. Am. Tol. Copt. Syr. Ar. P. Slav.
12. *καὶ ἰδοὺ) — καὶ A. a 28. β 2. γ 2. Compl.   Vulg. Copt. Syr. Arm.
    Arr. Slav. MS.
    *αὐτοῦ ἔσται) ἔσται αὐτοῦ a 15. Compl.   ἐστιν αὐτοῦ A. 21. 38. Syr.
13. *ἐγώ εἰμι) — εἰμι A. a 22. Compl.   Vulg. MS. Am. Slav. MS.
    *Α) ἄλφα A. a 7.
    *ἀρχὴ κ. τέλος, ὁ πρῶτος κ. ὁ ἔσχατος) ὁ πρ. κ. ὁ ἐσχ. ἡ ἀρ. κ. τὸ
    τέλ. a 13. β 2.   Vulg. Æth. Syr. Ar. P. Slav. MS.   So,
    only — ὁ (twice) A. 3. 7. 8. 9. 21. 22.   ὁ ἐσχ.) — ὁ Er.
14. *ποιοῦντες τὰς ἐντολὰς αὐτοῦ) πλύνοντες (πλυνοῦντες 38) τὰς στολὰς
    αὐτῶν A. 7. 38.   Vulg. Æth. Arm. (in m.)

still : ⸆and he that is filthy, let him be filthy
still :⸅ and he that is righteous, let him work
righteousness still : and he that is holy, let him
be holy still.   Behold, I come quickly; and my 12
reward *is* with me, to give to every man according
as his work is.   I *am* Alpha and Omega, the first 13
and the last, the beginning and the end.   Blessed 14
are they who wash their robes, that they may have
right to the tree of life, and may enter in through
the gates into the city.   Without *are* dogs, and 15
sorcerers, and whoremongers, and murderers, and
idolaters, and whosoever loveth and maketh a lie.

I Jesus have sent mine angel to testify unto 16
you these things in the churches.   I am the Root
and the offspring of David, *and* the bright and
morning Star.   And the Spirit and the bride say, 17
Come.   And let him that heareth say, Come.   And

---

e [εἶμι.]   *f* [A.]   *g* [ἀρχὴ καὶ τέλος, ὁ πρῶτος καὶ ὁ ἔσχατος.]
m +[τοῦ.]   *n* [Δαβὶδ.]   *o* [ὀρθρινὸς.]   *p* [ἐλθε.]

---

15. **δὲ*) — A. *a* 27. β 2. γ 4. Compl.   Vulg. Æth. Syr. Slav. MS.
   οἱ πόρ.) — οἱ Er.
   *ὁ φι.) — ὁ A. *a* 14. β 2. Compl.
16. **ἐπὶ*) — 4. 11. 12. 47. 48. Er.   Arm. Slav. MS.   ἐν A. 18. 21.
   38.   Vulg. Slav.
   ἡ ῥίζα) — ἡ Er.
   *τοῦ Δ.) — τοῦ A. *a* 21. (& 11. 39.)   Δαβὶδ) Δαυὶδ; (better orthography; so Compl.)
   *ὁ λαμπρὸς καὶ ὀρθρινὸς) ὁ λαμ. καὶ ὁ πρωϊνὸς A.   Vulg.   ὁ λαμ.
   ὁ πρω. *a* 23. β 2. γ 3. Compl.   Copt. Æth. Syr. Slav. MS.
   ὁ πρω. ὁ λαμ. *a* 5.   Ar. P. Slav. MSS.   ὁ λαμ.) — ὁ Er.
17. **ἐλθὲ* (twice) & ἐλθέτω) ἔρχου & ἐρχέσθω A. *a* 28. β 2. γ 4.
   Compl.

εἰπάτω, ^a"Ερχου.[|] καὶ ὁ διψῶν ^bἐρχέσθω·^{| c|} ὁ θέλων ^dλαβέτω[|] ὕδωρ ζωῆς δωρεάν.

18 ^eΜαρτυρῶ ἐγὼ[|] παντὶ ^fτῷ[|] ἀκούοντι τοὺς λόγους τῆς προφητείας τοῦ βιβλίου τούτου· ἐάν τις ^gἐπιθῇ ἐπ᾽ αὐτά,[|] ἐπιθήσει ὁ Θεὸς ἐπ᾽ αὐτὸν τὰς πληγὰς τὰς γεγραμμένας ἐν ^hτῷ[|]
19 βιβλίῳ τούτῳ· καὶ ἐάν τις ⁱἀφέλῃ[|] ἀπὸ τῶν λόγων ^kτοῦ[|] βιβλίου τῆς προφητείας ταύτης, ^lἀφελεῖ[|] ὁ Θεὸς τὸ μέρος αὐτοῦ ἀπὸ ^mτοῦ ξύλου[|] τῆς ζωῆς, καὶ ἐκ τῆς πόλεως τῆς ἁγίας, ^{n|} τῶν γεγραμμένων ἐν ^oτῷ[|] βιβλίῳ τούτῳ.

20 Λέγει ὁ μαρτυρῶν ταῦτα· Ναὶ ἔρχομαι ταχύ. Ἀμήν· ^{p|} ἔρχου, Κύριε Ἰησοῦ.

21 Ἡ χάρις τοῦ Κυρίου ^{q|} Ἰησοῦ Χριστοῦ μετὰ πάντων ^rτῶν ἁγίων.[|] ⌈ἀμήν.⌉

---

a [ἔλθε.]   b [ἐλθέτω.]   c +[καὶ.]   d [λαμβανέτω τὸ.]   e [συμμαρτυ-
k Rec.—   l [ἀφαιρήσει.]   m [βίβλου.]   n +[καὶ.]

17. *καὶ ὁ θέλ.) — καὶ A. a 23. β 2. γ 4. Compl.   Vulg. MS. Am. Tol.
Copt. Æth. Slav. MSS.
*λαμβανέτω τὸ) λαβέτω. A. a 24. β 2. γ 5. Compl.
18. *συμμαρτυροῦμαι γὰρ) μαρτυρῶ ἐγὼ A. B. a 24. β 2. γ 4. Compl.
Vulg. MS. Am. Copt. Æth. Syr. Arm. Arr. Slav. MSS.
μαρτύρομαι ἐγὼ 11. 48.   μαρτύρομαι γὰρ 34. 35.
*παντὶ) + τῷ A. B. a 16. β 2. γ 3.
τῆς προ. τοῦ) — τῆς & τοῦ Er.
ἐάν) εἴ Er.
*ἐπιτιθῇ πρὸς ταῦτα) ἐπιθῇ ἐπ᾽ αὐτὰ A. a 26. β 2. γ 4. Compl.
ἐπιθήσει) σαι a 10. β 2. γ 2. Compl.
ἐπ᾽ αὐτὸν) — A* Before ὁ Θεὸς a 6. Compl.   ἐπ᾽ αὐτῷ A**, 11**.
τὰς πλη.) τὰς ἑπτὰ π. a 6. Compl.   Arm. Slav. MS.
*ἐν) + τῷ A. a 17. β 2. γ 4. Compl. "rel. fere omnes." Sch.
19. ἐάν) εἴ Er.
*ἀφαιρῇ) ἀφέλῃ A. a 26. β 3. γ 5. Compl.
*βιβλίου) τοῦ β. A. B. a 25. β 2. γ 3. Compl.

let him that is athirst come. *And* whosoever will,
let him take the water of life freely.
I testify unto every one that heareth the 18
words of the prophecy of this book, If any one
shall add unto these things, God shall add unto
him the plagues that are written in this book;
and if any one shall take away from the words 19
of the book of this prophecy, God shall take
away his part from the tree of life, and from
the holy city, which are written of in this book.

He who testifieth these things saith, Surely I 20
come quickly: Amen; come, Lord Jesus.
The grace of the Lord Jesus Christ *be* with all 21
the saints. [Amen.]

ροῦμαι γὰρ.] [f] Rec.— [g] [ἐπιτιθῇ πρὸς ταῦτα.] [h] Rec.— [i] [ἀφαιρῇ.] [o] Rec.— [p] +[ναὶ.] [q] +[ἡμῶν.] [r] [ὑμῶν.]

---

19. *ἀφαιρήσει) ἀφελεῖ A. B. *a* 9. (& 39. 55.) ἀφέλοι *a* 14. Compl.
*βίβλου) τοῦ ξύλου A. B. *a* 27. β 3. γ 3. Compl. Vulg. MS. *Am.* Copt. Æth. Syr. Arm. Slav. MSS.
τῆς 3 last times) —Er.
ἐκ) —A. 10. 38. Er.
*καὶ τῶν) —καὶ. A. *a* 25. β 2. γ 4. Compl. Copt. Æth. Syr. Arm. Erp. Slav. MSS.
*ἐν) + τῷ A. *a* 15. β 3. γ 3. Compl.

20. *ναὶ 2nd) —A. B. *a* 7. (& 12. 20. 29.) Vulg. Copt. Syr. Arm. Arr. Slav. MSS.
Ἰησοῦ) + Χριστέ *a* 5. γ 2. (& 13.) Copt. Arm. Erp. Slav. MSS.

21. *ἡμῶν) —A. B. *a* 20. β 2. Compl. Vulg. MS. Æth. Ar. P. Slav. MSS.
Χριστοῦ) —A. 26.
*ὑμῶν) —A. Vulg. MS. *Am.* τῶν ἁγίων B. *a* 27. β 2. γ 6. Compl. Vulg. MS. Copt. Syr. Arm. Slav. MSS.
Ἀμήν) —A. Vulg. MS.

LONDON:

SAMUEL BAGSTER AND SONS,

15, PATERNOSTER ROW;

WAREHOUSE FOR BIBLES, NEW TESTAMENTS, PRAYER-BOOKS, LEXICONS,
GRAMMARS, CONCORDANCES, AND PSALTERS, IN ANCIENT
AND MODERN LANGUAGES.

ΠΟΛΛΑΙ μεν θνητοις ΓΛΩΤΤΑΙ, μια δ'Αθανατοισιν.

For EU product safety concerns, contact us at Calle de José Abascal, 56–1°, 28003 Madrid, Spain or eugpsr@cambridge.org.

www.ingramcontent.com/pod-product-compliance
Ingram Content Group UK Ltd.
Pitfield, Milton Keynes, MK11 3LW, UK
UKHW012346130625
459647UK00009B/566